Postfeminist E

This book challenges a contemporary postfeminist sensibility grounded not only in assumptions that gender and sexual equality has been achieved in many Western contexts, but that feminism has gone 'too far' with women and girls now overtaking men and boys – positioned as the new victims of gender transformations. The book is the first to outline and critique how educational discourses have directly fed into postfeminist anxieties, exploring three postfeminist panics over girls and girlhood that circulate widely in the international media and popular culture. First it explores how a masculinity crisis over failing boys in school has spawned a backlash discourse about overly successful girls; second it looks at how widespread anxieties over girls becoming excessively mean and/or violent have positioned female aggression as pathological; third it examines how incessant concerns over controlling risky female sexuality underpin recent sexualisation of girls' moral panics. The book outlines how these postfeminist panics over girlhood have influenced educational policies and practices in areas such as academic achievement, anti-bullying strategies and sex-education curriculum, making visible the new postfeminist, sexual politics of schooling.

Moving beyond media or policy critique, however, this book offers new theoretical and methodological tools for researching postfeminism, girlhood and education. It engages with current theoretical debates over possibilities for girls' agency and empowerment in postfeminist, neo-liberal contexts of sexual regulation. It also elaborates new psychosocial and feminist Deleuzian methodological approaches for mapping subjectivity, affectivity and social change. Drawing on two UK empirical research projects exploring teen-aged girls' own perspectives and responses to postfeminist panics, the book shows how real girls are actually negotiating notions of girls as overly successful, mean, violent, aggressive and sexual. The data offers rich insight into girls' gendered, raced and classed experiences at school and beyond, exploring teen peer cultures, friendship, offline and online sexual identities, and bullying and cyberbullying. The analysis illuminates how and when girls take up and identify with postfeminist trends, but also at times attempt to re-work, challenge and critique the contradictory discourses of girlhood and femininity. In this sense the book offers an opportunity for girls to 'talk back' to the often simplistic either wildly celebratory or crisis-based sensationalism of postfeminist panics over girlhood.

This book will be essential reading for those interested in feminism, girlhood, media studies, gender and education.

Jessica Ringrose is Senior Lecturer in Sociology of Gender and Education at the Institute of Education, University of London.

Foundations and Futures of Education

Series Editors: Peter Aggleton, Sally Power and Michael Reiss

Being a University
Ron Barnett

Education: An 'Impossible Profession'?
Tamara Bibby

Radical Education and the Common School
Michael Fielding and Peter Moss

Re-Designing Learning Contexts: Technology-Rich, Learner-Centred Ecologies
Rosemary Luckin

Schools and Schooling in the Digital Age: A Critical Analysis
Neil Selwyn

The Irregular School
Roger Slee

Gender, Schooling and Global Social Justice
Elaine Unterhalter

Language, Learning, Context: Talking the Talk
Wolff-Michael Roth

School Trouble
Deborah Youdell

The Right to Higher Education: Beyond Widening Participation
Penny Jane Burke

Postfeminist Education? Girls and the Sexual Politics of Schooling
Jessica Ringrose

Postfeminist Education?

Girls and the sexual politics of schooling

Jessica Ringrose

Routledge
Taylor & Francis Group

LONDON AND NEW YORK

First published 2013
by Routledge
2 Park Square, Milton Park, Abingdon, Oxon OX14 4RN

Simultaneously published in the USA and Canada
by Routledge
711 Third Avenue, New York, NY 10017

Routledge is an imprint of the Taylor & Francis Group, an informa business

British Library Cataloguing in Publication Data
A catalogue record for this book is available from the British Library

Library of Congress Cataloging-in-Publication Data
Ringrose, Jessica.
Postfeminist education? : girls and the sexual politics of schooling /
Jessica Ringrose.
    p. cm. – (Foundations and futures of education)
    ISBN 978-0-415-55748-1 (hardback) – ISBN 978-0-415-55749-8
    (paperback) – ISBN 978-0-203-10682-2 (e-book) 1. Feminism and
    education. 2. Sex differences in education. 3. Sex discrimination in
    education. I. Title.
    LC197.R56 2012
    370'.82–dc23   2012004442

ISBN: 978-0-415-55748-1 (hbk)
ISBN: 978-0-415-55749-8 (pbk)
ISBN: 978-0-203-10682-2 (ebk)

Typeset in Garamond
by HWA Text and Data Management, London

Printed and bound in Great Britain by
TJ International Ltd, Padstow, Cornwall

Contents

Acknowledgements   vii

1 Introduction: postfeminism, education and girls   1

2 Successful girls? Exploring educational media and policy 'scapes'
   and the postfeminist panic over feminine 'success'   12

3 Mean or violent girls? Exploring the postfeminist panic over
   feminine aggression   28

4 Sexy girls? The middle class postfeminist panic over girls'
   'sexualisation' and the protectionist discourses of sex education   42

5 Rethinking debates on girls' agency: critiquing postfeminist
   discourses of 'choice'   57

6 Towards a new discursive, psychosocial and affective theoretical–
   methodological approach   70

7 Sexual regulation and embodied resistance: teen girls entering
   into and negotiating competitive heterosexualised, postfeminist
   femininity   86

8 Girls negotiating postfeminist, sexualised media contexts   113

9 Conclusion: ways forward for feminism and education   139

Notes   151
References   158
Index   182

Acknowledgements

Like any project, this book is an assemblage of ideas and represents various intellectual synergies that have come together to shape its pages. This 'journey' started during my PhD at York University in Toronto where I developed poststructural and psychoanalytic research tools in my thesis on psychosocial understandings of feminist, anti-racist teaching and learning, that underpin this book – under the guidance of my PhD supervisors Lorna Erwin, Alice Pitt and Didi Kayatt, and through a particularly inspiring postgraduate seminar on feminist, poststructural methodology with Deborah Britzman.

Many of my ideas about girlhood femininities gained speed, however, when I took up a Social Sciences and Humanities Research Council postdoctoral research fellowship on 'Teen girls, femininity and aggression' at Cardiff University in Wales with Valerie Walkerdine in 2004. The research community at Cardiff was incredible, and through the 'Culture, subject, economy' research group headed by Valerie, the 'Gender and sexuality' research cluster headed by Debbie Epstein, and the 'Childhood studies' research group headed by Emma Renold I forged important writing and thinking relationships that wind their way through this book. Valerie has opened many doors for me and continues to be an enormous intellectual inspiration. Debbie Epstein has been significant in shaping my ideas about education, particularly about the 'successful girls' discourse, largely formed in discussion and early writing with her. My thinking and writing partnership with Emma Renold has been so inspiring and fruitful. I would like to thank her first for being the most fabulous friend and second for tirelessly talking through many of the ideas in this book with me through text, email, iPhone, landline and Skype conversations (thank goodness Skype eventually saved on the phone bills!), providing on-going emotional support during the writing process. Other members of the postdoc and postgraduate community at Cardiff University were Katarina Erickson (we have supported each other's book writing through Skype and Facebook, as she's back in Sweden) and Merryn Smith, an Aussie whose ferocious wit and debating energies I much appreciate.

In 2005, during my time at Cardiff I was asked to present and participate in the 'New femininities: postfeminism and sexual citizenship' ESRC seminar series, which was a critical event in my consciousness. It introduced me to notions of postfeminism, which became a linchpin to my thinking about contemporary Western culture. Rosalind Gill, one of the series organisers, has been a huge inspiration to me and my writing, and has introduced me to so many interdisciplinary colleagues and networks in media and feminist studies, leading to many exciting opportunities, including our follow-up seminar series 'Pornified: Complicating debates on the "sexualisation" of culture' (with Ros Gill, Meg Barker and Emma Renold).

Also during my time at Cardiff I was asked to present and participate in another ESRC seminar series, 'Girls in Education 3–16: Continuing concerns, new agendas' organized by Carrie Paechter, Caroline Jackson and Emma Renold. This seminar introduced me to key UK scholars working on gender, education and girlhood, and also to the vital work of the Gender and Education Association, of which I am now an executive member. I also met Institute of Education (IOE) scholar Deborah Youdell, with whom I now work and who encouraged me to put in a book proposal for this Educational Foundations and Futures book series. In 2006 I took up a lectureship in 'the Sociology of Gender and Education', which has been a productive platform for my interdisciplinary educational research. I'd like to thank colleagues from the former School of Educational Foundations and Policy Studies for supporting my work, and the IOE as a whole for giving me many postgraduate teaching opportunities that dovetail with my research interests; particularly my MA module Gender: Theory and Practice in Education, which has generated such stimulating debates and amazing student essays: particular thanks to Anna Wolmuth whose 2009 essay on UK sex education lesson plans informed my thinking in Chapter 4.

I'd also like to thank Marnina Gonick for inviting me to be a part of a series of American Educational Research Association Conference symposia on girlhood with Lisa Weems and Elizabeth Marshall that ran from 2007 to 2009, and which led to a special issue in Girlhood Studies 'What Comes After Girl Power?: Rethinking Agency and Resistance' (with Marnina Gonick, Lisa Weems and Emma Renold) that informs the thinking in this book. Many thanks to the two reviewers of the book proposal Madeline Arnot and Christine Skelton who believed in the book at its inception, and the series editors Peter Aggleton, Sally Power and Michael Reiss who commissioned the book. I particularly extend my gratitude to Michael who has offered unflagging editorial commentary and support in the final revision stages. Miriam David has been central to the writing of this book as its initial 'reader'. She has provided copious intellectual and moral support, having read and commented on each chapter along the way, for which I want to thank her profusely! Others who have been generous enough to read and comment on the proposal or versions of chapters over the past few years include Mary Jane Kehily, Claudia Lapping, Emma Renold, Gabrielle Ivinson, Meg Barker, Danielle Egan, Feona Attwood, Tracey Jensen and Ros Gill. Enormous thanks for your time and effort in helping me to make the book stronger. Special thanks also to: Rebekah Willet who took a risk and conducted a minimally funded research project on social networking with me, which forms the basis for Chapter 8; Adi Bloom, such a talented journalist who has made my gendered, educational research findings accessible for media consumption without sensationalising complex issues; Victoria Showunmi, a terrific friend and 'coach' at work who's always encouraging me to keep going; Laura Harvey, a brilliant champion of the 'feminist sisterhood' who helped me through a bit of 'writers block'; Mindy Blaise, my 'conference buddy' who's talked through book ideas with me in various international conference locations; Jette Koefed with whom I've written about 'affect' and sexual cyberbullying informing my thinking in Chapters 6 and 8; Fin Cullen, a youth-work- practitioner-academic inspiration, who advised on how to make my arguments about youth's social peer dynamics (at school and beyond) more salient to an educational audience; and Rebecca Coleman who has helped me to better understand the methodological relevance of Deleuze (and Guattari) and with whom I am editing a forthcoming collection: Deleuze and Research Methodologies (EUP).

Finally, no book can be written without the love and support of partners, family and friends. I want to give copious thanks to my dear husband José for putting up with me and helping me through the lows, highs and general drama of the writing process (e.g. through his laundry, cooking and many counselling sessions!). My mom, Karen, is the original feminist in my life who gave me the thinking tools to see and challenge injustices like sexism, and has always helped me to believe in myself, for which I'm profoundly grateful. And lastly, thanks to all the friends and family who have kept sending supportive vibes through the phone-lines, email and Facebook. As I explore in this book, these digital mediums are redefining our lives and a few words of encouragement on one's Facebook page can make the difference between a bad writing day and a good one!

1 Introduction

Postfeminism, education and girls

What is postfeminism and how does it relate to education?

This book explores postfeminist discourses that circulate in the media and popular culture and how this relates to educational policy and practice, ultimately shaping the sexual politics of schooling. This opening chapter explores what postfeminism means, what postfeminist educational politics are and why the idea of postfeminist discourses provides a useful analytical lens for looking at current debates around girlhood, gender, sexuality, education and schooling.

In brief, feminist commentators writing about postfeminism tend to position this phenomena as a set of politics and discourses grounded in assumptions that gender equity has now been achieved for girls and women in education, the workplace and the home (McRobbie, 2004, 2008; Gill, 2008; Tasker and Negra, 2007; Negra, 2009; Gill and Scharfe, 2011). Angela McRobbie (2004: 4), a key figure in theorising postfeminism, suggests it is characterised by a set of discourses that 'actively draw on and invoke feminism … in order to suggest that equality is achieved, [and] in order to install a whole repertoire of meanings which emphasise that it is no longer needed, a spent force'. Postfeminist discourse also promote the idea that women have now won total equality or even surpassed boys/men, so that feminism is attributed with having 'gone too far' and unleashed girls'/women's competitive and aggressive qualities and power (Taft, 2004). Moreover, girls'/women's over-success is positioned as having been won at the expense of men. Postfeminism as a concept describes, then, both the cultural diffusion of feminism into the public domain and a backlash against feminism, due to fears and anxieties over the shifting gender 'order' (Connell, 1987). Postfeminism encapsulates both a moment in time or a political era and a set of ideological beliefs or discourses that both incorporate yet ridicule feminism, as obsolete and out of touch (McRobbie, 2004). My goal in this book is to apply this lens to understanding gender and sexual politics within the contemporary domain of education.

To begin to illustrate the postfeminist cultural landscape and tenor of educational debate in the UK and internationally, I want to introduce a recent example that captures some of the core dynamics of postfeminism in relation to education. While media analysis by its very nature is easily dated, media stories and 'events' capture the political moment, but they also gesture both backwards historically and forwards to the future, the very type of temporal dynamic I have wanted to signal through the provocative signifier of 'post'-feminism in my title.

On 1 April 2011 a news story broke in the *Daily Telegraph*, 'David Willetts: feminism has held back working men' (Prince, 2011). In the article David Willetts, Minister for Universities and Science in the UK Coalition Government, is described as arguing in his recent book *The Pinch* that the rise of equal rights for women has left working class men struggling – 'as a result of better education for women, households now contain two people who are either both financially successful or struggling to get on'. There was a general uproar about the *Telegraph* article on feminist sites, blogs, tweets and Facebook profiles, debating whether the content of the article was actually an April Fool's joke, given the release date and its blatant sexism. But no, the content was taken directly from a briefing with journalists on his Coalition social mobility strategy. In response to questions about where to lay the blame for the lack of social mobility, Mr Willetts is quoted as saying:

> The feminist revolution in its first round effects was probably the key factor. Feminism trumped egalitarianism. It is not that I am against feminism, it's just that is probably the single biggest factor.

He went on to note:

> One of the things that happened over that period was that the entirely admirable transformation of opportunities for women meant that with a lot of the expansion of education in the 1960s, 70s and 80s, the first beneficiaries were the daughters of middle-class families who had previously been excluded from educational opportunities.

He then suggested:

> And if you put that with what is called 'assortative mating' – that well-educated women marry well-educated men – this transformation of opportunities for women ended up magnifying social divides. It is delicate territory because it is not a bad thing that women had these opportunities, but it widened the gap in household incomes because you suddenly had two-earner couples, both of whom were well-educated, compared with often workless households where nobody was educated.

To summarise, then, the minister is quoted here as suggesting that the feminist revolution was 'the single biggest factor' contributing towards economic decline in the UK, because women, who had previously had very few educational or vocational opportunities, were suddenly able to pursue a career. Instead of challenging inequality feminism has 'trumped egalitarianism'. Moreover middle class women's 'assortative' mating rituals have meant they apparently 'choose' successful men, thereby worsening social divides.

What is significant about this set of logics for introducing this book is they perfectly encapsulate a form of postfeminist discourse where feminism is 'taken into account' (McRobbie, 2008), whilst it is simultaneously blamed for social problems of women being overly-successful at the expense of (particularly working class) men. This is a form of divide-and-conquer tactic that works effectively to divert our attention from issues of post-industrial decline in the UK as a result of late modern global capitalism (shifting the jobs from UK manual labourers to more poorly paid developing world workers) and the knowledge economy. Ignoring the Coalition Government's 'wide-scale savage cuts in education, health and welfare ... on-going social and structural inequalities'[1] and an associated increase in women's and children's poverty, this is an interesting strategy where feminism becomes the straw woman for economic and social demise (Cullen, 2011). The postfeminist logics at work mean the universities' minister of the UK is effectively blaming feminism for entrenching class divisions and hierarchies and even overall economic decline in the UK.

Postfeminism panics: neo-liberalism and the crisis of feminine 'success'

As strongly evidenced in Willetts' comments, a key component of postfeminism is the positioning of girls as the primary benefactors and winners of globalisation in the twenty-first century (Aapola *et al.* 2005; Harris, 2004). Anita Harris's powerful thesis in *Future Girl* is that girls and girlhood has become a projective vehicle for contemporary desires about what is possible in the late modern world of complex globalised de-industrialised societies. Harris looks at Ulrich Beck's (1992; Beck and Beck-Gernsheim, 2002) important theses about individualisation and risk as defining features of advanced capitalist society where the subject becomes defined through their capacity to safeguard against risks as part of market competition (financial, social etc.). Harris argues this leads to a highly individualised DIY subjectivity, where young women are 'constructed as ideal flexible subjects; they are imagined as benefiting from feminist achievements and ideology, as well as from new conditions that favour their success' (Harris, 2004: 8).

Others have built upon this theorisation of late modernity to examine how neo-liberal governmentality is a key discourse through which globalisation and the scaling back of the welfare state operates.[2] Difficult to succinctly define, educational feminist Bronwyn Davies with David Bansel (2007: 248) suggests neoliberalism is characterised by 'the transformation of the administrative state, one previously responsible for human well-being, as well as for the economy, into a state that gives power to global corporations and installs apparatuses and knowledges through which people are reconfigured as productive economic entrepreneurs of their own lives'.[3] My interest in this book, touched upon throughout, is how neo-liberalism operates as a totalising discourse through which subjectivity is re-constituted in economic terms, where market values and commodification thoroughly saturate the construction of self and other. A heightened competitive market ethos infuses education, where educational actors of various scales become interacting economic units (or machines) of competition (from individual, to family, neighbourhood, school, local authority, region, nation state etc.). According to Stephen Ball (2008), two central subjectivities are established in neo-liberal discourse: the entrepreneur (who is innovative producer) and the chooser (the consumer who is free to make market choices). The neo-liberal ethos is to change, transform, adapt, reinvent and self-perfect towards the goal of marketability and consumption (Davies and Bansel, 2007) and this logic transfuses the dynamic of education and learning more generally, including self-help, spirituality, new age, fitness and health make-over genres, which hold specific pedagogical dynamics around perfecting the self (Ringrose and Walkerdine, 2008).

Gill and Scharff (2011: 7) have called for a closer examination of how neo-liberalism and postfeminism are mutually reinforcing discourses or logics and how neo-liberalism is 'gendered', suggesting both discourses thrive on a current of individualism and free choice, arguing women are to a greater extent than men figured in the dynamics of change, transformation and self-regulation invoked through neo-liberalism. As Tasker and Negra (2007: 2) describe:

> Postfeminist culture works in part to incorporate, assume, or naturalise aspects of feminism; crucially it also works to commodify feminism via the figure of the woman as empowered consumer. Thus postfeminist culture emphasises educational and professional opportunities for women and girls; freedom of choice with respect to work, domesticity, and parenting; and psychical and particularly sexual empowerment. Assuming full economic freedom for women, postfeminist culture also (even insistently) enacts the possibility that women might choose to retreat from the public worlds of work ... postfeminism is white and middle class by default anchored in consumption as a strategy ... for the production of the self.

In this book I explore how neo-liberal *educational* discourses and practices have directly contributed to postfeminist notions about female power and feminine success (Gonick, 2004; Gonick *et al.*, 2009). Aapola, Gonick and Harris (2005) usefully suggest, however, that girlhood is constantly articulated through competing modes of celebration *versus* crisis. I map out how educational debates, discourses and policies feed into and shape oppositional representations of girls as *either* empowered consumers/winners *or* vulnerable victims of sexualised society. I explore a series of crisis discourses or what I position as 'postfeminist panics' over girlhood and the implications of these and relationships to educational debates and policies.

Blackman and Walkerdine (2000), drawing on Cohen, define 'moral panics' as public anxieties that certain forms of behaviour are 'deviant' and pose a menace to the social order. Lynne Segal (1999) talks about 'gender anxieties' over shifting and destabilising feminine and masculine 'roles' and subject positions as this relates to transformations in contemporary late modern cultures characterised by de-industrialisation and the partial break down in conventional 'sexual contract' and gender roles in the private and public spheres as theorised over twenty years ago by Carol Pateman (1988). Moral panics and shared group anxieties are a useful framework for thinking about the affective dimensions and dynamics of how public discourses circulate and emote. It helps us understand the power of some *educational* discourses to grip the public imagination and individual psyches and enliven controversy and fear over the 'gender order' (Connell, 1987). I develop my arguments about postfeminist panics over girlhood in the first few chapters of the book. Chapter 2 outlines a panic about overly successful girls, Chapter 3 a panic around overly aggressive girls, and Chapter 4 a panic surrounding overly 'sexy' girls. Overall, I argue that these postfeminist panics about girls and 'girlhood today' work to reconstruct universal notions of girlhood and ideal and deviant types of girls. They also tend to gloss over on-going issues of sexism, sexual objectification and sexual violence facing girls at school and in the family and wider social spheres (Baker, 2008).

Postfeminist, educational 'entanglements'

Returning to unpacking and defining what postfeminism actually means, Rosalind Gill, another key thinker and writer on postfeminism, explains that while postfeminism has become a central term of feminist critique in recent years, it is often used fuzzily to indicate very different meanings (Gill and Scharff, 2011). Firstly, and perhaps most confusingly, postfeminism has been used as signalling an 'epistemological break' with other forms of feminism, so that it is aligned with postmodernism or poststructuralism and seen as a particular type of new feminist theory or analysis (Genz, 2006). Secondly, postfeminism has been used as synonymous with third wave feminism, and to distinguish it from second wave feminism (Gamble, 2001). Thirdly, postfeminism has been described as a media-generated 'backlash' discourse that blames feminism and women's gains for social ills, generating new forms of 'retrosexism' or 'new sexism', that suggest men are the victims of political correctness, affirmative action etc. Stephanie Genz (2006: 336) suggests that these various discrete boxes for understanding postfeminism are problematic, illustrating an 'unwillingness to engage in postfeminist plurality'. Gill and Scharff (2011: 4) argue, drawing on Angela McRobbie, that postfeminism represents more of a complex 'entanglement' with feminisms. They urge following McRobbie in a move to 'position postfeminism as an object of critical analysis *rather than* as a theoretical orientation, new moment of feminism or straightforward backlash' (ibid.). In this book I adopt this last way of thinking about postfeminism as a 'sensibility' or set of dominant discourses that infuse and shape the zeitgeist of contemporary culture.

Yet while the body of postfeminist inquiry has grown in areas of cultural and media studies, the ways these discourses are informing and informed by educational discourses have thus far been largely neglected (Harris, 2004; McRobbie, 2008).[4] I seek to redress this gap, exploring how postfeminist thinking infiltrates and shapes the political realms and policy domains of education. What is particularly interesting about the notion of 'post'-feminism for the 'Foundations and Futures of Education' book series is that it signals the time, space and movement of feminist activism, politics, theories and research methodologies. Rather than promoting the idea of postfeminism as a teleological development of feminist phases over time, or heralding the end or 'death' of feminism (Nurka, 2001), I use the notion of 'post' to signal different spaces and moments, the history and futurity of feminist engagements with education. Postfeminism is therefore a 'heuristic device' (Collins, 1998) used to trouble our ideas about what feminism has been, is and can be in relation to the sexual politics of education and schooling.

Postfeminist sexual politics and resistance

To briefly illustrate the contemporary context of sexist sexual politics under exploration in this book I want to introduce one further example. The second significant postfeminist political moment I want to consider began in 24 January 2011 when a Canadian Police Officer, Michael Sanguinetti, offered a routine 'personal safety' visit at Osgoode Law School at York University in Toronto. Sanguinetti began his talk with the disclaimer 'You know, I think we're beating around the bush here.' He went on to deliver the now infamous line 'I've been told I'm not supposed to say this – however, women should avoid dressing like sluts in order not to be victimised.' What Sanguinetti did not know was that several outraged young women in attendance[5] would go on to publicise his deeply misogynist comments globally, and organise the Toronto 'SlutWalk', a political march to protest the comments, which has now spread virally across major cities in a host of countries.[6]

Sanguinetti's comments illustrate the spatial and temporal elasticity of postfeminist politics because they express a form of retrosexism (Atwood, 2006) – what a woman wears can provoke sexual attack – yet his comments are offered in the contemporary moment as part of official guidance about personal safety during a police visit to a Canadian university campus in 2011. Sanguinetti's remarks highlight a state of sexual politics in dominant culture that legitimises rape and victim blaming. His comments also pithily illustrate one of the main points I will argue in this book, which is that despite the beliefs that women 'have it all', that ground gender equality mythologies, women are still subject to deeply sexist, widespread cultural mores that their bodies are the bearers of sexual (and other forms of) morality (McClintock, 1995) and strongly held socio-biological beliefs about relations between the sexes, that the female body holds the sexual power to overcome men's rationality (Gavey, 2005). Women's bodies remain the prime site of sexual regulation, which is why whether it is clad in a bikini or a burqa it is a site of controversy and discipline from men and other women (Werbner, 2007).

The international SlutWalks that arose in relation to these events are an important example of postfeminist politics and valuable in introducing this book because they help to signal new forms of political action that both respond to and resist sexist cultures of masculine violence, but also incorporate liberal feminist notions of sexual freedom, through the donning of nipple tassels at the marches, for instance (McCartney, 2011).[7] The SlutWalks illustrate both a continuation and a rupture from previous forms of feminist activism by aiming to reclaim or 're-signify' the injurious label of slut and turn it into a signifier of celebration and resistance (see Ringrose and Renold, 2012). This works to overturn the classed dynamics of sexual rivalry and regulation between girls and women as well (Attwood, 2007). In this book I will spend considerable time unpacking the form of heterosexualised power dynamics (Butler, 1990) through which women's and girls' bodies are regulated in class- and race-specific ways but also the ways that girls are resisting these dynamics through the same type of re-signifying dynamics apparent in the SlutWalks.

A central paradox explored in the book is if girls and women are so 'successful' and 'aggressive' at the expense of boys, as some media and educational discourses imply, why are girls and women still subject to oppressive sexual politics, including intensified (hetero)sexualised regulation (Gill, 2008) in both private and public spheres? The book disrupts the postfeminist mythologies that have been called the gender 'equality illusion' (Banyard, 2010), arguing that we are facing on-going and in some cases renewed and intensified forms of (hetero)sexist sexual politics in education and schooling. In response to the breakdown of fixed gender roles in society we find pushes towards re-stabilisations of binary construction of male and female (Braidotti, 1994), which I examine as manifestations of postfeminist dynamics. In light of this re-fixing of gender and sexual difference, I also seek to rejuvenate an older second wave feminist discourse of 'sexual politics' (Millet, 1968), as signalled in the title of the book, to take forward my thinking. I will argue, in direct contrast to postfeminist celebratory discourses of girlhood, that we are facing on-going and perhaps intensifying sites of sexual regulation of girls' bodies as the new contemporary conditions of sexual politics in schooling and beyond.

As noted, this book fills a significant gap in writing on postfeminism, largely dominated by media and popular cultural analysis by exploring how 'real' girls respond to and negotiate normalised and sometimes 'hidden' postfeminist cultures of sexism through two empirical research projects focused specifically on the dynamics of girls' friendships, peer cultures, intimacies and identities at school and online. I use innovative psychosocial theoretical and methodological tools to present research findings on teenage girls' own perspectives and responses to postfeminist discourses of girlhood, which intimately shape their experiences of education. I also explore how girls speak back to and disrupt sexual regulation by re-signifying and taking up sexual discourses, objects and symbols in new ways.

Organisation of the chapters

I begin to develop my arguments by exploring the relationship between media representations of girls and gender and educational policies and discourses, exploring mass postfeminist panics over girlhood in Chapters 2 through 4. Chapter 2 outlines a panic over 'failing boys' and 'successful girls', examining trends in educational debates on gender and achievement (Epstein *et al.*, 1998; Skelton and Francis, 2008). It demonstrates the mass circulation of educational discourses about girls' success in the public domain through an analysis of a global postfeminist 'mediascape' and processes of 'mediatisation' where media and educational policy mutually inform one another (Gerwitz *et al.*, 2004). I illustrate the 'discursive effects' (Foucault, 1980a) of a 'successful girl' discourse – its influence on wider globalised postfeminist politics and contemporary understandings of gender equality. I show how the mainstream press has promoted reactive educational arguments such as girls benefitting 'too much' from the feminisation of education, while boys are suffering. The failing boys panic is argued to have shifted understandings of sexism and gender equality from a feminist analysis of patriarchal power relations underpinning the social and schooling (Arnot *et al.*, 1999) to a postfeminist educational policy terrain that reinterprets 'gender gaps' and sexism to refer almost exclusively to the need to help boys catch up to girls in school. Internationally in Western (largely Anglophone) contexts boys are positioned as the new 'disadvantaged' (Lingard, 1998, 2003). The chapter draws on international research on government policies on achievement to illustrate the wide-reaching impact of this postfeminist panic. I also touch upon how the discourse of girls' success has been harnessed as a neo-liberal performance marker exported through development discourses where girls are viewed as a crucial human capital factor for stimulating economic growth in the global South (Gill and Koffman, forthcoming).

Chapter 3 continues mapping the relationship between media discourses on girls and educational policy and practice by exploring a related international postfeminist panic over mean, bad and violent girls, tracing how it impacts educational policy and practices around bullying (Owen *et al.*, 2000a). I look at claims that girls are becoming meaner and more covertly aggressive as well as bigger bullies than boys. This is argued to be a postfeminist discourse that reverses earlier claims of girls' vulnerability (Gilligan, 1982) to new universalising claims that girls are becoming more aggressive than boys (Crick and Rose, 2000). I explore international policy interventions around girls' aggression and bullying. In North America and Australia a host of new educational, psychological, therapeutic and disciplinary interventions have emerged to regulate 'relational' and 'indirect' feminine aggression (Simmons, 2003; Owens *et al.*, 2000a) coded as a white, middle class problem of irrational, pathological femininity. In the UK, however, despite growing psycho-educational research, policy and practices around girls' bullying and behaviour, the UK media largely ignores everyday issues of middle class, sexualised competition and aggression among girls (Ringrose, 2006a, 2008b), focusing instead on violent, deviant 'problem girls' (Lloyd, 2005) who are increasing being targeting and criminalised, as I document (Alder and Worrall, 2004). Education's role in these raced and classed splits is considered, including new ways of managing failure, through policies and practices of discipline within and beyond school.

Chapter 4 explores a paradox between the construction of girls as successful, neo-liberal winners, examined in Chapter 2, and another recently escalating postfeminist panic around girls and 'sexualisation'. While fears about girls' sexuality have long posed a moral problem in society (Jackson, 1982; Walkerdine, 1997), these concerns have recently heightened in the midst of an international moral panic over the 'too early' and 'hyper' 'sexualisation' of children and young people, particularly girls (Papadopoulos, 2010). I explore some of the media and popular culture content of the sexualisation debates, asking: how do the sexualisation debates invoke feminism; in what ways is the sexualisation debate cut through with explicitly postfeminist discourses? I also explore what the sexualisation discourses are saying about girls; questioning whether it offers any useful resources for understanding the pressures facing girls in society, at school. I will suggest the sexualisation discourse is profoundly racialised and classed and the call to a return to girlhood innocence is a protective discourse around middle class femininity and childhood (Egan and Hawkes, 2008, 2010). I also illustrate how the moralising trends in the sexualisation panic resonate with explicitly protectionist UK sex education (SRE) policies and discourses. I review some SRE policy and curriculum guidelines, which focus on disease and pregnancy and 'parts and plumbing', constructing sexual activity as a burden for young women to delay as long as possible, and reconstructing girls as passive sexual recipients of sex who are also, however, responsible for sexual conduct in heterosexual contracts (Allen, 2004). I argue that schools are not dealing with the most pressing issues presented by 'sexualisation' such as 'pornification' (Paasonen *et al.*, 2008) and new forms of digital sexual intimacy.

Chapters 5 and 6 set out new theoretical and methodological pathways for researching girls and gender and education in a context of postfeminist discourses of girlhood. Chapter 5 reviews key debates on 'agency' in relation to girls and femininity. I touch upon a need for 'intersectional' approaches (Mirza, 2009; Ali *et al.*, 2010) to map girlhood that account for raced, classed, sexualised and gendered (and other) differences, but question the notions of structure and agency in many educational accounts of the subject. I discuss the use of 'agency' in some gender and educational empirical research, critiquing how agency can be (implicitly) tied to notions of rational 'choice' and transparent accounts of the self and power in analysis of narratives from girls. Responding to this, I review how governmentality approaches rooted in Foucault (1980a) have helped in understanding new technologies of the self and in mapping discourses as relations of power that are regulative and work to govern subjectivities, with particular implications for young femininities (Rose, 1999a; Walkerdine *et al.*, 2001; Harris, 2004). I outline key postfeminist debates from feminist authors who argue we have to re-evaluate how we understand 'agency' in postfeminist, neo-liberal contexts where empowerment and choice discourses are appropriated and actually become a key 'technology' through which the self is lived, and femininity is constructed with oppressive effects (McRobbie, 2004; Gill, 2007; Baker, 2008).

Chapter 6 looks at recent attempts to build upon and enrich discursive traditions through psychosocial and affective methodological approaches. First I explore Butler's theories, which posit discursive re-signification as the process of transforming social norms (Butler, 1993). I also raise questions about discursive determinism as well as the subjective processes involved in re-signification. To answer these questions I explore a UK research tradition of psychosocial studies, explicating the work of Valerie Walkerdine (and colleagues) in particular, to consider how 'discursive positions' and contradictions are negotiated by subjects in very psychically complicated ways (Henriques *et al.*, 1984; Hollway and Jefferson, 2000; Walkerdine *et al.*, 2001). Dissatisfied with the psychoanalytic theory of desire as lack, however, I then discuss an 'affective turn' in social theory outlining the methodological implications of 'transcendental empiricism' found in Deleuze and Guattari (Hickey-Moody and Malins, 2007). I explore the methodological value of Deleuze and Guattari's philosophy for understanding change and possibilities of ruptures to formations of power. Key concepts such as 'schizoanalysis', 'assemblages', 'deterritorialisation', 'lines of flight', 'becoming', 'smooth and striated space' and 'molecularity' are explained for their methodological relevance in mapping girls' disruptions of heterosexualised (oedipal/conjugal), gendered power dynamics. Throughout the chapter I draw on methodological examples and data analysis to illustrate the explanatory power of the various approaches.

Chapter 7 responds to my chapters on postfeminist panics and sets the theoretical terrain and methodological strategies developed into motion, outlining a study on girls' friendships, conflicts and entry into teen heterosexualised dating cultures. The findings are based on focus group and individual interviews with racially and economically marginalised girls aged 12–14 attending an inner-city school in South Wales in an area of high economic deprivation. The chapter explores how diverse girls are coping with cultural and schooling environments that demand competitive aggression at so many levels, focusing on their negotiation of what I call the heterosexual playing field at school. The chapter challenges postfeminist notions about gender equality, illustrating concerns about boyfriends, appearance and sexual desirability have certainly not receded in importance (Kindlon, 2006) for most girls. My findings illustrate how the majority of conflicts at school relate to heterosexual regulation of girls bodies, and sexual status and identity in the peer culture, which intimately shape educational experiences, although these are often 'hidden' and part of the informal curriculum of schooling. A psychosocial analysis of girls' narratives explores the complexities of negotiating relationships and conflicts, particularly focusing on sexualised name calling and 'slut shaming'. The ways girls resist sexual regulation at school are traced as 'lines of flights' (Deleuze and Guattari, 1987) or rupturings of what Butler (1990) calls the 'heterosexual matrix'.

Chapter 8 continues to challenge the postfeminst panics around girls, particularly the panic over 'sexualisation', drawing on research on how older teen girls are negotiating postfeminist media cultures and performing new digital sexual identities online. I explore findings from a project that researched teens' (aged 14–16) use of social networking sites (SNSs) in two UK schools, illustrating how SNSs are increasingly mandatory spaces of peer relationships and intimacy that tend to extend and intensify peer relationship networks at school (boyd, 2008; Selwyn, 2008). SNSs are theorised as sexualised virtual spaces and assemblages through which girls are performing their sexual subjectivities, friendships and relationships. In contrast to postfeminist notions about gender equality in wider social spheres and schools, I illustrate again how girls continue to be defined by their bodies in class and race specific ways in online culture. I also challenge any simple divide between the online and offline, given how digital experiences thoroughly mediate young people's relationships and experiences at school. I consider examples of girls' self-sexualisation, and also sexual cyber-aggression, mapping how girls negotiate sexual regulation and expression online and offline in complex ways. Again I map how lines of sexual subjection are disrupted and resignified, illustrating 'lines of flight' from regulative, molar norms through analysis of girls' interview narratives and their digital, online representations and communications.

My conclusion, Chapter 9, centres on bringing the threads of the book together to summarise the implications of my discussion of postfeminist panics of girlhood for education. First I consider some media coverage of my own research in UK broadsheets which serves as a reminder of the negative affective force of postfeminist sentiments. The coverage highlights a vehement rejection of calls for feminism in schools, highlighting neo-conservative and neo-liberal drives towards 'real' and 'rigorous' schooling focused on academic priorities. Challenging this view, I argue we need to continue to work on explicitly feminist responses to the problems I've outlined in the areas of school achievement, behavioural issues, PSHE, sex and relationship and media education. I detail the need to deal with gendered and sexual inequalities as a comprehensive issue in schools. I consider which spaces of hope are opening up politically for feminism presently, and raise questions about which aspects could be harnessed and developed educationally to re-imagine the sexual politics of schooling.

2 Successful girls?

Exploring educational media and policy 'scapes' and the postfeminist panic over feminine 'success'

In opposition to the largely liberal feminist concerns to address issues of self-esteem and vulnerability in 'girls' during the 1980s and 90s, at the start of the current millennium we have been faced with a 'postfeminist' onslaught of discourses about 'girl power' and the increasingly commonsense 'presumption' of gendered equality in education and work (Foster, 2000; Harris, 2004; McRobbie, 2004; Taft, 2004). It has been widely argued (see Adkins, 2002; Francis and Skelton, 2005) that education, work and the labour market have been 'feminised'. In 1997 the UK left wing think-tank Demos noted the 'future is female', suggesting women were set to enter the labour market in huge numbers, suggesting the kinds of work which stress characteristics ascribed to femininity – service, empathy, communication, nurturance, to-be-looked-at-ness would be the ones in demand (in Walkerdine et al., 2001). Ten years later, a 'futurologist' for British Telecom, Ian Pearson, confirmed the worrying trends in the 'gender order' (Connell, 1987) with the headline 'The future is female' (BBC News, 23 April 2007b) which warned of a future dominated by female-oriented jobs that will 'displace' men. As discussed in the introduction to this book, in 2011 David Willetts, Minister for Universities and Science in the UK Coalition Government, was quoted as touting feminism as 'trumping egalitarianism' through a 'transformation of opportunities for women [that] ended up magnifying social divides' and worsening employment opportunities for (particularly working class) men (Prince, 2011).

The media cannot create this type of narrative on their own, however. The discourse of feminine success is co-constructed through and with educational research on girls. For instance, Harvard psychologist Dan Kindlon's book *Alpha Girls: Understanding the new American girl and how she is changing the world* (2006) outlines the mythical qualities of the new 'successful girl', suggesting the 'alpha girl' is poised to change the world, economically, politically and socially, as a new hybrid that embodies the best traits of masculinity and femininity. Kindlon suggests this new hybrid is somehow confident, assertive, competitive, autonomous, future oriented, risk taking, as well as collaborative and relationship oriented but not obsessed with boyfriends or her physical appearance. The UK broadsheet, *The Times,* wrote a story based on the book: 'Free at last: alpha teenage girls on top' (Allen-Mills, 2006, October 15):

alpha girls [are] the new breed of ... schoolgirl growing up free of gender stereotyping and ideological angst. They are the daughters of the feminist revolution, but they see no need to become feminists themselves because they know they are smarter than boys.

Mediascapes and mediatisation

Whilst any media analysis is in danger of becoming 'dated', my interest is to map some of the 'patterned constructions' of how gender and feminism (Gill, 2007: 268) are constructed in relation to education in the media and in turn how this informs educational policies and vice versa. In analysing the relationship between media and educational discourses, I draw on Arjun Appadurai's (1996: 9) notion of 'mediascape' and 'ideoscape' to develop the idea of a 'postfeminist mediascape'. As Appadurai (1996: 35–36) notes:

> Mediascapes refer both to the distribution of the electronic capabilities to produce and disseminate information (newspapers, magazines, television stations, and film-production studios), which are now available to a growing number of private and public interests throughout the world ... mediascapes ... tend to be image-centered, narrative-based accounts of strips of reality, and what they have to offer to those who experience and transform them is a series of elements (such as characters, plots, and textual forms) out of which scripts can be formed of imagined lives, their own as well as those of others ... These scripts can and do get disaggregated into complex sets of metaphors by which people live (Lakoff and Johnson 1980) as they help to constitute narratives of the Other and protonarratives of possible lives, fantasies that could become prolegomena to the desire for acquisition and movement ... Ideoscapes are also concentrations of images, but they are often directly political and frequently have to do with the ideologies of states and the counterideologies of movements explicitly oriented to capturing state power or a piece of it.

A poststructural reading suggests that mediascapes and ideoscapes are never actually separable, since media narratives are always infused with ideological or discursive meanings (Kenway and Bullen, 2008; Gill, 2007). So in this chapter I will use 'mediascape' to refer to how the media shapes gendered fantasies and scripts and affective states like anxiety and fear around a discourse of 'failing boys' in school. I also want to extend the metaphor of scape to refer to international policy 'scapes' of education. Policies are increasingly 'mediatised' or shaped and informed by the media (Fairclough, 2000; Levin, 2004). The media 'shapes public opinion by directing readers to adopt particular policy priorities and assign responsibility for political issues' (Cohen, 2010: 106). The media has a massive impact on how gender and educational issues will be discursively understood and addressed as a contemporary social phenomenon, and which issues will be prioritised and given resources (Blackmore and Thompson, 2004; Gerwitz *et al.*, 2004).

This chapter begins to illustrate how a postfeminist mediascape appears to influence the educational policy-scape, reinforcing regressive sexual politics. I map some of the 'discursive effects' (Foucault, 1980a) of an educational 'failing boy' moral panic (Epstein *et al.*, 1998) spanning two decades, which co-constructs a binary 'other' – the figure of the *overly* 'successful girl' who disturbs the natural 'gender order' (Connell, 1987). I start by briefly outlining the development of 'educational feminism' and the struggles to gain educational equality for girls in Western contexts and the subsequent reversal to 'recuperative masculinity' panics over under-achieving boys (Lingard, 2003). The point of the chapter is *not*, however to re-hash the well-worn debates over whether or not an abstract, universal category of girls *really* are doing better than boys through re-analysis of statistical schematics which compare 'data' on fixed rates and variables by gender. Gorard (1999), Skelton and Francis (2008), Younger and Warrington (2007), Ivinson and Murphy (2007) among others have gone to great lengths to deconstruct the statistical construction of a UK 'gender gap' in favour of girls. There have been endless debates over whether it can be proved or not. Rather my goal is to question the relevance of the comparisons and why they are news worthy. I illustrate how the media selectively pick up on educational truth claims about boys' failure, creating a dominant pattern whereby the figure of the failing boy is reified. I explore how this figure haunts educational policies on gender and I analyse the implications of these postfeminist constructions.

From education feminism to postfeminist education?

Education has been a core issue for women's activism for centuries (Gamble, 2001). Early proto-feminist texts like Mary Wollstonecraft's *A Vindication of the Rights of Women* (1792) dealt at length with questions of female education, partly in response to Rousseau's notion that what girls needed to learn was how to look after men. In the developed world, women's access to secondary and, especially, higher education in many cases continued to be limited until the twentieth century (Weiner *et al.*, 1997); at Cambridge, women were not granted full degrees until 1948. And access to education for girls is still a problem in many developing countries (Aikman and Unterhalter, 2005).

Educational equality became a primary goal of the women's movement in the twentieth century (Arnot *et al.*, 1999). In the UK, the Education Act of 1944, which established the principle of free secondary education for all, prepared the way (Weiner *et al.*, 1997) for a series of 'equal opportunity' laws put in place from the 1970s onward, including the Equal Pay Act (1970), the Sex Discrimination Act (1975) and the Race Relations Act (1976) (Arnot *et al.*, 1999). Arnot *et al.* (1999: 7) note that in the UK in particular, the development of what they call 'education feminism' was central to the post-war era of social democracy.

Second wave feminists explored how girls and women were marginalised in many aspects of education (Weiner *et al.*, 1997). In the UK, feminists focused on the sexist curriculum, the limited range of girls' subject choices, and female students' generally poor performance in mathematics and science (Kelly, 1981; Walkerdine, 1989; Riddell, 1989). Others (e.g. Weiner, 1985) looked at the school experience: matters such as sexual harassment, lack of space and attention in the classroom (Spender, 1982), and whether girls and boys should be educated together or separately (Arnot, 1984).

Arnot, David and Weiner (1999) argue that the educational feminism of this period launched a global social movement demanding not only a 'gender blind approach to education' but equality of outcome and gender equity in society. Programs intended to redress a 'gender gap' (Arnot *et al.*, 1999) to address sexism facing girls were established across the developed world. However, in the UK and Canada, for instance, the relative decentralisation of education meant that feminist education initiatives tended to be localised, with little sustained funding: 'deeper structural changes and substantive modifications to curriculum to incorporate women's knowledge and experience proved ... difficult to implement' (Eyre and Gaskell, 2004: 6). Modest improvements came as liberal feminists, in particular, entered the policy field and gained a certain amount of leverage. This was especially noticeable in Australia, where a class of what became known as 'femocrats' working with the national government grew and assumed influential positions (Eisenstein, 1996).

With their focus on 'equal opportunities' as a key indicator of progress for girls and women, liberal feminists expressed concern that most girls were choosing subjects such as home economics and languages, and that the few who did take maths and sciences tended to 'underperform' in those subjects. However, research at the time also showed girls were actually not under-performing in any subject at the primary level, and that they were outperforming boys in subjects like English at the secondary level (Walkerdine, 1989).

In England and Wales, equal opportunity in education was finally formalised in 1988 with the introduction of a National Curriculum. For the first time, girls and boys had to take the same core subjects until they reached school-leaving age. League tables (public statistical tables) were introduced to gauge performance across gender and other variables. Gender differences were thus systematically measured for the first time and it was found that girls were not only outperforming boys in language subjects but were also catching up in maths and sciences more rapidly than boys were catching up in languages. In 1995 girls had gained a head start over boys in mathematics and science by the age of seven: in mathematics 81 per cent of girls had reached the expected level compared with 77 per cent of boys; in science the percentages were 86 and 83 per cent respectively (Arnot *et al.*, 1999). According to Jackson (1998), by 1996 public debate increasingly reflected the new 'facts' of gender equality in the UK:

- In English girls outperformed boys at ages 7, 11, and 14; results in maths and science were broadly similar.
- Girls were succeeding in traditional 'boys' subjects such as technology, maths and chemistry (adapted from Jackson, 1998: 78).

Arnot and Phipps (2003) argue that these types of results were touted as representing one of the most important changes in the history of social inequality in the UK. Academics argued that claims about boys' under-performance and girls' over-performance were exaggerated and played upon by the UK press (Epstein *et al.*, 1998).[1]

Postfeminist fears over the 'feminisation' of schooling

UK mediascapes

Concern has continued unabated. Worries that the introduction of supposedly new, more feminine modes of testing (fewer 'sudden death' exams), and 'softer' subjects (like sociology or drama) has been bad for boys have emerged repeatedly (Phillips, 2002). In 2002 a columnist with the *Daily Mail* suggested that 'wholesale feminisation' had made the education system 'unfair and discriminatory against boys' (Phillips, 2002). Four years later, *The Times* published another story on how 'Boys are being failed by our schools', citing Dr Tony Sewell who once again blamed a 'feminised' system and teachers who, instead of encouraging the development of 'male traits such as competitiveness and leadership … celebrate qualities more closely associated with girls, such as methodical working and attentiveness in class' (Clarke, 2006). In addition to recommending recruitment of 'more male teachers, particularly to primary schools', Dr Sewell called for 'replacement of some coursework with final exams and a greater emphasis on outdoor adventure in the curriculum':

> We have challenged the 1950s patriarchy and rightly said this is not a man's world. But we have thrown the boy out with the bath water … It's a question of balance and I believe it has gone too far the other way.
>
> (*The Times*, 2006)

The 2008 *Daily Telegraph* 'The future is female …' article cited above similarly 'reveals' how women 'are poised to become the dominant force in the workplace over the next decade, paving the way for a dramatic feminisation of society'. Although the article is on jobs, the educational discourse of failing boys is ushered into the dialogue by a psychologist quoted as imploring the government to take action with boys: 'Ministers must take note of these figures and do more to support boys at school to stop them falling off the ladder.' Statistics on male primary teachers (13 per cent) are also cited to underscore how 'many fear the imbalance has left young boys without positive role models'. Sue Palmer, author of *Toxic Childhood* is also quoted as saying:

> the gender imbalance in education has gone too far and threatened to lead to a similar imbalance in the workplace … school is becoming increasingly feminised. We have the concentration in coursework in exams, schools becoming more and more risk averse, which is a female trait, and there is less emphasis on the physical outdoor stuff. Boys are turning off.

We see similar headlines in 2010: 'Eton head says UK education is failing boys', which cites the headmaster warning, 'British system of education is failing to give boys the help they need and has become too focused on girls'. The headline statement is used to support a political goal of single sex schools or classrooms because 'boys require a much more physical and active style of learning' (Ross, 2010).

Another article 'Girls think they are cleverer than boys from age four' (Shepherd, 2010) from a study on 'Gender expectations and stereotype threat' warns us about the dramatic effects of teachers' poor expectations of boys, urging teachers to stop using phrases like 'silly boys' and 'schoolboy pranks' for fear of its negative effects on boys' psyche and development. Robbie Hartley, an academic, is quoted as saying 'gender bias' is normative and it's 'acceptable to pitch girls against the boys'. While it seems that Hartley is actually arguing against girl–boy comparisons in order to resist gender stereotyping, what is clear is that the broadsheet picks up and runs with the gender dichotomy 'girls think they are cleverer than boys' as the headline. I will argue in my conclusions to this chapter that this is because postfeminist gender anxieties propel largely negative affects that make for sensational press and can sell news stories.

Beyond the UK

A similar pattern of postfeminist educational politics and media sensationalism emerged in Canada following the introduction in 1993 of the School Achievement Indicators Program (SAIP), which analyses achievement levels in mathematics, sciences, reading and writing. At that time, concern was expressed that boys were falling behind girls in literacy and reading (Davison *et al.*, 2004).[2] The Canadian government became concerned over results of new tests conducted by the Programme for International Student Assessment (PISA, 2003) reporting that 'girls performed significantly better than boys on the reading test ... in all ten Canadian provinces'. Although it was noted 'few significant differences were found' in maths and science, the government still pointed to the reading results as grounds for concern that 'boys [were] lagging behind girls' (Statistics Canada, 2004).

According to Bouchard, Boily and Proulx (2003), articles reporting boys' school-related problems became increasingly common in Canada's English-language press following the 1999 release of a report by the hyper-conservative Fraser Institute (a 'think tank') entitled 'Boys, girls and grades: Academic gender balance in British Columbia's secondary schools' (Cowley and Easton, 1999). Although the report drew attention to the fact that girls were still constrained in their choice of subject – 'stereotypical course preferences remain firmly entrenched' – the point picked up by the media was 'girls and boys do not, on average, fair [*sic*] equally well in our secondary schools' (Bouchard *et al.*, 2003). Finding that 'on average girls out-perform boys by statistically significant margins on nearly all of the Report Card indicators', the authors of the Fraser Institute report raised what they called 'a provocative question: Are girls actually learning more or are school based assessments systematically biased against boys?' (Cowley and Easton, 1999: 8).

Concern about the possibility of a bias against boys reinforced fears that too many teachers were women, and that testing methods and school environments generally were therefore too 'feminine', signalling the rise of what Bouchard, Boily and Proulx (2003) call a 'masculinist' discourse around 'school success by gender'. Before long a 'failing boys' panic had spread across Canada, generating a spate of articles with headlines like 'La misère scolaire des garçons' (Gagnon, 1999) and 'It's time to give boys our attention' (quoted in Bouchard *et al.*, 2003). Another story on 'The Gender Gap' (CBC News, 2003) described how girls have benefitted from a feminist 'cottage industry' of strategies including:

> Girls-only physics classes, math and science camps, and female role models aimed at closing that gap ... The efforts with girls worked. Today 30 per cent of engineering students at Canadian universities are young women. More women than men are applying to medical schools. The demographics are rapidly shifting ... across the developed world, countries are looking very closely at this issue, trying to figure out strategies and innovative policies and approaches that will work for boys.

The report also cites Doug Trimble, a 'respected principal', who launched his own boys' strategy:

> 'It's great what we've done for girls, but boys, we're not doing what we need to for boys in school,' Trimble says. '[It's a] common fact. People can't argue. Can't debate that one.'

We can see a postfeminist dynamic of reprisals against feminism and a new logic of 'misery' for boys touted as common sense, un-debatable 'fact'. Bouchard *et al.* (2003: 26) suggest:

> The cornerstone of the discourse is the women's movement has achieved gender equality and that, as a result of the battle waged by women, they have managed in the space of a few decades to catch up to men in virtually every field. Women have allegedly gone beyond equality and relegated men to second place, even in fields that were traditional male domains.

As another Canadian media story frames the issues:

> After decades of focusing on finding ways to ensure girls weren't kept behind on the basis of their gender, statistics show it's the boys who are falling behind ... barriers that once kept girls out of universities are crumbling ... many girls have developed good multi-tasking skills through balancing school, sports, work and volunteering, giving them an advantage ... While we've done a very good job of challenging stereotypes that limit girls' potential l... as a society we've allowed tired old myths of what it means to be a male to remain standing and now boys are paying the price.
>
> (Connell, 2005, emphasis added)

Taft (2004) explains that this type of postfeminist argument that boys are 'paying the price' follows the logic that 'girls and women are doing fine [and] feminism is unnecessary'; not only have girls attained 'all the power they could ever want' but (here as a result of feminist interventions such as maths and science camps, the emergence of strong female role models, and the apparent feminisation of school and work alike) they may actually 'have too much power in the world' today (Taft, 2004: 72).[3]

Indeed, the Canadian Council of Ministers of Education, which administers the SAIP, registered concern that women will *eventually leap ahead of men* in the education, jobs and earnings race' (cited in Froese-Germain, 2004). Canadian educational researchers note that the media-driven 'perception among some parents/ guardians and educators that boys in school are being shortchanged' was taken up by many provinces and school boards that made new curricular and instructional plans for improving boys' literacy a priority (Davison *et al.*, 2004: 50; Wallace, 2007). New pedagogical interventions have been implemented in Canada to redress male disadvantage including:

> calls for more male teachers in schools (and male role models in boys' lives generally), more books that boys can relate to, and 'active learning' strategies in the classroom ... same-sex schools and classrooms, a return to traditional values ... a more teacher-centered approach to instruction for boys, increased testing ... using computers to sustain boys' interest ... [and] injecting a healthy dose of competition into one's instructional approach ... [to] suit boys' learning style.
> (Seeman, in Froese-Germain 2004)

A similar dynamic emerged in Australia where authors like Jane Kenway (1997), Bob Lingard (1998, 2003) and Wayne Martino and Michael Kheler (2006) have analysed a 'what about the boys' educational discourse as 'one element of a broader masculinity politics which attempts to argue that men are the new disadvantaged and that masculinity is under siege and in crisis in the face of the putative success of the feminist reform project' (Lingard, 1998).[4] Lingard contextualises the panic over boys in Australia and elsewhere as linked to globalisation and rising inequality, bleak employment opportunities and job insecurity for many as the 'backdrop to the politics of resentment and backlashes of various types. For example, emergent backlash national chauvinisms and new racisms'.[5]

Australian research has also traced a particularly acute anxiety over feminisation of schools and a perceived lack of male teachers (Lingard, 1998; Martino *et al.*, 2009; O'Donovan, 2006). This is captured in a 2008 article reporting on the keynote address by Dr Leonard Sax, visiting US education expert at the National Boys' Education Conference:

> Dr Sax, executive director of the National Association for Single Sex Public Education in the US, is in no doubt 'we live in a sexist society'. He said some teachers at all-boys' schools were able to use the 'all-boys format to break down the gender stereotypes' ... Speakers will talk about teaching in the single-sex environment and discuss motivating and engaging boys ... Tracey Padley, whose three sons attend The King's [boys] School, said her children were encouraged

to be boys at the single-sex school. 'They're allowed to run around,' she said. 'They're allowed to climb and play. They can relax and be who they are without competing with the girls.' Alison Saleh, who also has three sons at the school, said boys' needs were different to girls'. 'When you have them integrated in the same classroom, their needs aren't necessarily being met.'

(Sydney Morning Herald, Oct 12, Price, 2008)

In a striking reversal of feminist discourses, 'sexist society' has come to exclusively refer to the barriers facing boys at school and a need for 'boys to be boys' is advanced (O'Donovan, 2006). The global 'flows' (Appadurai, 1996) of the discourse of the 'failing boy' is also evident in the US keynote speaker's address to the Australian audience, which levels the two vastly diverging national contexts as if each context is facing the exact same issues.

Thus a comparable dynamic to the UK is evident in Australia where the emergence of concerns about boys' educational achievement have now centralised the 'what about the boys' question on the political agenda. According to O'Donovan (2006: 482) the report 'Boys getting it right' (Gill, 2005) 'remains the most significant and influential contemporary statement on gender in Australian education'. The report invokes a 'crisis meta-narrative' and contends that boys 'exhibit different learning styles from girls that are not accommodated by schools', and boys are suffering from 'the absence of fathers, the lack of male teachers, inappropriate curricular and teaching strategies, the feminisation of curricula and assessment systems and the declining status of men' leaving boys the 'new disadvantaged group' (2006: 480–482). The report also cemented convictions of 'feminism having run its course' (O'Donovan, 2006) and boys as 'more adversely affected' and 'not coping *as well as girls*' with the changes wrought by globalisation ('Getting it right', cited in Gill, 2005: 109, emphasis added).

Becky Francis (2006) notes that while the USA was relatively slow to take up the issues around feminisation of education because of its focus on ethnic inequality, a generalised concern over 'boys' underachievement' has developed. A 2003 cover story in the US *Business Week* entitled 'The new gender gap' discussed 'alpha femmes' describing girls' achievement as 'a kind of scholastic Roman Empire alongside boys' languishing Greece' (cited in Froese-Germain, 2004). Another cover story from the *New York Times,* in April 2007, focused again on the problems of high-achieving 'Super girls', discussing girls' overarching success and the perils of balancing academic excellence (Rimer, 2007). Again we find the fantasmic figure of feminine success positioned as a direct consequence of feminism. Hoff-Sommers' *The War against Boys: How Misguided Feminism is Harming our Young Men* (2000) and a 2006 national survey finding that 'young boys [are] failing across the US' (Swicord, 2006) are also notable.

Effects of the 'failing boys' discourse on UK policy scape

In the 'seminal' 1998 edited volume *Failing Boys* (Epstein *et al.,* 1998), Michele Cohen wrote instructively about the complex representational politics of the UK 'failing boys' debate. She draws on historical data to argue that the longstanding idea of boys' academic superiority is a myth: 'boys have always underachieved and more importantly, this underachievement has never been seriously addressed' (1998: 20).[6] The reason that boys' underachievement had never before been identified as a problem, according to Cohen, was that historically their successes were attributed to their innate intellect and ability, while their failures were attributed to external factors such as 'femininised' teaching methods. In the case of girls the scenarios were reversed: successes were attributed to the same external factors (such as feminised teaching methods) that were injurious to boys, while failures were attributed to innate intellectual inability.[7] Thus Cohen argues it is historically inaccurate to suggest that underachievement among boys is something new. She points out girls' recent achievements have tended not to be valued for their own sake, but rather for what they seem to tell us about boys (that they are falling behind). Cohen also draws attention to the tendency to blame boys' problems on a feminised system created by feminists.

Yet, well over a decade after *Failing Boys,* the 'moral panic' over boys' 'underachievement' has continued to dominate contemporary UK policy debates on gender and education (Skelton and Francis, 2008), 'channeling debate into a narrow set of perspectives associated with the policy drive to raise "standards" in education' (Ali *et al.*, 2004: 1). I do not have space for an exhaustive policy review, which would also be futile in a context of 'policy overload' and 'fatigue' given the constantly changing policy landscapes described by Ball (2008). My intention is to illustrate how the gender gap logics and failing boy figure continues to haunt educational policies on gender, shaping the nature of reports and guidance thereby impacting allocation of resources and energies in schooling.

In the UK the impact of the failing boys' panic was visible in the four-year (2000–2004) Department for Education and Skills 'Raising Boys' Achievement Project' which was developed as a 'holistic' school resource, focused entirely on 'helping boys succeed' (Younger and Warrington, 2005). The focus on 'helping boys succeed' indicated a complete reversal of the 'closing the gender gap' discourse initiated by Arnot, David and Weiner (1999) which was developed to describe feminist struggles to fight sexism against girls in education. The gender gap has since come to refer in a 'common sense' way to the gap facing boys.

In the 2007 UK Labour government's policy document 'Gender and education: the evidence on pupils in England' (DCFS, 2007) the effects of the failing boys debate are clear. While claiming to be about 'gender and education' more broadly, the report is entirely preoccupied with achievement as evident in its own description 'the focus [of the report] is not solely on the "gender gap" and "boys' underachievement" but also acknowledges that, on the one hand, boys are also high attainers, and on the other hand, that many girls face significant challenges' (DCFS, 2007: 6). Here we see that the report wants to move away from the gender gap but has to continue engaging with it to either dispel or support its rationality. At some points the report tries to critique the common sense of the achievement gap facing boys, saying class and ethnicity can hold larger impacts on attainment, and at other points it goes on to support the gender gap logic and offer positive points about boy-tailored learning strategies in schools.

The most significant aspect of the report for my arguments is how discursively gender and education as a policy field is constituted only in relation to attainment gaps. Significant issues like behaviour and safety are raised in the report (school discipline problems, leaving and truancy) but only as key 'indicators' of racialised (black) and working class boys' 'failure to attain'. Every issue is reduced to the outcome of attainment. What happens conceptually is that gender as a relation or as a culture or as an identity is never able to be addressed. Gender is only considered valuable for what it can tell us (or not) about achievement (Connell, 2010). The report makes 'failing' black boys and white working class boys the object of social intervention, which otherises and pathologises these groups of boys and masculinities and reifies an image of boys' failure, which I return to in the final section of this chapter. Discursively it also privileges the 'poor boys', mentioning white working class girls struggling with attainment but never analysing or elaborating these trends so that the overall assumption remains that of girls as more successful.

The report therefore reveals the narrow conception of what constitutes a 'gender' issue in the current UK educational policy domain. The wide spectrum of gender issues facing girls and boys (differently according to race, class, culture and location), such as sexism, heterosexism and homophobia in schooling and popular culture (Francis, 2005; Renold, 2005); gendered violence and issues of sexual bullying (McNeil and White, 2007; Ringrose and Renold, 2010); gender-specific dynamics of exclusion (Osler and Vincent, 2003); gendered behavioural issues (like self-harming or eating disorders) (Crudas and Haddock, 2005) are never adequately addressed (Mendick, 2011). They are left to other policy domains, while ostensibly they should be a relevant 'gender and education' issue in their own right.

The 'Gender and education' report is commendable for at points trying to dispel some of the assumptions embedded in the gender gap discourse. But the next set of governmental guidance in 2007 on gender for the early years, is once again, however, specifically targeted at young boys and achievement (3–7 years). The instructions, titled 'Confident, capable and creative: supporting boys' achievements' (DCSF, 2007) were a series of prescriptions (with supporting case studies) for teachers to re-masculinise boys and 'unlock', through careful diagnosis, their academic potential by drawing out their innate masculine learning styles. The report warns that 'boys [with] their natural exuberance, energy and keen exploratory drive may often be misinterpreted' (DCSF, 2007: 3). Urging practitioners to make sure 'boys' learning journeys are reflected on and celebrated with the child, parents and peers' (DCSF, 2007: 22). Here again, then, we find a melancholic attachment to the figure of the victim boy within government guidance focused on essentialised understandings of masculinity and gender (Renold and Ringrose, 2011). Unsurprisingly, the most recent policy guidance from the UK Coalition Government Department for Education website, confirms the trend:

> The Department has introduced a range of strategies to address the gap in gender achievement and to raise the performance of all pupils. The National Strategies, at primary and secondary … provide support for techniques to tailor teaching and learning to the needs and interests of boys. Helpful techniques for boys

include setting clear objectives to help them to see exactly what they have to learn, and interaction with the teacher in the whole-class sessions keeps boys motivated and involved.

(Department for Education, 2010b)

A recent UK Coalition Government White Paper (Department for Education, 2010a) illustrates, however, a contradictory, but perhaps even more worrying trend to empty out gender concerns almost completely from the educational policy landscape. The report opens with a sweeping foreword by Michael Gove:

> Throughout history, most individuals have been the victims of forces beyond their control ... Opportunities for women outside the home were restricted. Wealth governed access to cultural riches. Horizons were narrow, hopes limited, happiness a matter of time and chance. But education provides a route to liberation from these imposed constraints. (p.6)

In a report on the implications of the 2010 White Paper, my colleagues and I (David, Ringrose and Showunmi, 2010) have explored how it celebrates a culture of 'hyper-performativity of schools, teachers and pupils' and a 'competitive ethos' focused on individualised attainment, suggesting the White Paper 'reads like an exemplary neo-liberal recipe for DIY self-hood' (Harris, 2004, in David *et al.*, 2010). Via de-centralisation, devolution, and the championing of individual students, parents, teachers and schools as the various units of educational entrepreneurialism, we see the brave new schooling world of the 'Big Society'.

Key aspects of the White Paper surround 'improving discipline by trialling a new approach to exclusions', 'a transformed curriculum with rigorous assessment and qualifications', 'more academies and free schools', and more 'school-led improvement, replacing top-down initiatives'. What is most striking, however, is the White Paper does not even use the variable gender, focusing for instance on issues of homophobic bullying, whilst neglecting the cultural context of gender and sexism for girls in schools altogether. Perhaps another effect of the melancholic gender war has been this most recent rendering of gender as a non-issue for educators – another manifestation of the postfeminist equality myths under scrutiny in this book.

Measuring gender equality? Using and abusing feminism

Globalisation has resulted in massive restructuring of education systems where improving student achievement is seen as a crucial part of the effort to make the nation state marketable (David, 2004). In this climate, schools are under increasing pressure to produce an 'effective' suitably skilled and adaptable, 'employable' work force (Morely and Rassool, 1999). Efforts to improve school 'effectiveness' by setting quantifiable goals and measuring performance are consonant with 'neo-liberal' governments' emphasis on individual attainment and flexibility as the keys to both educational and career success in globalised contexts of social, economic and political transformation and instability (Hursh, 2005; Olssen and Peters, 2005;

Lauder *et al.*, 2006). According to Sherene Benjamin (2003), the international preoccupation with testing has produced a 'techno-rationalist' culture of 'curricular fundamentalism' in which schools and teachers are required to aim for specific, quantifiable versions of 'achievement'. Assessment-driven policies promote a culture of performativity, standards and effectiveness in schooling at the student, teacher, school, regional and national levels (Ball, 2008). Internationally, the results of 'high stakes' (Apple, 2006) standardised tests are used to lend weight not only to neo-liberal discourses of 'excellence' (Lucey and Reay, 2002) but also to governments' claims of success at addressing issues of social exclusion and inequality.

In this climate, comparative evidence showing that girls outperform boys on standard tests can be used for 'proof' (or not) of gender equality (David, 2004). In this way a liberal feminist formula of inserting girls and women into a highly class and stratified society can be shown to have 'worked' (Bryson, 1992). Girls' high test scores can be used as evidence, a measure that shows they have conquered social barriers. This works discursively to legitimate the system and to suggest that feminist goals have been attained, since what counts as success is reduced to high attainment on a test score. Test scores by gender becomes an equality tick box, like other affirmative action politics, greatly reducing what we understand gender to be in school. As Mendick has suggested (Mendick, n.d.), 'the boy's underachievement debate controls how we understand gender and education. It makes us pay more attention to some things and forget about other things.' It creates lenses for seeing and categories of knowing what is a gender issue or not.[8] This is why we are now able to see the UK Coalition Government effectively 'phasing out' gender from their policy papers, as one of my students recently put it. By constructing test scores as 'the' measure of equality, gender equality can effectively be treated as 'sorted'.

Thus one of the most significant implications of the postfeminist successful girls discourse for this book is how it has shifted and reduced understandings of gender and education away from any understandings of wider issues of *sexism*. We have witnessed a shift from a feminist stance that understands complex socio-cultural patriarchal power relations as underpinning social institutions like schooling (Spender, 1982) to what I am calling a postfeminist educational policy terrain that understands 'gender gaps' and 'sexist society', to refer almost solely to the need to help boys catch up to girls in school (Skelton and Francis, 2008). Universal categories of girl and boy set up a binary conception of gender where boy can be set against girl. There is a 'sex war' mentality and a see-saw pendulum (boys' failure vs girls' success and vice versa) (Jackson, 1998). Naturalised gender differences (like boys learn differently) are re-asserted, and there is a denial of other forms of gendered and sexualised difference and power shaping educational experience (Ivinson and Murphy, 2007). The construction of naturalised, universal gender and sex differences is a key dynamic of postfeminist politics (Gill, 2007) here playing out through the educational achievement debates.

More than two decades of anti-racist, postcolonial, black, critical race, feminist and sociological theory and research has challenged the statistical rates of comparing universal categories of 'identity' in educational policy. Comparing all girls vs all boys ignores the way gender is differentiated by other 'intersecting' or 'articulating' axes of experience and identity, or the many other social discourses that produce inequalities of social class, race and ethnicity (Mirza, 1992; Gillborn and Mirza, 2000; Youdell, 2006; Archer *et al.*, 2007; Ali *et al.*, 2010). Gender treated as a stand-alone variable without reference to economic and cultural factors of class and/or race can easily be used to prove either inequality or equality, comparing abstract bodies in a form of 'bio-politics' of social control that create new knowledges and norms as theorised by Foucault (1982). Critiques of statistical analysis and a genuine 'intersectional approach' is, however, difficult for policy makers to engage as we saw above in my brief analysis of gender and education policy documents, as policy makers are often tied to having statistically relevant evidence about rates of attainment (Shain and Ozga, 2001).

I will argue throughout this book that an intersectional analysis, via a poststructural lens, which analyses how class and race shape experiences of gender and sexuality, is crucial for deconstructing postfeminist discourses and panics. In the UK, schooling outcomes of success and 'excellence' are still largely the preserve of middle class students who benefit from the 'cultural capital' of their parents (Lucey and Reay, 2002; Skelton and Francis, 2008). The 'failing boys/successful girls' discourse obscures the reality that middle class white boys continue to succeed at school alongside their female counterparts, while many working class and BME (Black minority ethnic) boys *and* girls face significant gaps vis-à-vis more 'socially privileged' groups (Crozier and Reay, 2004; Gillborn, 2008). Walkerdine, Lucey and Melody (2001: 112) in their book *Growing up Girl* analysed how exam results from high-achieving girls at high-achieving schools have obscured the degree to which achievement is always a 'class related phenomenon', arguing that attainment figures based on gender alone serve to hide the class component of girls success. They also describe how girls and feminism get blamed for social problems like deindustrialisation:

> It was formerly relatively easy for boys to obtain employment that did not require high levels of literacy, a particular accent or stylish attractiveness ... However, fewer of those kinds of jobs exist in affluent countries and so boys are now being pushed to remake themselves as literate, adaptable and presentable: it is this that has produced a crisis for 'working-class masculinity' and it is this that sets girls' educational achievement as a particular problem in the present ... It is as though the success of girls has somehow been responsible for the dramatic and distressing changes that have happened over the last twenty or so years.
>
> (Walkerdine *et al.*, 2001: 112)

The crisis of working class masculinity continues to form a central discourse in the postfeminist mediascape. The recent focus on specifically white, male middle class poor performance in school, both in policy reports as I have outlined (DCSF, 2007) and occasionally in the press (Richardson, 2008), is perhaps laudable but the media consistently positions this 'problem' as resulting from girls' successes, preventing nuanced analysis of deindustrialisation, globalisation and accompanying processes, as we saw in the more recent headlines too. Apparently it is easier simply to blame feminism. Girls, women and the feminine can be held accountable for all manner of cultural effects. This dynamic of feminist and girl and woman blaming is profoundly *postfeminist* because it comes in the wake of cultural shifts enabled by feminism, yet seeks to recuperate these in the most simplistic and oppositional of ways.

Finally, however, whilst feminism is often blamed for male disaffection in the West, a contradictory effect of the successful girl and girl power discourses is how the simplistic story of girls success in Western context is being deceptively employed to fuel a story of girls' over-arching success in both the global North and South where 'governments and NGOs also look to the minds and bodies of young women for whom education comes to promise enormous economic and demographic rewards' (McRobbie, 2004: 6; see also Harris, 2004). Offra Koffman has called this dynamic the 'girl effect' in development discourses which suggest that the liberation of girls is the human capital pathway to national debt resolution and salvation (Gill and Koffman, forthcoming). Koffman's work examines the notion that 'adolescent girls hold the key to ending world poverty' which she argues 'underpins the initiative titled "The Girl Effect" promoted by a coalition of organisations including Nike, the UN and the World Bank'. For instance in the promotional materials girls are discussed as an 'untapped resource' who have 'the unique and indisputable potential ... to end poverty for themselves and the world'.[9] In this way the UN Millennium Development Goals for gender equality are being used strategically to erase the complexity of cultural issues relating to gender, education and development (Unterhalter, 2007) and girls' potential educational success is formulated as a magic bullet for economic prosperity. The supposed 'successful girls' transformation in the West is heralded as having the potential to transform Third World debt and poverty and supplanted onto the Global South (Gill and Koffman, forthcoming).

Conclusion

There are then, multiple, contradictory effects of the failing boys' discourse, which has generated gendered fears and anxieties and an accusatory, shadow binary construction of the educationally overly 'successful girl'. These logics can be used to promote a story of losing boys and winning girls, which has manifested as masculinity crises in the West, and fantastical solutions to problems of globalisation and economic disparity in the global South. Perhaps most pertinent for my arguments in this book is how the narrative can also be used to position gender as a non-issue in Western education today, which ends up neglecting the sexual politics of schooling for girls.

Indeed, Anita Harris (2004) and Aapola, Gonick and Harris (2005) have argued that one of the most powerful effects of the myth of the successful 'can-do' girl is the construction of a binary other, the 'at risk', failing girl who does not meet the idealised tenets of feminine success. As I proceed I will continue to deconstruct the postfeminist panic that girls are either overly successful, and its corollary that there are no longer any salient gender issues to address in UK schooling. I will explore two further sites of panic over risky and 'at risk' girls, including anxieties over girls' excessive aggression and violence in Chapter 3 and fears about girls' unruly sexuality in Chapter 4. I demonstrate that the situation facing contemporary girls of varying class and race backgrounds is certainly much more complex than entering gender-neutered school environments, or embracing some easy, there for the taking, educational and therefore life 'success'.

3 Mean or violent girls?

Exploring the postfeminist panic over feminine aggression

Having explored the discourse of successful girls in Chapter 2, this chapter explores how this established narrative of girls' success, power and adaptation relates to constructions of girls' aggression and their capacity to act out, and be direct both verbally and physically. I continue to explore a shift away from constructions of girls as vulnerable victims toward an ever-increasing onslaught of stories about girls' power and powerfulness (Aapola *et al.*, 2005; Projansky, 2007). Here I focus on a related international postfeminist media driven panic over girls as 'increasingly aggressive' and mean as well as bad and violent (Gonick, 2004; Batchelor, 2009).

First I look at the sensationalised mediascape that argues that girls' aggression is increasing, asking: how is it that girls' aggression can be repeatedly positioned as novel and shocking? Next, I explore psychological developmental discourses of female aggression and adolescent girls' aggression, in particular, which suggest that if indirect or relational aggression is measured girls are as aggressive as *or more* aggressive than boys. I suggest these discourses are postfeminist in that they reverse earlier claims of girls' vulnerability into claims of mean-ness and powerfulness.

In North America and Australia a host of new educational, psychological, therapeutic and disciplinary interventions are emerging to regulate simplistic notions of feminine aggression (Owens *et al.*, 2000a; Simmons, 2003) while the international mediascape mobilises anxiety over the social 'costs' of an aggressive, feminine subject that has entered into the public sphere. I look at the complex, contradictory ways in which feminism is implicated in the postfeminist construction of the new problem of girls' aggression: how feminism is positioned as responsible for unleashing 'too much' girl power in the form of mean, successful girls (Taft, 2004). I also look at how UK psycho-educational research and policy around bullying and behaviour has incorporated naturalising assumptions about girls as indirectly aggressive (Besag, 2006).

Finally, I explore how, in contrast to successful but mean girls, violent girls are constructed as abject 'losers', through class-based logics of deviance, and are subject to disproportionate discipline (compared with boys) (Lloyd, 2005). I argue that we are witnessing a complex, contradictory media-led representational terrain where some (middle class) girls are positioned as at-risk feminine subjects who express aggression pathologically, as indirect, mean bullies, for instance, which put them in need of psycho-educational interventions (Aapola *et al.*, 2005). 'Other' girls (primarily working class), meanwhile, are represented as risky out-of-control subjects, in need of greater legal interventions.

The sensational mediascape of girls' aggression

Having researched the issue of girls' aggression since the mid-2000s, it is possible to track the media coverage of this issue during the past decade as continuously evoking stories and images of girls' aggression as increasing, shocking and disturbing – a 'crisis' (Gonick, 2004). Girls are repeatedly positioned as becoming worse or more aggressive than boys. In 2002, headlines suggest 'Girls are now bigger bullies than boys' (McVeigh, 2002); in 2006, *The Guardian* asks again: 'Are girls worse bullies than boys?' (Leach, 2006). The issue of 'girl-to-girl cruelty', depicted as on a massive upsurge in 2002, is positioned as an 'epidemic' in 2008 (McVeigh, 2002: 1; Talbot, 2002; Asthana, 2008). For example, the *New York Times* magazine headline story 'Mean girls' (2002), which was picked up in the UK *Observer*, outlined how girls' cleverness makes them 'like sharks', dangerous, 'crafty' and 'evil' masters of 'intricate rituals of exclusion and humiliation' and as manifesting 'insidious cruelty' in their drive towards power, practices boys are 'not smart enough' to engage in (Talbot, 2002: 6; Hill and Hellmore, 2002). In the 2008 *Observer* article 'Crackdown on schoolgirl bullying epidemic' (Asthana, 2008), an educational psychologist, Valerie Besag, is quoted[1] as warning that '"vicious" and "manipulative" girl-on-girl bullying' is wrecking lives. Girls' aggression is positioned once again as 'far more damaging than the ways that boys intimidate each other' with '12 or 13 year old, girls' said to behave 'like "dodgem cars"' with 'bitchy behaviour … women's last barrier to triumph in the work place' that 'schools have a duty to eradicate'. Here schools are set up as places that must manage and 'eradicate' feminine pathology in the form of bitchy aggression.

Similarly, since the mid-2000s reports on girls as the prime motivators and victims (of each other) of cyberbullying have grown exponentially, emphasising that girls (more than boys) are using new technologies such as texting, instant messaging and social networking sites to wreak havoc on one another. Stories like 'Teen girls turn to cell phones, instant messaging to intimidate', from the *Rocky Mount Telegraph*, underscore this trend, telling us 'Fourteen-year-old Tricia Smith will probably never know who called her a whore 350 times in one day. But her intuition – and a growing body of research – tells her it's another girl' (Oliviero, 2004). Another headline 'Internet gives teenage bullies weapons to wound from afar' was again first-page news in the *New York Times* in 2004 (Harmon, 2004). This time we learn about a girl who received 50 text messages per hour, a 'barrage of electronic insults', like 'stuck-up bitch', from her girl 'cyberbullies' after she reported to her teacher that her pencil-box full of make-up had been stolen. The same headlines repeat in 2006: 'Are girls worse bullies than boys?' This report tells us 'research suggests that girls are adopting increasingly sophisticated methods of bullying – taunting, alienating and using SMS and instant messaging as forms of social intimidation. It makes the traditional violent methods used by boys seem almost comforting' (Leach, 2004). In 2007 we are told 'Girls more likely to suffer cyberbullying' (*The Guardian*, 2007). In 2009 headlines report: 'Teenage girl is first to be jailed for bullying on Facebook' (Carter, 2009), which outlines how Keeley Houghton was jailed for posting 'Keeley is going to murder the bitch' about another teen girl on her Facebook profile. Here girls are positioned as both risky and at risk of hyperaggression, particularly from one another.

Incidences of 'bullycide' which appeared in the early 2000s (Lawlor, 2002) continue to be widely reported as in a recent example: bullies 'jeered at leap girl as she lay dying' where Rosimeiri Boxall jumped to her death out of a window to escape girl bullies (Evans, 2009). Stories about increases in 'girl gangs' and girls who 'murder' (Leach, 2004; Twohey, 2004) that circulated in the mid-2000s are replicated repeatedly: 'Violent girls making the headlines' (BBC News 2008); 'Menace of the violent girls: Binge drinking culture fuels surge in attacks by women' (Slack, 2008); 'The feral sex: The terrifying rise of violent girl gangs' (Bracchi, 2008). The most recent headlines focus on the 'riot girls' of the London 2011 riots (*The Metro*, 2011), describing working class girl 'yobs' and 'chavs', as I will explore in more detail in the final section of this chapter (Haydon, 2011).

In the popular cultural domain more generally, during the 2000s multiple Hollywood films depicted teen girls' aggression and violence, for example *Mean Girls* (2004), *Thirteen* (2005), *Odd Girl Out* (2005). TV chat shows (*The Oprah Winfrey Show*, 2002), 'documentary' news programmes (BBC *Panorama*, 2005, 2009) feature length documentaries (*Rats and Bullies*, 2004), and radio programmes (CBC *It's a Girl's World*, 2004) worked to further internationalise and universalise discourses of girls' increasing aggression, exploiting public anxieties over teenage girls in crisis (Aapola *et al.*, 2005).

These repetitions evoke the question: why are issues of girls' aggression repeatedly and hysterically positioned as new and shocking? What is it about girls' aggression that continues to make it newsworthy? What I will suggest is that these sensationalised media headlines play on our emotional investments, cultivating affect – a sense of moral outrage and fear over changing forms of femininity, particularly disruptions to the status quo. Media reports present a plethora of confusing figures of mean bullies, violent offender girls gone 'wrong', and also victim girls (who typically suffer, however, at the hands of other girls), which need to be unpacked. At first sight these headlines may appear to signal the same type of story, that of girls' aggression gone awry. But the shock-driven media machine is drawn to different types of issues. First it focuses reports on girls' mean-ness to other girls (often positioned as the pathological cost of a too successful femininity competing with and manipulating other girls). Second it focuses on more extreme gender transgression, such as the violent 'ladettes' or 'riot girls' who belong to gangs, drink and use physical violence (meaning they are becoming too masculine) (Jackson, 2006). I will argue that these two discourses around mean and violent girls are highly classed. 'Meanness' is constructed as a middle class norm of repressive and pathological femininity, whilst girl violence is marked out as low class, becoming too masculine, and deviant. Stories of girls' aggression constitute a complex and contradictory representational terrain that centres on staking out the limits and possibilities of what it means to be feminine. I start by examining the discourses and research paradigm that has naturalised the indirectly aggressive mean girl.

The invention of indirect and relational aggression

Girl violence and aggression can only be repeatedly constituted as surprising and disturbing because violence has traditionally been coded male (Motz, 2001). As Burman *et al.* (2001: 1) suggest 'theories of female delinquency and violence ... have tended to be constructed out of existing theories based on male experience' contributing to 'patterns of female invisibility'. Put simply, if violence (read as direct aggression) is constructed as masculine, this sets up the feminine as non-violent and indirect.

Research on girls' 'relational' and 'indirect' aggression has responded to and attempted to reverse claims of essential female nurturing. Researchers from Sweden questioned whether 'males are in general more aggressive than females' (Bjorkqvist and Niemela, 1992: 4). The research looked at issues of motivation to aggress, claiming 'laboratory studies reveal that females behave as aggressively as males when they are not in danger of being recognised ... [a] fact that gives support for the view that women are as aggressive as men, as far as the motivation to hurt is concerned (ibid.: 14). This work was situated as a feminist challenge to the male bias in studying aggression, which has constructed a passive, 'non-aggressive' female, and as a corrective to preoccupations with whether males are more aggressive than females that ignored analysis of how females aggress (ibid.: 6, 13). Through the development of a 'peer nomination questionnaire, the Direct and Indirect Aggression Scales or DIAS, which included 12 items representing indirectly aggressive behaviours' Bjorkqvist sought to disprove earlier male-biased research and determine 'the gender and developmental differences in quantities of these behaviors' (Owen *et al.*, 2000a: 68), arguing that women aggress in qualitatively different ways that are indirect.

These claims about female indirect aggression were then taken up in the USA by developmental psychologist Nicki Crick (Crick, 1996; Crick and Grotpeter,1995) who used the term 'relational' aggression a few years later to examine young girls' use of relationships to hurt and psychologically injure those they are close to. Crick also used a 'peer nomination instrument to measure gender differences or to correlate indirect aggression with various measures of social psychological aggression' (Owens *et al.*, 2000a: 68). Crick and Jennifer Grotpeter (1995) argue that 'relational aggression' is the deliberate manipulation on the part of a child 'done with the intention of damaging another child's friendship or feelings of inclusion within a social group' and to 'thwart or damage goals that are valued by their respective gender peer groups' (Crick and Grotpeter, 1995: 710, 711). They claimed that relational aggression is engaged in with much higher levels by girls than boys, and includes a range of behaviours such as excluding another child from a play group as a form of retaliation, intentionally withdrawing friendship as a way of hurting or controlling a child, and spreading rumours about a child to persuade peers to reject her (Crick and Grotpeter, 1995: 711). Nicki Crick's research is said to have 'revolutionised the field's understanding of sex differences in psychopathology ... [and] taught us that girls also experience adjustment difficulties in childhood ... and that girls manifest an array of mental health problems in childhood, including those of an externalising nature (e.g., relational aggression)'. As psychology professor Carol Dweck of Columbia University is cited as saying, 'Crick has completely changed the field of aggression from an exclusive emphasis on boys and physical aggression ... [which] now takes seriously the fact that girls can have a problem with aggression and that aggression can involve an assault on other children's relationships' (in Mount, 1997: 2).

From a critical sociological perspective, Crick's psychological, developmental approach is inherently normative and essentialising. She has written articles arguing that relational aggression is a predictor for antisocial personality features among girls like engagement in illegal activities. She has argued that while overt aggression among males decreases as they get older, girls' relational aggression increases in adolescence and into adulthood, when stealing boyfriends and spreading rumours increases. Moreover, she suggests boys have to learn about relational aggression from girls once they have more sustained intimate relationships with them during and after adolescence (Crick and Rose, 2000: 158), although boys who display relational aggression are argued to be 'significantly more maladjusted than relationally aggressive girls', so there is some implication that masculinity might be at risk in displaying these types of feminine qualities (ibid: 164). Taking gender equivalency logic to its extreme in the form of a reversal, Crick suggests females may actually be the *more* aggressive gender in adolescence and adulthood (ibid: 158).

Martha Hadley's (2003: 340) review of this research has also pointed to problems with asserting a 'gender normative position' on aggression, which misses socio-cultural contexts as well as individual differences. My interest is in the naturalisation of the notions of indirect and relational aggression as a *feminine developmental issue and problem*. Chesney-Lind and Irwin suggest that the psychological literature on adolescent aggression 'came in part as a backlash to years of feminist research claiming that women are more nurturing, caring and relationship oriented than men' (2004: 49). Particularly in the work of Crick the novel discovery of relationally aggressive girls arises out of prior representations of girls' moral goodness, nurturing, sacrifice, silence and victimisation and vulnerability (Gilligan, 1982). Thus the developmental psychology reverses ideas about feminine passivity and nurturing, taking as its central claim that 'girls may be as aggressive as boys if gender specific forms of aggression are considered' (Moretti *et al.*, 2004: 3). But the truth claim that girls are as aggressive as boys can only be made in this debate by positing a distinctly feminine and indirect form of aggression different from that of boys (Bjorkqvist and Niemela, 1992). Girls' aggression is depicted as 'indirect', 'relational', 'social' and 'psychological' and expressed through a 'hidden culture' and 'secretive syndrome' claimed to be 'spiraling out of control'[2] (Crick and Grotpeter, 1995; Simmons, 2003).

Relational aggression is also naturalised as the logical extension of feminine repression, which has a pathologising dynamic where the feminine is set against a neutral, normal male version of aggression. As feminists we need to ask questions about where this research direction leads. What are the discursive effects of claims that girls are naturally relationally aggressive, and if this is accounted for are actually more aggressive than boys? What is the point of the construction of new gender differences and comparisons?

New strategies to manage feminine aggression

My interest in this section is to illustrate how the truth claims about indirect and relational feminine aggression have spread and become 'common sense' in both popular culture and educational domains. We are seeing the spread of technologies of psychological and pedagogical regulation in response to a perceived crisis over femininity and girls' aggression. Experts on feminine aggression and new regulative techniques have emerged – new therapies, health and educational programmes and parenting strategies have developed to manage the problem. Research on feminine indirect and relational aggression, what is also called psychological and social bullying, has grown among psychologists, criminologists and educationalists internationally in Europe, the USA (Putallaz *et al.*, 2007), Australia (Owens *et al.*, 2000b; Shute *et al.*, 2002), Canada (Pepler *et al.*, 2003) and the UK (Besag, 2006). Implementing the psychological research on indirect aggression, educational researchers in Australia (Owens *et al.*, 2000a, b) have been particularly influential in normalising understandings of girls as indirectly aggressive, positing that girls' aggression 'interfere[s] with the close personal relationships that are of paramount value to peers' (in Hadley, 2004: 342). But as Hadley (ibid.) has suggested, these approaches normalise this 'condition' without asking why or searching for deeper social meanings (see also Brown, 2003). The adoption of notions of girls' indirect aggression into educational literatures on bullying has fed into much wider state-funded policies, programmes and schemes to diagnose and treat girls' problematic (pathological) behaviour, depicted as on the increase and as universally generalisable to the vast majority of girls (Besag, 2006; Smith and Sumara, 2003).

I am interested in how understandings of these naturalised and individualised feminine conditions feed easily into a postfeminist cultural and media domain where the research on indirectly aggressive girls is repeatedly cited and normalised. The internet is now awash with references to relational aggression, including a Wikipedia site on 'relational aggression' oriented toward 'field building' which cites key authors in the field (including Nicki Crick). The site lists 'gossip, lies, betrayal, isolation, exclusion and humiliation' as the hallmarks of relational aggression, suggesting 'relational aggression is more common and more studied among girls than boys'.[3] In the context of privatisation and philanthropic organisations of the USA the discourses of girls' indirect aggression has thrived. The Ophelia programme, for instance, which was founded on Mary Pipher's (1995) theories of girls' self-esteem as in crisis particularly in transitions to 'womanhood', now positions itself as 'the' site for resources on dealing with 'relational aggression' and also offers club and camp packages[4] (Gonick, 2006). The Ophelia Project works to raise awareness about what it calls an 'epidemic of relational aggression'[5] and markets new therapeutic techniques, educational texts and psychological strategies on its web page. From speakers who travel the USA talking in schools to educational liaisons who will assist in the start up of anti-aggression programmes, for those parents who can pay to manage their girls' pathology, resources have developed to calm growing anxieties.

Faux-feminist solutions to girls' pathological mean-ness are increasingly popularised through such websites as well as mass marketed books like Rachel Simmons' *Odd Girl*

Out, The Hidden Culture of Aggression in Girls, which was the subject of an entire episode of Oprah Winfrey dedicated to exploring girls' relational aggression in 2002, and turned into a Hollywood movie in 2005. The book has since been updated with a new chapter focused on cyberbullying and relational aggression that promises to 'help girls handle the dangers of life online' (Simmons, 2011). Rosalind Wiseman's *Queen Bees and Wannabes* (2002) led to the creation of the 'Empower Program' for girls with courses to analyse 'the social hierarchy of the school … the cycle of gossip, exclusivity and reputations … [and] to help liberate girls from it' (Talbot, 2002: 8). Wiseman's programme, which received hefty grants from organisations like the Liz Claiborne Foundation, is reported to be in 'high demand, especially at some of the tonier private schools in the Washington area' (ibid.). The *Mean Girls* movie, based loosely on Wiseman's text, further popularised pop-psychology interventions for dealing with girls' manipulative, indirect, catty aggression, as scenes in the movie model psychological interventions for tackling girl mean-ness (Ringrose, 2006a).

These mediascape representations of girls' aggression are postfeminist, typically positioning the crisis over aggression as feminism gone wrong and holding feminism accountable for the fostering of girls' aggression. It is as a result of too much power that girls are striking out, competing with one another with long-term 'costs'. This is apparent, for instance in the Canadian documentary radio series on girls' 'social bullying' called *It's a Girls World: How Girls Use their Power to Hurt Each Other*.

> New evidence suggests that women pack up their social baggage from childhood and tote it to the office with their briefcases. Professional relationships among women at work are mired in the same dynamics that propelled them into hurtful behaviours in their younger years. Now the stakes are higher – their career is on the line. More than that, the male-dominated organizational structures of the workplace … foster resentment, cut-throat competition and power struggles among female bosses and their employees. After four decades of feminist efforts and hard won parity with men, a woman's success may well come at the expense of her own sex.'[6]

This narrative suggests that feminism has created problems of women aggressively competing in the public sphere, effectively erasing the male-dominated nature of institutional power into which women have been expected to 'insert' (Bryson, 2002). The idea is that girls and women compete with each other because of inherent, manipulative competitive urges and we can see how the mean girl discourse relates directly to the discourse of successful girls. We are told we are seeing the social repercussions of girl power that has entered into the public sphere through feminist gains for women. This success cannot be handled, it is implied, by the pathological feminine subject.

It is through the complex interface of the media, popular culture, research and policy scapes that a discourse of girls' indirect aggression is increasingly cited, normalised and becomes commonsensical. In Canada, for instance, popular media sources such as Simmons' *Odd Girl Out* (2004), the Ophelia website, *Mean Girls* (2005) and the Canadian documentary *It's a Girls World* (2004), are listed as anti-bullying resources on the Upper Canada school board site.[7] As noted, the discourse of relational and indirect female aggression represents big business in the USA and is completely normalised in US policy and guidance on bullying. For instance, American guidance on cyberbullying indicates the naturalisation of girls as indirectly aggressive: 'Many teens today, especially girls, use technology to bully others ... because they feel protected by the Internet. It's much easier to type mean words to someone than to say them in person, but that doesn't make them any less hurtful'.[8] In this example there is a photo of a light-skinned, possibly 'black', ambiguously racialised girl on a bed texting.[9]

An American school board report 'How girls hurt: The quiet violence in your schools' (Vail, 2002: 1) pictures a close-up of a blond girl's face then describes indirect aggression as follows:

> Look at the pretty girl with the honey-blond hair, the one always in the middle of an adoring orbit of friends, the one with the seemingly endless supply of outfits from Abercrombie and Fitch. She has everything, all right, but popularity isn't always what it seems. She and other adolescent girls live in a world where best friends can become enemies overnight, where one look from another girl can mean the difference between isolation and belonging. It's a world where no one tells you why you can no longer sit at the lunch table with your friends, where secrets are traded like currency.

Here we find reference to a largely white, middle class femininity, and it is this very proximity to these idealised feminine characteristics which guarantee her repressive tendencies, her indirectness, penchant for secrets and hidden rage. In this school board guidance, as in the postfeminist mediascape, the mean girl is treated as the logical conclusion of inserting the feminine into the masculine rational worlds of education and work where feminine lack and indirectness adds up to feminine pathology.

Naturalising middle class mean girls: the UK media and policy context

In the UK we have explicitly classed stories of 'little miss perfect' (Rowland, 2006) who tyrannises others in the playground or from her computer. But she is actually from a posh and privileged background and uses her cultural capital to manipulate those around her: 'With bunches in her hair and impeccable vowels, you might imagine they are a schoolteacher's dream. But children of well-heeled middle class families have been dubbed the latest playground tyrants.' This article suggests 'well-to-do parents over-indulge them, mean(ing) they often have no respect for the authority of teachers, and are frequently among the main protagonists in playground bullying'. Although 'children' are cited, the protagonist is actually female (bunches in her hair), invoking the discourse of girls as increasingly manipulative feminine bullies. Another article 'What turns the nice child into a bully' similarly examines how nasty bully girls are 'middle-class "poppets"' and how nice, middle class girls demand adoration like 'queen-bees' (Palmer, 2006). We find a similar naturalisation of a middle class successful, so therefore manipulative and dangerous, construction of femininity as in the US popular literature (*Queen Bees and Wannabes*) and films (*Mean Girls*).

UK researchers and advocacy groups have explicitly engaged with and promoted the notion of girls as indirectly aggressive in their research on gender and bullying (Duncan, 1999; Smith and Sumara, 2003; Woods and Wolke, 2003; YWCA, 2002; Besag, 2006). Much early research on bullying and school policies was actually 'gender blind', though focusing on boys (Rigby, 1998). Now when policy reports do address gender there is a total naturalisation of category of boy and girl, and reference to scientific claims that girls 'psychologically' bully, incorporating notions of girls' 'indirect' aggression, while boys' are said to aggress physically. This can be seen in the DfES report, *Gender and Education: The evidence on pupils in England* (DCFS, 2007) which in a single page referring to behavioural issues, claims simply 'girls are more likely than boys to have been the victim of psychological bullying for example, being upset by name calling (37% compared to 23%) or excluded from a group of friends (19% compared to 5%)' while 'boys are more likely than girls to have been the victim of physical bullying, for example, being threatened with violence (23% compared to 18%) or to have experienced violence from other students (24% compared to 12%)'. There is no qualification upon these supposedly self-evident facts that girls experience 'psychological bullying' while boys experience 'violence'. On the DfE 'Healthy Schools' website links to the bullying guidance has similarly naturalised gender norms of aggression, self-evidently asserting that 'boys and girls exhibit different bullying behaviours'[10] with girls experiencing depression and self-esteem issues and boys the fall-out from violence. These indicators are taken at face value as measurable, generalisable truths, but this has effects as I map below.

In 2009, definitions of sexual bullying were added to the *Teachernet* web resource, suggesting bullying could be related to sexual orientation and stating that 'Sexual bullying may be characterised by name calling, comments and overt "looks" about appearance, attractiveness and emerging puberty. In addition, uninvited touching, inuendos and propositions, pornographic imagery or graffiti may be used'. These represented a more nuanced and complex look at the practices of aggression, however, this guidance has now been removed, and the official report brief on bullying on the DfE website reverts to naturalised assertions about girls' and boys' bullying, suggesting again that

> Girls are more likely to be bullied in psychological ways (such as name calling and social exclusion), and because these are more common types of bullying this means that girls are more at risk overall. However, boys are more likely to be bullied in more physical ways (being forced to hand over money or possessions, being threatened with violence or experiencing actual violence).
>
> (DfE, 2010)

The only cyberbullying report on the DfE website likewise suggests 'Girls were significantly more likely to be cyberbullied, especially by text messages and phone calls, than boys', yet offers no further guidance (Smith *et al.*, 2006).

Here we meet the dynamic I've been exploring throughout that girls' aggressive behaviour puts other girls 'at psychological risk'. While it is useful to point out the difficult effects of bulling for girls, the construction of girls as 'psychological' bullies sets up new norms, which then inform how gender relations are read and understood. What I would like to suggest is that a naturalisation of girls' and boys' patterns of aggression (girls as indirect, boys as violent) reinforces norms of girls as simply pathologically repressive and mean and boys as always physically violent. One effect of this is that it upholds conventions of appropriate feminine behaviour from girls as repressed and passive, which are coded through racial and classed ideals of femininity (Walkerdine, 1991; Hadley, 2003; Walkerdine and Ringrose, 2006; Ringrose and Walkerdine, 2007).

A second implication of naturalised assumptions that girls are indirect, mean bullies is the finding that this has led to a lack of resources or strategies for addressing the socio-cultural gender, classed and raced dynamics of bullying for girls in schools (Lloyd, 2005; Ringrose, 2008b). Audrey Osler has suggested that girls are separated into two camps, those that are 'not a problem' who face issues of an 'internalising' nature (Osler *et al.*, 2002; YWCA, 2002) vs those 'problem girls' who act out and disrupt norms of feminine aggression (Lloyd, 2005; Jackson, 2006). Osler and her colleagues (2002), in the only major UK study to address how issues of bullying relate to school exclusion, found that schools constructed issues facing girls as less important than managing the behavioural problems of boys, leading to major difficulties in addressing the 'invisible' and 'hidden' 'psychological' effects of bullying for girls (Osler *et al.*, 2002: 21) and an 'institutional failure to tackle issues facing girls effectively' nationally (Osler and Vincent, 2003: 5). Further research indicates that issues like self-exclusion (Osler and Vincent, 2003), self-harming (YWCA, 2002), eating disorders, and depression (Crudas and Haddock, 2005) among others facing girls are being neglected. Thus, naturalising discourses about normal girls as indirectly aggressive has not led in the UK to greater resources for coping with peer sexual bullying and violence in schooling (Duncan, 2006; Maxwell *et al.*, 2010). The bullying guidelines fail, for instance, to acknowledge the much higher statistical proportion of girls who are subject to unwanted touching up and sexual bullying (McNeil and White, 2007; Maxwell *et al.*, 2010; Ringrose *et al.*, 2012).

What is also striking is that Osler and her colleagues found that when girls did misbehave in school, disruptive girls were treated much more harshly and they were excluded more easily than boys. These 'problem' girls were also disproportionately from particular racialised and working class 'groups'. Echoing findings about much higher rates of school exclusion for racialised, black boys (Gillborn, 2004, 2008), black girls are more than four times more likely to be excluded than white girls (Osler *et al.*, 2002).[11] Zero-tolerance policies[12] around bullying or violence in the UK may leave few resources for coping with violent or 'problem' young people. Both girls and boys are pushed out of the school system into the category of 'youth offending' and directed to pupil referral units (Conolly, 2008). Also important, however, is behavioural needs research, which indicates that because boys' behaviour is seen typically as more disruptive than girls, boys tend to receive more than two-thirds of support available for behavioural problems like bullying and violence (Cruddas and Haddock, 2005). It is these findings that disruptive, overtly aggressive girls receive fewer resources but also are subject to more intensive scrutiny, discipline and regulation, that I discuss next as a way of concluding the chapter. I will suggest that the media promote discourses about violent girls as aberrant and deviant, as transgressing the ideals of femininity. I will suggest the classed and raced discourses about violent girls are also profoundly postfeminist and relate to fears of the return of the repressed female and disruptions of the natural gender order.

Deviant, low class, violent ASBO girls

Across Western contexts we have faced increasing reports that girls' violence is on the rise (Chesney-Lind and Brown, 1999; Leschied *et al.*, 2000). The news media have been heavily implicated in popularising fears over new categories of violent girls – explicitly classed figures, constructed as abject laddettes who are binge-drinkers and/ or belong to violent gangs of dispossessed youth and wreak havoc on civic society by becoming too much like boys (Jackson, 2006). The article 'The feral sex: the terrifying rise of violent girl gangs' (Bracchi, 2008), for instance, reports on a 13-stone 'girl gang member' who plays for the local girls football team and 'is never out of a chav T shirt and tracksuit bottoms'. The girl in question attacked a retired school teacher to 'look good' and gain 'respect' in front of her group. The article reports that 'sometimes beneath a cap or "hoodie" it is hard to tell one sex from another anymore – girl from boy, or boy from girl'. The writer also worries that you do not have to 'grow up in a sink estate, come from a broken home, get excluded from school, be promiscuous, binge drink or play violent computer games' to be immersed in this culture any more, although the implication is that these aspects will contribute to the likelihood of this happening.

In ways similar to the rationales offered for indirect feminine aggression, claims about girls' violence have also been positioned as misplaced girl power. As Batchelor (2009: 400) suggests in her article which critiques the media production of fears over rising girl violence:

> Typical accounts suggest that 'girl violence is on the increase in an alarming way' (Lambert, 2001), fuelled by a 'ladette' binge-drinking culture (Clout, 2008) in which 'young women are aping and mimicking the traditional behaviour [of] young men' (Geoghegan, 2008). This so-called 'masculinization' is often portrayed as 'the dark side of girl power' (Prentice, 2000), an unfortunate by-product of young women seeking equality with young men (Batchelor, 2007; Chesney-Lind and Irwin, 2008).

Indeed, another story about a Cardiff schoolgirl who attacked a chip-shop worker, attracting 'thousands of hits on … YouTube', describes girls becoming involved in violence as a kind of 'twisted feminism' – 'these girls think physical violence empowers them. It is feeding their aggression and they are misinterpreting it as some kind of feminism' (BBC News, 2008). In this story, another schoolgirl sentenced for kicking someone unconscious in north London is reported to have been trying 'to reinforce her aura as boss' in front of her gang. The male principal suggests 'it's a bit like the Spice Girls' "girl power" thing. Kicking and lashing out is seen as a way of empowering yourself, but it's not'. He also warns girls: 'And it's not a way of attracting boys either like some girls might think. Boys might find aggressive women in music videos attractive, but they don't want to take them home and marry them.'[!] While the rest of this article goes on to explain that the size of the female prison population and the number of girls carrying weapons have actually dropped, the main discourse promoted in the article is how feminist goals of equality between girls and boys have motivated 'feral' bids for power from girls.

The notion of a virulent spread of the 'ASBO (anti-social behaviour order) girl' was evident through a UK 'documentary' reality TV programme *ASBO Teen to Beauty Queen* (Five TV). The show featured ASBO girls from working class neighbourhoods in Manchester who compete to become the UK's first entrant to the Miss Teen International beauty pageant held in Chicago. The girls are to transform from resistant trouble makers – bad girls, utterly defiant of middle class femininity propriety – into subjects who can perform as appropriately passive aggressive competitors for the title of beauty queen. This show follows on the heels of others like *Ladette to Lady* (ITV1), concerned with remodelling working class, 'chav' girls (those who smoke, drink, are single mothers and on welfare benefits) into something more respectable, palatable and *productive* for a middle class public (Skeggs, 2005; Ringrose and Walkerdine, 2008; Tyler, 2008).

Another recent media flurry over working class girls' violence came in the wake of the 2011 London Riots. *The BBC* and *The Metro* coined girl participants 'riot girls' and a BBC audio clip of 'Croyden girls'[13] at a riot scene spread internationally in audio through a YouTube clip on 'London riots chav girls' and transcript, reporting the 17-year-old girls saying the rioting was 'good fun' and 'showing the police we can do what we want, and now we have' as they drank looted Chardonnay at 9am.[14] BBC News Nottingham ran the headline 'girl aged 11 admits damaging shops'. While the story is reporting on over 100 people getting arrested it focuses on the 11-year-old girl 'who cannot be named' that pleaded guilty to criminal damage and 'told the court she did not think she would be caught' (BBC News, 2011). We are told the girl is in foster care and that she was given a 'referral order much longer than normal because of the seriousness of the incident'. Like other images of 'criminal girls', she is pictured in a hoodie in the article, the ultimate sign of an ASBO gender-bending gang girl (Ringrose, 2006a).

Feminist criminologists have gone to great lengths to complicate the simplistic story that rates of female violence are increasing by suggesting that it is changes in criminalisation – the reporting and handling of girls' aggression – that are actually leading to higher statistical rates of female offending (Worrall, 2004). In the UK, despite media sensationalism over chav girls, the most recent government reports suggest that rates of young women offending remain very low (Girls and Offending summary, Youth Justice Board, 2009).

In the USA, poor and culturally marginalised and typically ethnic minority and racialised girls associated with gang activity are increasingly criminalised and bear different consequences of the new forms of regulation and discipline that accompany shifts in categorising girls' behaviour (Chesney-Lind and Irwin, 2004). In the UK, feminist criminologists have described a shift from the 'welfare route' to the 'justice route', where in contexts of neo-liberal governance less public money for welfare interventions (including school-based programmes) result in higher levels of sentencing (Alder and Worrall, 2004). This is evident in the rapidly increasing criminalisation of girls via new technologies like the 'anti-social behaviour orders'. The Youth Justice report also found that girls were being prosecuted for 'school offences' such as 'fighting with other girls' at school, which would have been managed differently in the past (Youth Justice Board, 2009: 7). It is these shifting categories of girlhood aggression, violence and criminality that at least in part result in the 'perception that violence among young women is increasing' despite the data which show that while there is an 'increased number of convictions for girls and young women for violent offences it is not possible to directly attribute these to a real increase in actual offending' (ibid.).

Given rates of young female violence are not significantly rising, my questions are: Why does the figure of the violent girl hold such allure in the mediascape? What is it that marks out girls' looting in the London riots as so newsworthy, rendering boys' presence less remarkable, more expected? My argument is that these are postfeminist gendered anxieties about shifting formations of femininity and masculinity, where some girls can be positioned as risky, failures and symbols of society gone wrong (see also Harris, 2004). These gendered politics are intertwined with class and race politics: the ASBO and 'chav', 'riot girls' signify the terms of girls' abject failure. The 'riot girls' defy the call to neo-liberal success and adaptation (Aapola *et al.*, 2005), refusing to perform the tightrope balancing act of performing masculine productivity and success on the one hand and feminine passivity and sexual desirability on the other (with mean-ness a problematic but normalised by-product). The shock value is derived from assumptions about femininity and passivity spiralling into 'twisted' irrational violence (Worrall, 2004). The ASBO girls are deviants, whose qualities cannot be reconciled with the newest versions of successful, neo-liberal feminine subjectivity, the successful but mean girl.

To conclude, the figures of mean and violent girls therefore actually signal complex differences among girls with vastly different familial, community, educational and economic contexts under which aggression and violence are constituted, expressed, understood and ultimately regulated. Where girls' indirect aggression is naturalised and normalised as the logical expression of a pathological repressive femininity within the institutional spheres of school and work, girls' violence is depicted as deviant – as normative female development gone awry.[15] Girl violence is also seen as erasing the differences between girls and boys, therefore placing femininity and masculinity and the 'gender order' in crisis (Connell, 1987).

Both the mean and violent girl figures highlight postfeminist gender fantasies and panics. The successful, adaptive but necessarily pathological femininity that comprises the mean girl is positioned as a nuisance at school and in the workplace, but as largely inflicting pain on other girls and women – competitive women become their own worst enemy, unable to handle full, equal inclusion in the public domains of school and work. The overtly aggressive girl presents a bigger 'anti-social' 'problem' because she is outward-facing, directly aggressive and violent; she disrupts, is loud and bad, rude and nasty, and too masculine. Constituted as threatening and anti-productive members of society, girls who act out overtly and violently are subject, therefore, to very different regulatory rules and are more harshly disciplined; so particular girls are in danger of being pushed out from and either informally (through the peer group) or formally (through the school policies) excluded from spaces of schooling (Osler *et al.*, 2002) and subject to criminal sentencing and banned from the public spaces of the street (Worrall, 2004).

As I continue, I will respond to these problematic postfeminist constructions of feminine aggression through my qualitative research with young working class girls in the UK. In Chapter 7, I explore how tween and teen girls understand and challenge the postfeminist discourse of girls as mean and examine what happens when anti-bully interventions are organised around expectations for feminine niceness and passivity. In Chapter 8, I look at what happens when working class girls transgress the normal boundaries of indirect, mean girl into physical violence. Through my theoretical, methodological and data chapters I also think about how anger and aggression can be re-positioned as positive dimensions of feminine subjectivity (Brown, 2003; Austin, 2005) as potentially positive 'lines of flight'.

4 Sexy girls?

The middle class postfeminist panic over girls' 'sexualisation' and the protectionist discourses of sex education

As has been argued so far in this book, the UK media and popular culture tends to depict the UK as a society that is 'postfeminist' and situates girls and 'women' as liberated and empowered in the wake of decades of gender equality legislation and educational and workplace gains. Chapter 2 explored how girls' success is positioned as there for the taking, an educational discourse about 'can-do' girls, where overly successful girls pose a risk to boys and masculinity. Chapter 3 looked at how concerns about femininity were also rife in constructions of overly aggressive at-risk and risky girls, in ways that were cut through with class and race meanings. This chapter explores another contradiction in relation to the 'successful girl' thesis; namely, if girls are so successful, that is they have escaped the oppressions of their 'sexed' body, why do we have a competing moral panic surrounding girls sexuality and 'sexualisation', particularly in the Anglophone, global North?

This chapter explores a third contradictory site of postfeminist moral panic or 'crisis' (Aapola *et al.*, 2005) over girlhood by examining the controversial debates over the 'too early', premature sexualisation of girls (Egan and Hawkes, 2008). I look at an affective wave of public anxiety and concern over child 'sexualisation' evident in a swathe of official government reports from a range of countries as well as popular books and media coverage. I ask psychosocial questions about the sexualisation panic and its objects of inquiry: What is this discourse actually saying about girls? Who is being worried about in which ways? Who is the desired object of protection? What are the implications for which girls? How do the sexualisation debates call up feminism? Does the sexualisation debate offer useful insights for understanding young people and sexuality, or more specifically the different pressures facing differently classed and racialised girls? And, critically for the purposes of this book, what are the implications of this debate for education? How does the debate relate to educational provision and schooling around gender and sexuality?

Through media analysis, I argue that public anxieties over 'sexualisation' illustrate familiar historical trends and worries about controlling girls' sexuality (Jackson, 1982; Jackson and Tinkler, 2007), which correspond in important ways to the classed and raced discourses of the problems of overly aggressive girls mapped out in the previous chapter. I also identify the sexualisation panics as *postfeminist* because they often position sexualisation as a moral problem resulting from too much and too early sexual liberation for girls on the back of feminist gains. I argue that concerns over girls and sexualisation relate to maintaining classed and raced moral boundaries and regulating appropriate norms of feminine sexuality.

Next I will illustrate how the desires to return to an age-appropriate feminine sexuality in the sexualisation discourse resonate explicitly with the way sexuality is engaged with in schools. Sex and Relationship Education (SRE) policy and guidance in the UK is organised around principles of sexual risk and protection in highly gendered ways. For instance, there is a focus on disease and pregnancy and 'parts and plumbing' that constructs sexual activity as natural for boys, and a risky burden for young women to delay as long as possible. Girls are also positioned in typical SRE guidance as passive sexual recipients who are nonetheless responsible for delaying and managing sexual conduct in heterosexual contracts.

Finally, I will spell out the implications for education of the sexualisation debates and policy reports, arguing that despite raising a range of important issues around sexuality, gender, commercial culture and young people, sexualisation panics are closing down discussion through moralising, class-based discourses around age-appropriate sexuality. The sexualisation debates have neither offered a platform to critically engage with the dominant trends around risk and protection in SRE, nor addressed wider issues of sexism and gendered power dynamics in schools (Coy and Garner, 2012; Ringrose and Renold, 2011).

Too much too soon?: mapping public anxieties over child 'sexualisation'

The dangers of girls' sexuality have recently been brought to a fevered pitch through debates on child and girl sexualisation in a range of countries. In Australia, a high profile report on 'corporate pedophilia' looked at the 'adultification of children' and 'direct sexualisation' of girls (Rush and La Nauze, 2006). In the USA, a report on the sexualisation of girls was commissioned in 2007 from the American Psychological Association (APA). In Canada, the government commissioned research focusing on 'sexualisation of girls as a root cause of dating violence'.[1] In the UK in 2009, the Scottish Government commissioned a report on sexualised goods aimed at children (Buckingham *et al.*, 2009). In 2010, the Home Office conducted a Review on the Sexualisation of Young People (Papadopoulos, 2010). These have been followed up by a review of the reviews (perhaps an unsurprising audit) by the neo-liberal UK Coalition Government: the Bailey Review 'Letting children be children' (Bailey, 2011).

Across these international contexts, public debates over sexualisation have tended to become polarised between those who condemn sexualisation and call for greater regulation of young people's use of various media and those who critique the 'sexualisation thesis' as part of a moral panic that robs children of their rights, sexuality and agency (Bray, 2008). There were numerous critiques launched of the APA report, which despite attempting to address issues of sexism ended up by suggesting that sexualisation was wholly negative for girls, reinforcing discourses of girls as victims and neglecting pressing issues of feminine rights around sexuality and pleasure (Lerum and Dworkin, 2009). In the UK, with the release of the Sexualisation of Young People review, there was a dichotomy between popular support for the awareness about corporate sexualisation that the report generated in the media and stringent academic critiques of the research findings, methodology and recommendations. Critiques ranged from attacks on the 'glamorous' celebrity psychologist, Linda Papadopoulos, who led the report (Murch, 2010) to the content itself.[2] Critics suggested that the report lacked social and historical analysis of 'inequality', and had 'nothing useful to say about the ways in which children and young people might engage or participate in the contemporary media landscape, sexual or not' (Smith, 2010: 178; Murch, 2010). It was suggested that the report was simplistic, relying on an under-theorised, over-generalised buzz word 'sexualisation' which 'may distract attention from other, more fundamental – and perhaps more intractable – social problems' such as the 'inherent inequalities of a hyper capitalist society' (Buckingham and Bragg, quoted in Murch, 2010). Most significantly, by positing, rather than 'questioning', '"sexualisation" as a driver of violence against women', the report was said to generate 'a politics of alarm' and a 'common-sense rhetoric of distress for the "lost innocence of childhood"', offering only a 'scary futurology of increasing sexualisation' (Smith, 2010).[3] Most recently, the Bailey Review 'Letting children be children' has been critiqued as an age-appropriate set of guidelines to responsibilise parents about the 'risks' of sexualisation through a range of strategies and techniques to regulate sexual attitudes and behaviour of their children. A feminist critique has been the trend to focus on age appropriateness rather than sexism, meaning young people should simply wait until they are older to enter into sexualised culture.

While I will discuss the specific implications of the UK reports and policy debates on sexualisation for education below, here I want to map the sheer volume of interest in the 'sexualisation' phenomena as part of the postfeminist mediascape, and to look at how 'sexualisation' becomes a common-sense discourse with a set of implied meanings. While the directional dynamic of affectivity between the popular press and popular publishing and academic research and government policy (the flow of effects and nature of impact) is always difficult to pinpoint (Ball, 2008), the official government concern over child sexualisation needs to be located within a veritable flood of books on sexualisation in the child behaviour and parenting publishing market. I want to explore what these books and news articles say about sexualisation vis-à-vis girls.

Popular books on sexualisation and effects on children include, for example: *The Sexualisation of America's Kids: And How to Stop It* (Wright, 2001); *Hooked: New Science on How Casual Sex is Affecting Our Children* (McIlhaney and McKissic Bush, 2008); and *The Sexualisation of Childhood (Childhood in America)* (Olfman, 2008). A central focus is on what is positioned as '*premature* sexualisation', evident in the book *So Sexy So Soon: The New Sexualized Childhood and What Parents Can Do to Protect Their Kids* (Levin and Kilbourne, 2009).

There are also books that look specifically at sexualisation and commodification of girls. These texts include *The Lolita Effect* (Durham, 2008), which critiques the corporate production and normalisation of a market organised around precocious, sexually available young femininity. Others include *Girls Gone Skank: The Sexualisation of Girls in American Culture* (Oppliger, 2008), which draws out the explicitly classed dynamics of girls taking up 'dirty' sexuality, since 'skank' is defined as: filth: any substance considered disgustingly foul or unpleasant,[4] with girls' sexual innocence under threat from 'skank' formations of feminine sexuality. Maggie Hamilton's *What's Happening to Our Girls?: Too much, Too soon, How our kids are overstimulated, oversold and oversexed* (2009), makes similar arguments, featuring teen girls in high heels, mini-skirts and halter-tops on the book cover, and asking of readers:

> Why are girls as young as five years old concerned about their looks and addicted to shopping? Why are they having sex and binge-drinking so young, responding to chat-room predators, and bullying their peers via email and text messages? Why are depression, cutting and eating disorders on the rise, and why, with so much choice, do so many just want to marry young and have babies?

Here we find a ménage of 'crisis' (Aapola *et al.*, 2005) discourses facing girls, ostensibly stemming from the 'over-sexing' of girls from an early age, effects of which appear to include binge-drinking, depression, cutting and eating disorders. We also see age-appropriate discourses of sex and fertility, which I will return to in the final section of this chapter, when I consider sex education provisions.

The quasi-academic book *Getting Real: Challenging the Sexualisation of Girls* (Tankard Reist, 2009) attempts to bridge the journalistic and academic market, includes some academic research, and is organised around a feminist critique of sexual objectification of girls and women in popular culture. However, this frequently ends up slipping into seemingly class-based moral outrage about 'sexualisation'. For instance, complaints about girls being bought 'slutty bratz dolls' and 'wearing inappropriately skimpy clothes and tops' (Hamilton, 2009: 56) mean that the useful feminist critique of oppressive bodily practices for women (Tankard Reist, 2009) and compelling research on the medicalisation of girls' sexualisation (Klein, 2009) in the book end up being overshadowed by invocations to a discourse of childhood innocence. The preface, for instance, argues for 'the right of children to be children' (Hazelhurst, 2009: 1).

Further books looking at corporate marketing and girlhood include: *Packaging Girlhood: Rescuing Our Daughters from Marketers' Schemes* (Lamb and Brown, 2006). The market also includes books aimed at older teens, which trace the effects of early sexualisation for later romantic relationships, such as *Unhooked: How Young Women Pursue Sex, Delay Love and Lose at Both* (Stepp, 2007). Some suggest that sexualisation is a form of sexual bullying of girls, such as Azam in her book *Oral Sex Is the New Goodnight Kiss: The Sexual Bullying of Girls* (Azam, 2009). Azam's book also focuses on the classed and racialised economic risks facing girls, highlighting and sensationalising gang-based teen prostitution rings and teen girls' involvement in pimping other girls. But this ends up morally condemning and pathologising the girls involved, rather than shifting the gaze and extending a critique of sexism across social spheres that continue to make the sexual contracts of men buying girls' sex for money viable.[5] Unsurprisingly, some books suggest a return to sexual modesty, innocence and appropriate femininity to counteract the sexualisation trends, such as *Girls Gone Mild: Young Women Reclaim Self-Respect and Find It's Not Bad to Be Good* (Shalit, 2007).

A further market explores the relationship between sexualisation and the porn industry, developing the notion of society being 'pornified' to theorise the normalisation of pornography and its supposed negative impact on family and relationships (Paul, 2005). There is a swathe of books discussing the effects of pornography on society including *The Porning of America: The Rise of Porn Culture, What It Means and Where We Go from Here* (Sarracino and Scott, 2008) and *Pornified: How Pornography Is Damaging Our Lives, Our Relationships, and Our Families* (Paul, 2006). This genre includes Levy's *Female Chauvinist Pigs* (2005), which actually offers an important critique of middle class women's consumption of economically marginalised women's sex labour through their consumption of activities like lap dancing, although this can reduce the problem to class divisions between women, without extending a wider political economic critique of the largely male owned and operated sex industries.

Natasha Walter's (2010) *Living Dolls: The Return of Sexism*, the eagerly awaited follow up to *The New Feminism* (1999), spectacularly showcased Walter's retreat from her earlier beliefs that feminism had won the battle for equality to her realisation that the decade following the millennium had brought a renewal of sexism and sexualisation:

> I once believed that we only had to put in place the conditions for equality for the remnants of old-fashioned sexism in our culture to wither away. I am ready to admit that I was wrong. Empowerment, liberation, choice. Once the watchwords of feminism, these terms have now been co-opted by a society that sells women an airbrushed, highly sexualised and increasingly narrow vision of femininity.[6]

Walter's book explores the normalisation of the sex industry and glamour modelling and its encroachment into middle class families, offering persuasive investigative journalism-type findings from women in the sex industry and the male purveyors of lap clubs, for instance. The worry, however, is often aimed at the effects for those women who have not traditionally been part of the sex industry falling prey to its allure. Indeed, the Amazon marketing indicates the intertextual referencing of these populist texts, given that one promotional endorsements reads: 'If anyone doubts the need to protect girls from the toxic, hyper-sexualised, disempowering environment they're now growing up in, they should read [Walter's] *Living Dolls*' – Maggie Hamilton, author of *What's Happening to Our Girls?*[7]

My conceptual point here is that we need to think psychosocially about who is being worried about in what ways in these texts. What are our own deeply held feminist desires around protection? And who are we trying to protect? Can sexualisation as a banner offer a conceptual route into critical analysis of gendered and sexual power relations (Gill, 2011)? We need to guard against drawing renewed binaries around good and bad femininity, and the age-old logic that sex work is okay for some (low class) women (Skeggs, 2005) and that others (middle class girls and women) need to be sheltered and protected (Walkerdine, 1991; 1999). Egan and Hawkes have extended an important critique of the discourses arising from sexualisation texts as constructing a 'hypodermic' narrative where the media operate as a vector for 'corruption' and 'victimisation' (2008). These authors point to the sensational market generated by these texts, which are productive of new surveillant gazes upon girls and women, voyeuristic looks into the secret sexual worlds of young people with the aim to 'discover', 'shock' and re-draw moral boundaries around feminine sexuality (Renold and Ringrose, 2011). Unfortunately the news media and popular texts seem largely driven to generate sensationalised class- and race-based panic and fear over 'sexualisation', as I elaborate further below.

Lost youth: sexualisation and the popular press

A consistent stream of UK news headlines for the past 5–6 years has fed the moral panic over the sexualisation of girls. The article 'The truth about tweens' (Dobson and Hodgson, 2006) reports on 'shocking evidence of premature sexualisation of girls' using internet chatrooms. This article suggests that parents are unaware of sexual chatting and that the girls involved are 'at risk for pregnancy and for sexually transmitted diseases', despite the researchers not knowing if the girls were actually engaging in sex or merely 'talking sex' online. The focus of the article is exposing 'sexually precocious behaviour in young girls'.

In 2007 similar concerns revolved around the release of the American Psychological Association's report on sexualisation of girls. The BBC News reported 'sexualisation "harms" young girls', drawing on the APA report to argue sexualisation can lead to 'lack of confidence, depression, eating disorders and a negative effect on healthy sexual development'. While the article offers an analysis of sexual objectification of girls, its analysis of the problem as having specific psychological, cognitive and health effects for all girls reduces the issue once again to one of inherent risks of sexuality facing girls, neglecting the complex classed and raced construction of girls' sexuality, and the complexity of issues different girls might be facing.

In 2008, *The Times* article 'I'm single, I'm sexy and I'm only 13' (Deeley, 2008) again proclaimed sexualisation was taking a toll on girls' 'mental health' suggesting that 'teenage girls are being swept up by reality TV style tits-out culture, becoming more willing than ever before to bare all'. The article drew on a poll of UK teenagers by 'Lab TV website' which found that Jordan was top of the list of good role models, with 63 per cent saying that lap dancing would be a good profession.

Here we meet one of the central contradictions about girlhood that I am exploring in this book. On the one hand, girls are encouraged to believe a universalising narrative about the possibility of overcoming sexual difference to compete in a sexism-free, gender-neutral meritocratic world and rise up to hold key positions of social, political and professional power alongside men. On the other hand, girls are presented with celebrity culture and what looks like increasing opportunities to use their bodily and erotic capital for money. It's important to think about how these discourses are drawn around class lines. Feminists have long pointed to the informal exchange of sex for economic benefit underpinning the sexual contract of marriage through patriarchal law (Delphy and Leonard, 1992), but historically prostitution and sex work have been associated with working class femininity (Walkerdine, 1991; Skeggs, 2005).

It would appear that the extension of sex work as an economic possibility for middle class girls (63 per cent of girls in general considering lap dancing) is what underpins a great deal of the moral outrage here, rather than a feminist concern to address the political economy of sex work, prostitution and pornography with transparent fair labour conditions, for instance (Brock, 1998; Jeffreys, 2009). While I will argue that feminists would do well to engage critically with the continuing dynamics of sexual objectification and exploitation that organise the sex industry, this form of analysis is *not* the basis of the media panic over sexualisation. Rather, it is fuelled by a desire to return to a mythical time/space of sexual innocence for some (middle class) children and girls. Moral outrage over 'loss of innocence' appears to be what is driving some of the media accounts, and what makes these debates newsworthy.

This is evident in the headline 'Lost youth: turning young girls into sex symbols', an edited extract from Durham's popular text, *The Lolita Effect*, which points to the sexualisation of ever younger girls in Western contexts (Durham, 2009). The opening passage narrates a story of a five-year-old showing up to Durham's house on Halloween in 'tube top, miniskirt, platform shoes and eye shadow', declaring 'I'm a Bratz'. The reference here is to the racialised and eroticised 'slutty' (Hamilton, 2009) Bratz dolls that have overtaken Barbie as doll of choice in the girls' toy market (Renold and Epstein, 2010). Durham says that she had a 'dizzying flashback to an image of a child prostitute I had seen in Cambodia, in a disturbingly similar outfit'. The author explores the ever younger sexualisation of girls and the commercial motivation behind selling products enabling women and girls to perform sexualisation, but the critique slips back into an individualising, moralising concern for her own daughters, and the need to create 'safe and supportive spaces for [white, middle class, majority world ...] girls to understand their sexuality on their own terms and in their own time'. While Durham's concern about potential sexual exploitation of vulnerable girls is crucial, we are offered no way to understand how concerns around sexualisation affecting her daughters are different from girls who work in the international sex trade or child prostitution; there is no space for worrying about the Cambodian child prostitute who lurks as a pitiful yet 'lost' figure in Durham's text.

What is also relevant is how 'sexualisation' can be staged in the postfeminist terms I've outlined as the direct result of feminist gains for women. The article 'Rebelling against a culture of porn' (*The National Post*, 2007), reviewing *Girls Gone Mild* (2007) in the Canadian *National Post*, asks the incendiary question 'Which is the greater oppression – sexual virtue imposed by the patriarchy, or sexual libertinism imposed by the matriarchy?' In this bizarre formulation, the reporter suggests that radical feminists are behind 'girls gone wild' as the new sexual 'good' positioned as 'another form of cultural tyranny ... except now the oppressors are post-morality theorists and "desperate housewife" moms urging public "hotness" rather than stern, moralistic fathers suppressing it'. Rather than foregrounding the sexism and objectification in popular media cultures (like, for instance, the increasing demand for body modification surgery), the article positions sexually 'liberated' mothers as responsible for over-sexualising their daughters, which is argued to have led to 'lap dancing ... [being] considered a more desirable profession than a teacher'. The article argues that

Girls Gone Mild (2007) by Wendy Shalit is a response to 'bad girl culture', which looks at 'promiscuity's harsher toll on women than men'. It suggests that 'radical feminists' despise the author as a 'precocious politically incorrect "modestynick" who herself remained cheerfully chaste until marriage'. Radical feminists are then equated with Hugh Hefner as the article also reports that 'Playboy scornfully dubbed her "A man's worst nightmare" and *The New York Observer* caricatured her as an SS officer'. Finally, the article blames 'loose' mothers spawned by the feminist revolution, like Erica Jong, for over-sexualising themselves, leading to daughters rebelling against 'permissive mothers'. In this depiction, girls' activism against sexism (such as campaigns to stop 'sexualising' merchandise) is reduced to intergenerational in-fighting between women and a rebellion against ageing feminists! The article shows how anti-feminist sentiment enters into the debates on sexualisation with feminists constructed as unleashing 'bad girl', excessive sexuality. A turn back to girls' 'natural restraint' is proffered as the solution, as the article concludes: 'free will choosing principled modesty because it confers self-esteem? Now that's true sexual liberation'.

By analysing these international media reports, we can gauge some of the potentialities of the critical debate opened up by the sexualisation discourses, but also problems and weaknesses. As Egan and Hawkes (2010) have suggested, the sexualisation discourses position girls' sexuality as both risky and at risk, mobilising widespread fear, anxiety and moralism. They suggest that the lack of understanding about what the generalised notion of 'sexualisation' actually is 'moves feminist thinking away from a deconstruction of dominant patriarchal culture and vilifies [girls'] sexuality as opposed to sexism'. As I've illustrated, the media discourses are concerned primarily about the 'premature' and 'age-inappropriate' sexualisation of girls which ends up weakening the possibility of a critique of the sexual objectification of women generally. The sexualisation discourse is drawn around class-based moralising lines and tends to invoke fears over contaminating forms of sexuality infringing upon constructions of appropriate girlhood sexual innocence and purity.

This trend to attack classed markers of sexual excess (Skeggs, 2005) has escalated in the news media in the wake of the most recent UK government Bailey Report, aptly named 'Letting children be children'. In the lead up to the report, during calls for evidence and after its release, the popular press seized upon the calls against sexualised goods and clothing, in highly classed discussion of the dangers of 'sexualisation'. The *Daily Mail's* 'Cocktail parties in stretch limos, catwalk shows and fake tattoos: The disturbing sexualisation of little girls revealed' (Tozer and Horne, February 2011) explores the Essex-based 'Party Pampering' company, which provides make-over limo cocktail parties for 6–12 year olds, critiquing the company's use of make-up, fake tan and tattoos, glitter, and faux cocktails with this age group. The article quotes Reg Bailey, Chief Executive of the Mothers' Union who led the government report:

'I want to know whether parents think that there is too much sexualised imagery day to day, and if this makes it seem like the norm to children,' he said. 'I think that many, many parents will be concerned by the prospect of children not being allowed to be children and being expected to grow up way before their time ...

The saddest thing to me, as a parent, is what this is saying to children – that they only see themselves as needing to look pretty.'

Dr Katherine Rake, Chief Executive of the Family and Parenting Institute, is also quoted:

'This type of activity is giving girls an image of themselves which is based solely around their physical appearance,' she said. 'That puts huge pressure on them to conform to some kind of unachievable standard. This results in low self-esteem, eating disorders and all sorts of psychological and health issues.'

What is interesting is that an Essex-based company providing what might be seen as 'working class' child-based entertainment is targeted in the article as an example of sexualisation of children. The signifiers of pretend alcohol (mocktails), 'heavy' make-up and fake tan, among others, are flagged as sites of particular danger to young people. Again the discourse of children growing up 'too fast' is presented as an age-appropriate, moralising discourse for parents to make responsible marketing choices for their children. There is an important slippage as well in Bailey's comments that he is sad about 'children', although the discourse about 'pretty' obviously refers to girls, indicating the actual gendered discursive locus of concern is around the inappropriately sexualised girl's body (Renold and Ringrose, 2011), with issues related to boys largely shunted to the sidelines (see Egan, 2011).

The construction of innocent and safe childhood has long been critiqued as a middle class construction (Cook, 2005), but it is critical that we gender this debate and expose the powerful discursive threads that point to how it is particularly *girls'* bodies that are under an increasingly microscopic gaze. Some girls' bodies are defined as being more 'at risk' and are surveyed more closely. We see classed fears over unbridled female sexuality as a threat to the moral order of society since, as Egan and Hawkes also suggest, the sexualisation debate 'reproduces … patriarchal and moralising beliefs about the … pathological nature of female sexuality – particularly the sexuality of poor and working class women' (Egan and Hawkes, 2008: 294). Unpacking the discourse of pre-mature sexualisation, it seems that the projected focus of anxiety surrounds the letting loose of an unbridled, classed female sexuality that is dirty and degenerate (seen especially in popular moralistic texts like 'Girls gone skank'). Historically dangerous, licentious sexuality has been constructed as the purview of working class women (Walkerdine, 1991; Ringrose and Walkerdine, 2008) that may potentially contaminate an idealised, sexually innocent, or at least 'coy', purer guise of, middle class feminine sexual subjectivity.

On the one hand, then, sexualisation debates are totalising and universalising discourses (Egan and Hawkes, 2008), constructing a story about precocious girlhood that at once erases class, race and cultural specificity, but on the other hand the discourse is actually constructed through moralising cautionary tales about working class sexuality and excess seeping into middle class life: Bratz dolls out-selling Barbie, parents buying their kids 'pamper parties' and sexualised items (e.g. Playboy Bunny merchandise), a classed dynamic which I explore further in my empirical chapter on girls and 'sexualisation'. Finally, in desiring to return girls to a mythical state of sexual innocence and purity the sexualisation discourse denies spaces for expression of sexuality from girls, reading every expression of sexual identity or practice from girls in deterministic and reductive terms as evidence of victims of sexualisation (see also Lerum and Dworkin, 2009). This relates in important ways to dominant trends in sex and relationship education in schools. In the next section, I explore resonances between the recent moral panic on sexualisation and older discourses of risks of inappropriate feminine sexuality that have long informed sex education. My aim is to show how the public sexualisation debates are in many cases simply reinforcing older discourses of sexual risks for young people and girls in particular.

Girls, risk, protection and sexuality in schooling

Historically, sexuality has been a tricky educational issue with schools having to mediate between the specific cultural backgrounds, influences and norms of local parent cultures and nationally mandated curricula on sex education (Rasmussen, 2006). Traditionally, in the UK sexuality was bracketed off as a discrete topic in secondary education as a health discourse which dealt with the reproductive functions. Sex education was modified to sex and relationship education (SRE) in 2006 in an attempt to address issues of sexual *relationships*. The Labour government attempted to change policies to address aspects of sexuality in primary schooling, perhaps in response to the developing discourses over premature sexualisation, and pressures for schools to address these trends. Yet, to date, SRE been only partly compulsory in England, meaning few schools will timetable more than 6 hours per year (Wolmuth, 2009) and some parents can opt out of sex education due to cultural and religious preferences, for example. Near the end of its term the Labour government announced plans to make SRE compulsory for all students by 2011, yet at present, according to the 2010 report 'Sex and relationship education: Views from teachers, parents and governors':

> the law requires that primary schools must decide whether sex and relationship education (SRE) should be included in their school's curriculum and, if so, what the educational provision should consist of and how it should be organised. Secondary schools, meanwhile, must provide SRE (including education about HIV and AIDS and other sexually transmitted diseases) and must teach human growth and reproduction as set out in the national curriculum.

To date, then, SRE is not compulsory in primary schools, and secondary schools have only certain areas targeted as compulsory. SRE and Personal, Social and Health Education (PSHE) curriculum is currently undergoing yet another 'review', leaving its status uncertain. Thus it inhabits a perpetually shaky space in the formal school curriculum and increasingly it is the individual school's responsibility to manage the curriculum and pedagogy of SRE, making its delivery ad hoc, and its status de-valued (Alldred and David, 2007). The 2010 Sex and Relationship Education report also suggests:

Current SRE provision in the UK lags behind that of many developed countries and a 2007 survey by the UK Youth Parliament of over 20,000 young people found that shockingly 61 per cent of boys and 70 per cent of girls aged over 17 reported not receiving any information at school about personal relationships.[8]

Moreover, it found:

90% of parents and 93% of Governors thought schools should be involved in providing SRE, but that 80% of teachers do not feel sufficiently well trained and confident to talk about SRE. Only 9% of school leaders rated the teaching materials available to them as 'very useful'. More than one in four school leaders and a fifth of governors believe that current SRE in schools is failing children by preparing them for the future 'not well' or 'not at all well'. (ibid.)

Part of the problem has been the bracketing off of sexuality as a 'special' area that is removed in policy and curricula from other gender concerns (such as the gender agenda). As Stevi Jackson famously suggested in 1982, sex education is like a 'remedial programme made necessary by society's attitude to children as a special category of people and sexuality as a special area of life'. Also significant is how gender equality issues get separated off from sexuality in sex education provision in the formal curriculum of schooling (Epstein and Johnson, 1998). As I illustrated in Chapter 2, gender is constructed in dominant educational discourses and policies (e.g. the UK 'Gender Agenda') as the crude bodily distinction between numbers of girls and boys in school and gender is compared by performative success by gender in test scores. In this way, gender issues can be constructed as an equality box (performance by test score due to some girls' high performance on exams) that has been ticked (as with other affirmative action discourse that takes equal female representation to have eliminated sexism) (Bryson, 1992). This works to eclipse ongoing issues of gendered and sexualised power relations in schools, for instance, gendered dynamics of instruction, and less time spent with girls than boys in lessons (Francis, 2005).

Researchers both in the UK and internationally have criticised sex education programmes as refusing to engage with the 'realities' of sexual relationships and gendered power dynamics among young people (Kehily, 2002), and consistently reducing sexuality to an issue of parts and plumbing and disease which is influenced by a 'protectionist' discourse: that adults have the responsibility to protect children from the risks of sexuality (Allen, 2004; Alldred and David, 2007). For instance, the DfES SRE guidance document from 2000, which is still used explicitly, states that:

The key task for schools is, through appropriate information and effective advice on contraception and on delaying sexual activity, to reduce the incidence of unwanted pregnancies. (p.16)

Even if we examine more updated regional-specific SRE guidance for Year 9 in London,[9] we find that five of the six lessons focus on risk and three on contraceptive methods. Lesson 2, 'Recognising and managing risk' will teach young people to 'assess and manage the element of risk in personal choices and situations,' suggesting a discussion focus on 'sexual activity, human reproduction, contraception and pregnancy, and sexually transmitted infection and HIV'. Lesson 3, 'Reasons to have sex or delay' is also organised around risk in 'decision making', encouraging discussion of 'informed choices', and 'personal, social and moral dilemmas and choices'. Lessons 4, 5 and 6 focus on contraceptive methods, condoms and STIs respectively, foregrounding the primary focus on preventing pregnancy and disease, although condoms are the only contraceptive focused on in explicit detail in the guidance.

To summarise, these SRE provisions centre on risks of diseases, teen-age pregnancy and safe-guarding against poor personal sexual 'choices'. The body is fragmented into discrete 'risky parts' to be managed. Debbie Epstein and colleagues have found this focus on protection and risk makes discussion of desire and pleasure difficult in the sanitised space of schooling (Epstein and Johnson, 1998). Epstein has written incisive critiques of the nature of the relationships promoted in SRE where heteronormative relationships organised around heterosexual penetrative sex are privileged and normative, yet risky and appropriately delayed. Thus she and others have suggested that SRE advocates an a-sexual or non-sexual, heterosexual relationship in the singular (Epstein *et al.*, 2003).[10]

This has particular implications for girls. Michelle Fine (1988; Fine and McClelland, 2006) has suggested that there is a 'missing discourse' of female desire writ large in sex education, organised around health and reproductive danger. In the US context this risk has typically been contained through abstinence education, going much further than other developing countries in advocating the delay of sexual intercourse till marriage and positioning women as moral regulators of sexuality by positioning their bodies as risky sexual objects to protect from predatory male sexuality (Ibid; Aapola *et al.*, 2005). Louisa Allen, writing in the New Zealand context (2004: 183), suggests that there is a total absence of a viable discourse of 'erotics' in sex education, indicating that young women are particularly disadvantaged since they are 'already socially constituted as possessing lower levels of sexual desire and being able to experience sexual pleasure less easily than young men'. In the UK context, the SRE curriculum, as we've seen, continues to promote a discourse of health and disease particularly for young women, who learn about periods, sanitary towels and penetrative sex and pregnancy: both girls and boys may learn the mechanics of putting a condom on a replica of the phallus (SRE Core Curriculum for London, 2009). Discussions of male sexuality thus contain overt reference to male arousal – erections and condoms – and the curriculum also contains references to 'wet dreams' which positions the sex drive as higher and more out of control for boys than girls and positions girls as at risk or/and moral regulators of such predatory and drive-based sexuality (Allen, 2004; Wolmuth, 2009). However, while the mechanics of female reproduction (periods) are present, the mechanics of female arousal are often not (Reiss, 1998). This is a *crucial distinction* since reference to male orgasm is present in the SRE curriculum, but reference to female orgasm is typically not: this remains a taboo site. Male arousal and sexual pleasure is therefore a condition of possibility (Foucault, 1982) in the SRE curriculum, which foregrounds the phallus–condom–vagina assemblage of parts (Renold and Ringrose, 2011), whilst female sexual pleasure is mystified and repressed. Female sexuality is reproduced as a passive hole to receive the penis, as I explore further with empirical data with girls in Chapter 8.

From this brief sketch, we can see immediate resonances between SRE and the current panic on premature child sexualisation. Both discourse are organised around notions of sexual risk and age-appropriate sexual experiences and construct normative accounts of 'healthy sexuality' focused on delaying sexual practice and self-sexualisation (from girls particularly), constituting those who do not manage a healthy sexual self as deviant. The resulting educational problem, as I elaborate further in my conclusions to this chapter, is that SRE continues to offer little guidance addressing gendered and sexualised *relationships* in the new sets of social conditions discussed in this book; this includes new digitally mediated intimacies in school peer networks and new 'technologies' of 'sexiness' (Gill, 2008; Evans *et al.*, 2010) that construct new idealised femininities, masculinities and new performative pressures for girls and boys.

Conclusions: implications of the sexualisation debates for education

Returning to the official government discourses of sexualisation I raised at the beginning of this chapter, the UK reports on sexualisation have had different aims and have had different things to say about education. The Scottish Parliament report has been lauded for undertaking rigorous research and offering a 'thorough review of literature',[11] but focused on exploring parents' and children's views on sexualised goods and did not explicitly aim at interventions through strategies for education. Nonetheless, the role of the school did come up as a key concern for parents:

> Parents felt they needed some support in their efforts to deal with this issue. Some expressed a wish for schools to address the issue of sexualisation with young people – partly because they recognised that doing so themselves could be ineffective, or easily dismissed by their children … However, parents felt that they often did not have a voice in schools, including on issues such as holding proms or policies on uniform, make-up and so on that had direct and significant consequences in this area. (2009)[12]

A crucially important aspect of this report is its recommendation for further research and exploration of educational resources to address this issue.

The Sexualisation of Young People report (Papadopoulos, 2010) has been criticised as I documented above (Smith, 2010). It was seen as biased, using 'cherry picked' data and failing to distinguish academic research from PR campaigns.[13] It has also been critiqued for reducing the issues around sexualisation to an age-appropriate dialogue of sexually regulating girls who were constructed as victims in relation to predatory males (Renold and Ringrose, 2011; Barker and Duchinsky, 2012). Despite these weaknesses, it contained an important feminist strain, in that the Home Office had worked with women's organisations and feminist groups to outline some of the core issues of sexism underpinning corporate 'sexualisation'. It also had important recommendations surrounding the need for raising awareness around issues of sexualisation in education including: introducing 'gender equality' training and modules into Social and Emotional Aspects of Learning (SEAL) education; developing a 'whole school' approach to tackling gender inequality, sexual and sexist bullying and violence against women and girls; developing lessons on 'sexualisation', advocating that gender stereotypes and pornography be included in DCSF's revised Sex and Relationships Education (SRE) guidance for schools (Papadopoulos, 2010: 14–15). This represented a significant set of recommendations which would have opened space for analysis of gender stereotypes and sexism within the spaces of schooling.

However, any feminist voice articulated in the Sexualisation of Young People review were largely undercut by the Bailey review, which focused its concerns again on issues of parenting, family values and responsible marketing. The emphasis has shifted from analysis of gender and sexism to age-appropriate rules around sexual activity, and delaying entry into what is assumed to be inevitable sexualised adult culture (Coy and Garner, 2012). There are references to the need for media literacy in the Bailey review but no joined-up analysis of how we might work on issues of sexualisation across PSHE and SRE in particular. The Bailey review has vague unsubstantiated recommendations, and completely neglects any curriculum-specific attention to PSHE or SEAL programmes, which have been weakened by the Coalition Government's intensified focus on academic performance, as I discussed above.

Despite, then, heightened attention to sexualisation in the public domain, the governmental policy reports do not seem to have been able to generate a clear angle of intervention around 'sexualisation' or around sexuality in schools that might help to unpack power dynamics organised around gender, race and class. Mary Jane Kehily has suggested that there is a perennial problem of gaps between official sex education and the '"lived" experience of sexuality among pupils' (Kehily, 2002: 71), but this gap seems particularly problematic given the intensifying moral panic on sexualisation, and we may be seeing a turning back of the clock into neo-conservative tendencies around sex education (Coy and Garner, 2012). Indeed, in the lead up to the release of the Bailey review, sex education emerged as a renewed space of controversy in the UK in mid-2011 when Nadine Dorries of the Coalition Government introduced a new sex education bill which had as a particular focus teaching abstinence to girls aged 13–16, and advocated stricter controls on abortion, echoing US sex education policies.[14] Perhaps we are seeing some of the discursive effects of the sexualisation panic coming to fruition via the conservative politics of the Coalition, where girls' bodies are again positioned as a key biopolitical site for controlling the sexuality of the nation state (McClintock, 1995; Weeks, 2003)?

To bring the findings from this chapter together, then, I have argued that it tends not to be concern over sexual objectification or sexual regulation of girls' and women's bodies that underpins either the public panic over sexualisation *or* sex and relationship education. Rather, the public sexualisation panics as well as SRE provisions in schools are concerned with premature, too early and unhealthy sexuality, particularly precocious girlhood sexuality. It follows that the focus has not been on developing strategies to enable girls to develop sexual pleasure as equal actors in sexual relationships nor on fostering critical capacities and understanding of girls' sexual rights (Lerum and Dworkin, 2009) as sexual beings through literacy with anti-sexist understandings of the social. Instead, the concern is psychosocially oriented towards pushing girls back into an (adult, middle class) fantasy space of sexual innocence to 'protect' girls. In effect then, many of these sexualisation panic discourses are deeply sexist (Gill, 2011), repressing and avoiding gendered power dynamics in society instead of offering resources that would help young people cope with them in educational contexts.

There are deeply individualising trends evident in the Bailey review, which aims to take the issue of sexuality out of school and the public domain, pushing responsibility onto parents, and particularly mothers. We saw that the media chastise working class mothers as sexualising their daughters by buying the wrong goods and promoting self-sexualisation, while middle class mothers are constructed as pushing feminist sexual libertinism onto their daughters (Lerum and Dworkin, 2009), inciting the moral demise of society. Through this neo-liberal individualisation trend, the dynamics of corporate marketisation and profit which shape social norms in adult culture and discussion are lost sight of. Those engaging with the sexualisation debates should be wary about how the discourse can actually harness feminist concerns over girls' welfare as victims of male sexual violence, or concerns about the political economy of the pornography and sex industries (Sarakakis and Tsaliki, 2011), appropriating and twisting feminist concern with gender and sexual power into a moralising, 'panic'-type discourse, which ends up constructing some girls' sexuality as inherently problematic and pathological, and all girls as at risk of 'catching' these problems.

In responding to these dilemmas, academics have consistently pointed out that we actually have very little qualitative research about how children or girls are negotiating their sexual identities in the contexts of the assumed shift that is called the 'sexualisation' or 'pornification' of culture (Atwood, 2009; Bragg *et al.*, 2011; Gill, 2009, 2011; Smith, 2010). Rosalind Gill has specifically argued the need for an intersectional-based research and analysis that 'pays attention to gender, class, age, sexuality and racialisation within practices of sexualisation' (2009: 142). Better understandings of the links between 'sexualised' identities and young people's experiences in school are also needed (Ringrose, 2010a). This is exactly the type of complex empirical picture I aim to paint in my empirical chapters, where I explore how differently raced and classed girls manage complicated sexual politics of school-based peer networks via their online sexual identities (for instance, using classed symbols like the Playboy Bunny in complex ways, drawing upon middle class discourses of girlhood innocence to defend implication as dirty and trashy). Then, in my concluding chapter, I explore what we can do in schools to address these issues, considering possibilities for re-igniting an appropriately complex feminist political, pedagogical response to the dilemmas of sexism facing girls in contemporary culture (Gill, 2011).

5   Rethinking debates on girls' agency
Critiquing postfeminist discourses of 'choice'

So far in this book I have been mapping some of the dominant contemporary postfeminist discourses and moral panics surrounding girlhood. To review, I position these panics as 'postfeminist' because they have emerged in a trail of assumptions about gender equality in society and vehement disinvestment and disavowals of feminist thinking in public consciousness (McRobbie, 2008). I explored how postfeminist anxieties relate to fears over feminine excess (Walkerdine, 1991), including concerns over girls as too academically successful, too indirectly mean or overtly aggressive and too sexual. Some central contradictions arise out of these moral panics over contemporary girlhood. These form the central paradoxes I am exploring in this book: if girls are so (un-problematically) successful, why is there a moral panic over their forms of relating and relationships; and assertions they are too aggressive in the wrong ways, as mapped in Chapter 3? If girls are apparently freed from their sexed bodies and enjoying unprecedented success at school, work etc. (Kindlon, 2006), why does heterosexual desirability and competition for male attention still rate as so important in Western and global popular culture to the degree that it has motivated a moral panic over girls at risk of hyper-sexualisation, as mapped in Chapter 4? Are we really living in gender equal times? How can we go about theorising these complex contradictory discourses about success, aggression and sexuality and girls' agentic capacities to maneuver these discourses?

In an incisive review of 'Girlhood today' Catherine Driscoll suggests: 'The girl is an assemblage of social and cultural issues and questions rather than a field of physical facts, however much of the girl's empirical materiality is crucial to that assemblage' (2002: 14). Driscoll also suggests researching 'girlhood' is challenging because 'girl studies is always suspended by its object between the apparently universal category of "girl" and the pervasive cultural distinctions between girls' (ibid.: 27). This is a problem of the global and local that can only be resolved through a multiplicitous theoretical framework that offers rich analyses of power operative at multiple levels in the social and attends to historical and cultural specificity and considers how specific girls are affected or informed by these contradictory discourses. Driscoll also suggests that two central challenges of girls' studies include overcoming the relative (in)significance of girl culture in academic debate, in this case challenging its insignificance in educational research, but also policy and practice. The second issue is finding adequate ways to understand regulative discursive constraints that define and constitute the 'girl' and girls' own 'power, which renders as a particular problem the theorisation of girls' agency' (ibid.: 14).

Theorising girls' agency is at the heart of girlhood studies (as theorising women's agency is key to feminist/women's studies) and agency is a key organising concept in the field of gender and education, which is concerned with understanding constraint and possibilities around girls and boys (gendered) ability to achieve, aspire and perform and enjoy 'well-being' in various educational spheres. The predominance of the concept of agency in current understandings of gendered identity and subjectivity in the overlapping areas of research informing this book, make it crucial to unpack it in order to unfold how I want to re-think female subjectivity and subjectification, as well as the possibilities of psychosocial movement (at the level of subject and social) in this book. This chapter sets out then to review some key debates on agency in relation to girls and femininity. I insist discussion of agency and choice needs to be placed in the context of postfeminst discourses of girlhood.

Debating agency

A great deal of contemporary theorisations of agency across the fields of cultural, gender, girlhood and educational studies relates strongly to sociological and cultural studies work such as Paul Willis (1977) and his Marxist theorisations of agency and resistance as reproductive of class cultures, in a structural reproduction formation where working class resistances further entrenched marginalisation from the middle class norms. Early now 'seminal' feminist critiques inserted the girl subject into these cultural studies to explore the distinctive realms of girls' agency in the private sphere, such as Angela McRobbie's (1991) work on bedroom culture. Anthony Giddens' (1984) classic formulation of structure and agency and structuration theory has proven a staple of sociological research based on a dialectic between that assumed rational, conscious actor and structuration processes that constrain the agent (Shilling, 1992). Pierre Bourdieu's work (e.g. Bourdieu and Wacquant, 1992) is also a dominant framework for understanding agency in relation to habitus and field and cultural and other forms of capital, and debates have abounded as to whether the theory 'freezes' agency (Harker, 1984) through reproductive determinism or allows scope for theorising agentic practice across multiple spaces and sites of education and schooling (Reay, 2004).

Debates over how to understand the relative play of agency vs regulatory structural or discursive constraints have been central to many fields of inquiry. In childhood studies and youth studies, for instance, there are protracted debates on how to characterise children and young people's relationships to socio-cultural constraints, as well as to pop-culture and mass media, in ways that recognise their agency (Nayak and Kehily, 2008). According to some commentators the entire field of childhood studies is caught up in a theoretical battle between understanding children or young people through the dichotomy of 'exploited/empowered' (Cook, 2005: 158). As David Buckingham (2000) notes, a problematic binary of the competent consumer child versus the child in need of protection is created in debates in relation to both a commercial media market and the pedagogic arenas.

As suggested by Driscoll above, these debates have been particularly protracted in relation to girls, culture and girlhood studies, since feminist concerns with women's rights compound with concern for children's rights into a messy terrain over-ridden by binary formulations of relative girl-child 'empowerment' vs 'victimisation' in relation to a wide range of issues such as sexual violence, (Kelly, 1988), how girls are affected by popular and media cultures (Kearney, 2006) and how they can engage in education across global sites (Unterhalter, 2007). Debates over agency are therefore central to gender and educational research. The binary of empowered vs exploited girl plays out within all the realms of educational debate I've explored in the book so far – at a basic level in relation to questions of how girls are able to 'act' and 'be' in a phenomenological sense (Young, 1990; Paechter, 2009) – and at other levels in relation to their intellectual achievement or success in school, in relation to acting out aggression, and in regard to their sexual behaviour.

Throughout my media analysis chapters on postfeminist panics I have explored how the categories of girlhood are cross cut with axes of social differentiation and power, including gender, race, class, age and sexuality, if we explore femininity through an 'intersectional' framework (Archer *et al.*, 2007; Ringrose, 2007b).[1] I have advocated an 'intersectional approach', which I view as an explicit engagement with race, class, gender, sexuality, age, ability (etc.) as axes of power that organise educational experiences (Ringrose, 2007b). Intersectional theories, are, however, caught up in a theoretical battle over structure and agency and how to theorise 'axes' of power and difference (Yuval-Davis, 2006: 203) and how to theorise structural constraint vs agency. For instance, Heidi Mirza has debated Black girls' and women's relative agency in racist educational structures (Mirza, 1992; 2009). In a recent conference plenary roundtable with Suki Ali, Heidi Mirza, Ann Phoenix and myself on Black British Feminism, we explored and asked questions about the nature of the subject being formulated in accounts of 'agency and structure' in intersectional approaches (Ali *et al.*, 2010: 53). We explored the limits of structural versions of intersectionality as Ali (ibid.: 652, 655) argued:

> the idea that all structures impact equally, always, on individuals in the same way, is problematic, and a mutual constitution of certain kinds of inequalities is a more productive way of thinking about that … One is not abandoning a structural analysis and the sense that material conditions matter to those debates, at the same time is looking to deconstruct how those operate, and to look at the performative and discursive aspects of those encounters, which are really important.

The speakers also questioned the limits of a rational, choosing, humanist 'agent' and the limits of this conventional 'sociological' mode for understanding the relationship between 'the psychic and the social' (Phoenix in Ali *et al.*, 2010: 653).

These issues underpinned the now classic debate over poststructural theories between Alison Jones and Bronwyn Davies in the journal *Gender and Education*, where they debated problems in 'invoking a humanist subject (a choosing agent)' and the quandary presented by the agentic subject: 'that we can have our cake and eat it too; we are both constituted and yet can choose what we might be constituted as' through discourses (Jones, 1997: 266). Becky Francis (2001a: 73) has critiqued what she says is a postmodern reduction of agency apparent in Foucauldian thinking (see also McNay, 2000) suggesting in response to a discussion of 'discursive constraint' that 'thankfully we are not without agency. We can choose to talk to, form relationships with, and read about the experiences of people with different material characteristics', suggesting also 'it is our ability to choose different discourses which enables us to go beyond our personal material realities and envisage the world from other perspectives, enabling sympathy and rapport' (2001b: 176).

Questions about what agency means and the limits of this construct were also the focus of a special issue my colleagues and I (Gonick, Renold, Ringrose and Weems, 2009) edited for *Girlhood Studies*, 'Rethinking agency and resistance: What comes after girl power?' Contributors explored issues of agency in girlhood in relation to class (Hey), religion (Byers), popular culture and music (Weems, Whynachats, Gonick) and Race (Rajiva), grappling with the complexity of how to theorise the relationship between girls' 'agency' and 'choice'. As Jessica Willis (2009: 98) argued in her paper, 'Girls reconstructing gender: agency, hybridity and transformations of "femininity"' discussions of agency in research on girlhood need to 'build upon feminist scholarship that contests the location of persons as either determined or voluntary subjects' and foreground 'both dominant cultural discourses and the relational contexts in which meanings are produced'.

In this chapter, I raise questions about the contemporary usefulness of the concept of agency, if we do not simultaneously deconstruct the neo-liberal discourse of the 'choosing' rational subject. Agency can be under-theorised and treated as a self-evident concept in some gender and educational research. I will think about the possibilities and limitations of the agency concept through detailed discussion of one piece of fascinating research on girls' sexual agency and empowerment. Then I will revisit Foucauldian thinking and key interventions in governmentality research and feminist debates that explain how postfeminism is a set of powerful, contradictory discourses that shape the formation of subjectivity through a discourse of female choice and empowerment (Gill, 2007; McRobbie, 2008).

Rethinking agency, narrative voice and power

As I have noted, it is striking when reviewing gender and educational literature that the concept of 'agency' is frequently used as a self-evident and unqualified construct (Francis, 2001a, b; Francis and Archer, 2004; Archer *et al.*, 2007; Gordon, 2006; Hains, 2007). For example, in an electronic journal keyword search of 120 educational articles for 'girls' and 'agency', most introduced the notion of agency without explicitly attaching it to a theoretical framework – its meanings were implied rather than demonstrated. Only a handful actually defined agency or systematically grounded the notion in a robust theoretical discussion. Many appear to be based in a common-sense sociology version of structure and agency, perhaps unconsciously grounded in Giddens or Bourdieu.

In a recent article exploring 'agency' in research on girls, gender and sexuality, Claire Maxwell and Peter Aggleton (2010) raise similar questions about the apparent lack of thinking about the meanings of agency in theoretical and methodological work in research on girls' and young women's sexual relationships. They do engage in a robust discussion, aptly noting that agency is a 'slippery' term in a great deal of educational research (Hitlin and Elder, in Maxwell and Aggleton, 2010: 327). Maxwell and Aggleton argue that key theoretical interventions around agency have come from educational scholars working within what they define as two traditions – deriving from Bourdieu and Butler. They review research using Bourdieu's theories and concepts such as 'cultural capital' and 'field' which they suggest illuminate 'the complex intersections of power relations and individual agency' (Allard in Maxwell and Aggleton, 2010: 329). They also outline Butler-inspired research that has looked for possibilities of young women using 'discursive resources' and having gendered 'misfires' as important ways girls' 'side step' social positionings, highlighting the concept of 'discursive agency' (Youdell in Maxwell and Aggleton, 2010: 328). Maxwell and Aggleton suggest that through their review of research literature 'agency is usually evidenced in moments of (active) resistance or re-signification' (ibid.). They argue that they aim to go beyond this approach to find 'sustained agentic practice, as well as explore possible reasons for such practice becoming embedded' (ibid.: 331) .

In their search for what they have called 'a third way' (p. 331), Maxwell and Aggleton also engage with my own work with Emma Renold, which has attempted to elaborate on Butler and the useful focus on discursive subjectification and re-signification (or transforming of social norms) that has come with up-take of Butler in some educational research (e.g. Rasmussen, 2006; Youdell, 2006; Davies, 1997). My work with Renold has also tried to use tools offered by Deleuze and Guattari and associated post-humanist feminist thinkers who draw on this approach, to try to think outside the individualising, neo-liberal category of the rational, acting agent, offering ways of thinking about movement through and between bodies, and I will outline this approach in greater detail in the next chapter. Significant here is that Maxwell and Aggleton suggest our research findings are problematically driven by 'binaries', arguing 'Renold and Ringrose find that ruptures can be swiftly followed by reterritorialisation (often of other forms of dominance, differentiation and Otherisation)' (ibid.). Maxwell and Aggleton suggest our analysis is 'interesting', but because we explore ruptures of dominant discourses in fantasies it does not evidence agency. They argue they want to get beyond the binaries of agency, that is the push and pull between whether subjects are constrained by discourse or exercise agency in their actions, saying 'we wish to avoid, as we see it, the constraints of analysing empirical data within a specific theoretical framework, we have approached the reading of young women's conceptualisations of power in a relatively open manner' (ibid.: 332).

These authors offer an important overview of key thinking around agency in educational research on girls, but after outlining the variety of approaches they appear to retreat back into problematic assumptions that: 1. the researcher can move beyond binaries around agency and constraint; 2. the researcher can search for and find evidence of genuine agency through a 'third way'; 3. interpretations of agency do not have to be grounded in a 'specific theoretical framework' guiding the research (ibid.: 332). In contrast to our (Renold and Ringrose, 2008) approach exploring micro ruptures to dominant and normative discourses, Maxwell and Aggleton (2010: 327, 331) argue their teen girl participants were able to 'feel powerful' and illustrate 'sustained agentic practice' over time in several different ways including 'being powerful in relationships', by 'taking power back' specifically from their boyfriends as described by several of their research participants:

> Because I'm quite like a strong person and I can't cope with like weak people that agree with me and stuff like that – I just get really, really irritated … like I was seeing this guy a few weeks ago and then, like … he supposedly really likes me, but he kept agreeing with everything that I said and it was just all like … no don't take the piss out of me, I just couldn't really cope with it so I sort of stopped that [the burgeoning relationship]. (Letitia) (ibid.: 337)

> I just hate people that have no backbone, and I'd much prefer … I want my boyfriend to be like [to] get angry with me if I do something and not be scared of me …'cos I can be quite scary … I much prefer someone that has a bit of a backbone and says 'Oh shut up'. (Iona) (ibid.: 337)

> Towards the end [of the relationship], I just stopped fancying him and we stopped having sex, and he made a comment … [and] we got in a massive fight, I said, 'I'm not having sex with you for a couple of weeks, 'cos we got in a fight', and he said, 'Oh that doesn't make any difference, that's not much change.' So I thought, 'Well that's it.' And then we were in bed together just going to sleep and then he thought I was cheating on him with X, the guy from the holiday actually … which I wasn't. And we got in a fight and he hit a wall and put a hole in the wall. And so I thought, 'Right, you're getting aggressive around me, it's not on', so I broke up with him. (Mercedes) (ibid.: 337)

Maxwell and Aggleton suggest that these accounts represent evidence of the girls being powerful and evidencing agency via their 'strong personalities' (ibid.: 337). They suggest girls showed an 'agentic response' in ways that indicated a 'systematisation of insight, at the discursive if not conscious level' and that this was 'central to developing more sustained agentic practice' (ibid.). I find the narratives fascinating and agree that mapping how narratives of rational decision making emerge is crucial, but also think we need to ask how a 'systematisation of insight' might relate to a coherent set of contemporary discourses (e.g. of girl power and choice) the girls are drawing upon to narrate the self as powerful.

For me, the article raises several crucial questions, which relate to the wider field of researching feminine agency and subjectivity and theorising voice in narrative: Does girls' agency simply mean the capacity to speak and think? How should we account for how narratives are shaped through gendered power and dominant, historically locatable discourses of girlhood (Driscoll, 2002)? Do we need to look at the relationship between specifically raced and classed girl participants and dominant social discourses of masculinity and femininity (Gonick *et al.*, 2009; Weems, 2009)?[2] For instance, are Letitia and Iona invested in a version of hard and powerful masculinity that commands in a relationship, re-inscribing an idealised binary version of masculine and feminine behaviour organised around binaries of male strength and female passivity (Holland *et al.*, 1998)? How do we analyse the dynamic where the girl/woman withholds sex in relation to sexual conflict and the male reacts with violent aggression (Barter *et al.*, 2009)?

To take one further useful example, Maxwell and Aggleton consider the narrative of Natalia who 'did not enjoy oral sex' because 'it just makes me feel sick':

> *Natalia*: Er … no I hate … going down on the guy [giving oral sex], I don't like that at all, I don't think that's very nice.
>
> *Claire*: Do you like a guy going down on you?
>
> *Natalia*: Yeah it's all right, I just cannot stand doing something to him. It just makes me sick and my old boyfriend didn't actually mind, so he was like, 'I don't care', so that was nice.
>
> *Claire*: So it was alright. So did you kind of say to him, 'Listen, I don't like this at all'?
>
> *Natalia*: Yeah, but X [another ex-boyfriend] was really up for me doing it, and that's why I didn't like go out with him anymore, I was just like, 'No thanks'.
>
> (ibid.: 339)

Because Natalia's decision to not perform oral sex has been 'sustained across a number of relationships' the authors argue it is an example of 'sustained agentic practice': 'young women who recognised certain conditions or experiences they were unwilling to have repeated, and incorporated the lessons learned into their future practice – pointing to possibilities for sustained "agency in action"' (ibid.: 339). But what I find interesting is the way in which the account also hints at subjective struggle. As well as agency it seems to point to a complex binary between the intense pressures many young women are under to perform these sexual acts and the way they manage these.

I want to contribute to and build upon this type of analysis to think further about the nature of the subjective struggle involved for the teen girls in my own research and I want to place this struggle in the context of the dominant cultural discourses through which these 'choices' are forged. These are questions that feminists will feel it is imperative to explore and understand, which means moving beyond any empiricist desire to privilege the research subject's (in this case the teen girls') narrative 'voice' or description of decision making or 'power' as a neutral or transparent account of the self (Orner, 1992).

Maxwell and Aggleton (2010: 341) usefully state that they desire to free themselves from pre-conceived theoretical positions and the 'binaries' surrounding theories and discussions of agency (i.e. agent/victim). Each one of us working in the field of girlhood studies face a similar struggle. However, I would suggest we cannot free ourselves of these binaries around agency but must explicitly engage with them and unpack how they over-determine subjectivities. To do so I aim to re-formulate the terms of debate away from 'agency' which has limited analytical purchase, by elaborating a dynamic of discursive regulation and subjective negotiation and movement, as outlined in the following chapter (Ringrose, 2007a, b, c). Poststructural feminists (e.g. Weedon, 1987; Lather, 1991; St. Pierre and Pillow, 2000) insist we cannot disinvest from our implicit theoretical frameworks and epistemological vantage points. They have long critiqued claims of empirical neutrality as an impossible 'God trick' (Haraway, 1991). What we need to develop, then, is an explicit reflexivity and awareness about which theoretical and political approaches we are 'invested' in (Benjamin, 1998; Ringrose, 2007b) and when we come down on one side of the binary of empowerment vs victimisation, elaborate and justify our thinking about why. I argue we need to map the dominant discourses informing the social terrain, which I outline as postfeminist. I will argue it is only then, against this theorisation of power and a systematic analysis of how narratives are forged through discursive regimes of power (Popkewitz, 2002), that we can explore how subjects negotiate and manage these social 'conditions of possibility' (Foucault, 1980a; Walkerdine *et al.*, 2001).

Questioning 'choice'? Foucault-inspired governmentality research and postfeminist discourses of femininity

Since the 1980s, educational accounts drawing on the theoretical resources of Foucault have flourished, with researchers suggesting it has now become a dominant trope, perhaps minimising other ways of viewing social reality (Dillabough, 2009). However, the type of Foucauldian analyses that have proven particularly important to the hybrid field of youth studies and girl studies are post-Foucauldian governmentality theories (Rose, 1999b) of social governance and complex forms of bio-power in late modern societies, dominated by discourses of social risk but also individualism (i.e. Harris, 2004). As I explored briefly in my introduction to this book, a governmentality approach is based in Foucauldian theories and documents a shift from a repressive to a disciplinary society where norms come to be established through statistical measures (bio-power), and these norms are internalised and enacted through surveillance of self and others. Governmentality theorists suggest that neo-liberalism is a primary discourse through which subjectivity is governed at present; where subjectivity is reconfigured through primarily economic terms, and market values and commodification thoroughly saturates the construction of self and other (Fimyar, 2008). This approach is particularly important for educational empirical research methodologies since it goes beyond a concern with discourse at the level of language or representation, through a Foucauldian concern with discourse as 'dispotifs' or webs of signification that instantiate or constitute material practices in education (see Ball, 2008) through processes of interpellation, which subjectivate subjects in the 'real' (Youdell, 2006, 2010), as I will explore further in the following chapter.

Anita Harris's (2004) work has applied a governmentality framework and analysis of 'risk' and individualisation (Beck, 1992; Beck and Beck-Gernsheim, 2002) in girlhood studies to theorise femininity (see also Aapola, Gonick and Harris, 2005).

Harris and her colleagues have comprehensively and incisively shown how late modern capitalism and neo-liberal social trends have resulted in a form of individualised self-hood and self-responsibilisation with modern, Western girls viewed as harnessing and benefitting from these 'girl power' trends. Harris argues that choice is a new technology of young self-hood where young people are encouraged to construct 'choice biographies' (Beck, 1992) so as to narrate experiences as part of a 'do-it-yourself assemblage' (Harris, 2004: 8). The DIY self is 'responsible for life chances, choices and options ... within ... risk environments' (Harris, 2004: 8). This general logic of youth identity dovetails with feminist discourses of empowerment so 'young women are ... doubly constructed as ideal flexible [choosing] subjects ... imagined as benefiting from feminism achievements ... as well as from new conditions that favor their success' (ibid.). Girls are constructed as 'successful "choice biographer[s]" negotiating one's path in the midst of a ... web of choices' (Aapola *et al.*, 2005: 63).

Writing around similar issues in the UK context, Angela McRobbie (2004, 2008) has developed a powerful critique of agentic girlhood as a key postfeminist discourse (see also Banet-Weiser, 2007). As I have been exploring in this book, McRobbie describes postfeminism as a set of defensive gender discourses and politics in our contemporary era, that position feminism as having achieved its aims and as therefore now not only obsolete but regressive and backward, which suggests that women have unlimited choice and options to 'succeed'. What she argues, using a governmentality inspired framing, is that nowadays 'the dynamics of regulation and control are less about what young women ought not to do and more about what they can do. The production of girlhood now comprises a constant stream of incitements and enticements to engage in a range of specified practices which are understood to be progressive but also consummately and reassuringly feminine' (2008: 57). McRobbie explores choice discourses as a new form of 'postfeminist masquerade', where girls have been allowed entry into civil society, but must compensate for the adoption of masculine 'phallic' traits, by emphasising their femininity.[3] She argues this is a new 'sexual contract' involving intensified technologies of bodily perfection and visual display to be constituted as a feminine subject which includes adopting new hyper-sexualised forms of feminine sexuality understood as empowering choices.

In relation to education and work, the postfeminist masquerade 'exacts ... a kind of compromise, [the girl] takes up her place in the labour market without going too far. She must retain a visible fragility and the displaying of a kind of conventional feminine vulnerability will ensure she remains desirable to men' (ibid.: 79). McRobbie argues 'it becomes increasingly difficult to function as a female subject without subjecting oneself to those technologies of self[4] ... new norms of appearance and self-presentation expected not just in leisure and in everyday life but also in the workplace ... (and we must add here in schools)' (ibid.: 60). In light of these arguments McRobbie insists we have to radically re-theorise agency within a postfeminist context where 'choice' discourses of the 'can-do', empowered girl are dominant motifs of understanding the self and others. Crucially for my arguments McRobbie maintains postfeminist culture results in a 'double failure', which cannot account for the complexity of subject formation:

in its over-emphasis on agency and the apparent capacity to choose in a more individualised society, it has no way of showing how subject formation occurs by means of notions of choice and assumed gender equality coming together to actually ensure adherence to new unfolding norms of femininity. That is choice is a modality of constraint.

(McRobbie, 2004: 10–11)

Rosalind Gill has also been a key cultural commentator on postfeminism, also taking a Foucauldian approach to explore new disciplinary technologies of the self and femininity. She has likewise argued we have to reformulate our ideas of agency in relation to dominant discourses whereby empowerment and 'choice' are appropriated and actually become a key 'technology' through which the self is lived, with oppressive effects. How exactly we can understand agency within this set of constraints has been an issue of dispute in media studies in a well-known debate between Gill (2007) and Duits and van Zoonen (2006, 2007) over girl's 'choice' of clothing in a contemporary media context where 'sexualised' styles, that Duits and van Zoonen call 'porno-chic', predominate. Duits and van Zoonen (2006: 105) define 'porno-chic' as a term to describe 'the representation of porn in non-pornographic art and culture … the postmodern transformation of porn into the mainstream cultural artifacts … [including] mainstream fashion'. Duits and van Zoonen challenge the way that girls' adoption of either 'porno-chic' or headscarves is treated by media studies scholars as an external imposition, rather than a legitimate 'choice' and they call for 'research that examines girls' own everyday experiences and their definitions', which can challenge a view of girls as 'objects rather than actors', and treat girls as 'capable and responsible agents producing "speech acts" with their choice of clothing' (2006: 115).

Gill suggests (2007: 68), in counterpoint, that there is a need to question the terms 'agency', 'autonomy' and 'choice' employed by Duits and van Zoonen, which Gill argues remain 'trapped in the individualising, neo-liberal paradigm'. Drawing on McRobbie, Gill suggests, that 'choices' to wear items of clothing deemed 'porno-chic' are 'made in a context in which a particular kind of sexualised self-presentation has become a normative requirement for many young women in the West' (2007: 68). Gill insists we need to complicate our understandings of female agency in contemporary 'postfeminist media contexts'. Through a review of dominant advertising tropes, Gill argues we have witnessed a discursive shift away from the victim-feminist construction of a passive, dominated female sexuality as 'object' to the normalisation of depictions of women as sexually empowered subject, as in control, knowledgeable, and making confident choices around their sexuality. Gill proclaims, however, that this 'performance of confident sexual agency' is actually central to a new 'disciplinary technology of sexy' which has 'replaced "innocence" or "virtue" as the commodity that young women are required to offer in the heterosexual marketplace' (ibid.: 68). Duits and van Zoonen respond to Gill's 'reply' in a 'rejoinder' by insisting again on the 'imperative to examine which tactics girls use in their everyday lives to "make do" with all the forces that bear on them' through on-the-ground research, critiquing (it is implied) Gill's academic position that theorises girls' subjectivity from afar, or what they refer to as 'the remote shores of feminism' (2007: 166).

In a later paper, Gill (2008: 40) solidifies her arguments about the contradictory ground of female agency and 'choice', suggesting for girls and women 'compulsory sexual agency [is] a required feature of contemporary postfeminist, neoliberal subjectivity'. Combining the ideas of 'compulsory' with 'sexual' and 'agency' is a conceptual or heuristic device Gill undertakes to further destabilise taken-for-granted notions of free will and choice that underpin humanist theories of agency, and to suggest we are witnessing a new hegemonic discourse of feminine empowerment. She suggests the 'performance of confident sexual agency' has shifted to become a key regulative dimension or 'technology' of femininity. Enacting idealised 'sexy' femininity across mainstream 'postfeminist' media and advertising is now the norm so that girls and women are 'required to be skilled in [and take pleasure in] a variety of sexual behaviors' (Gill, 2008: 53).

It is just this form of analysis we need to bring to bear on teen girls' and young women's accounts of how they manage incitements to perform oral sex, for instance. But to present these pressures as a form of 'compulsory sexual agency' also places girls' capacity for sexual decision making in doubt, and does not offer us insight into how actual girls are engaging with and negotiating such discursive shifts around femininity. Compulsory seems to imply a regulative framework, where nuance and negotiation is absent. Indeed, Gill's (and often McRobbie's) analysis remains at the level of media representations of women in advertising and in popular culture. I agree with both Duits and van Zoonen (2007) and others' call for empirical research on girls' sexual agency in postfeminist contexts (see also Albury and Lumby, 2010). It is up to researchers first to ask questions about whether we are seeing instances of new dominant postfeminist discourses in the particular media contexts they are studying; and second to use empirical analysis of 'real' girls' experiences to explore what the 'performative' (Butler, 1993) strategies of girls might be as they use and make sense of 'sexualised' discourses in these media contexts.

Conclusions

Overall, the Foucauldian, governmentality inspired approach has been crucial in setting out the ways that globalised, neo-liberal, entrepreneurial discourses have shaped new forms of feminine DIY 'choice biography' subjectivities (Harris, 2004; Raby, 2007; Ringrose and Walkerdine, 2008). These issues are being taken up in a range of empirical educational research on how postfeminism is shaping constructions of contemporary girls and girlhood (Gonick, 2004; Ringrose and Walkerdine, 2007, 2008; Baker, 2008, 2010; Gonick *et al.*, 2009; Ringrose and Renold, 2011; Griffin, 2011). I want to conclude with a particularly persuasive account, found in Joanne Baker's (2008) deconstructions of the discourse of 'choice', that underpins neo-liberal subjectivity and has implications for women's and girls' capacity to make sense of and address domestic violence. Baker argues that in the Australian advanced neo-liberal state there is a:

promotion of the hyper-responsible self and denial of imposed constraints and limitations [which] is a covert technique through which to govern where individuals are persuaded to make meaning of their life as if it were the outcome of individual choices made in furtherance of self-interest and self-actualisation … Furthermore, some feminist ideas about empowerment, independence and choice for women have been co-opted for the promotion of seductive neo-liberal discourses of social mobility and democratic meritocracy ([Harris, 2004] and [McRobbie, 2008]). The concepts of self-production and rational choice so fundamental to neo-liberalism are fused with palatable elements of a liberal feminism.

(Baker, 2008: 54)

By drawing on McRobbie's and Gill's powerful critiques of humanist theories of rational agency and choice discourses in neo-liberal political contexts, Baker has tools to explain why young women suffering domestic abuse now position their experiences as 'choices' to stay in violent relationships, but also how those in dead-end jobs or unable to access university position these issues as choices because this is the dominant framework through which they are able to interpret their experiences (Baker, 2010). Baker explains in her discursive analysis of choice as a political concept: 'there was extensive and indiscriminate reference to concepts of choice by nearly all the participants, regardless of their social and economic circumstances' (ibid.: 58); 'choice was often used as an overarching and un-contextualised principle to illustrate the way in which purposeful and determined behaviour would bring rewards in the new meritocracy that young women envisaged' (ibid.: 57). A critique of choice discourses means Baker draws very different conclusions about girls' and women's assertions of empowerment from those of Maxwell and Aggleton (2010):

Notions of neo-liberal choice and assumptions about de-traditionalisation and liberation converge to create new modes of subordination which work at a psychological level to regulate women. Crucially, these new modes of subordination do not rely on the exclusion of women or overt directives as to how they 'should' behave. Rather, modernisation is signified by their participation through individual choice (in a fundamentally unchanged social structure).

(Baker, 2008: 62)

Baker goes on to assert that the beacon of choice actually acts as a 'decoy for domination'. Baker's analysis is crucial for breaking through an empiricist investment in girls' narratives of choice, power and empowerment as transparent accounts of agency. She illustrates just how problematic the emblematic banner of choice can be for girls and women today.[5]

I am deeply invested in this radical critique of 'choice' discourse as a starting point for any exploration of girls and women in contemporary postfeminist, neoliberal times. In this chapter I have argued we need to grasp new forms of governance, via individualising trends of self-reflexive feminine person-hood before we can go further to deconstruct the implied un-moving and fixed nature of such 'domination'.

I illustrated how the governmentality lens offers an important frame for disrupting normative, postfeminist discourses of agentic 'choice'. This frame allows us to see the mechanisms and technologies of power in disciplinary society through which we understand ourselves to be free (Rose, 1999b; Harris, 2004; Baker, 2008). It has enabled the theorisation of new disciplinary technologies of femininity, what McRobbie (2008) calls the 'postfeminist masquerade' of oppression masquerading as empowerment, and what Gill (2008) has called 'compulsory' displays of confident sexual agency, which are now de-rigueur manifestations of successful feminine subjectivity. These analyses raise new questions about how we can explore girls' voices and narratives as I will demonstrate in my data chapters which follow.

I also wondered during my discussion, however, whether sometimes these Foucauldian approaches can err too far on the side of discursive determinism. This returns us to binaries that plague debates on agency raised by Maxwell and Aggleton (2010). To my mind what is needed is an approach that outlines the conditions of regulation and governance – that maps how power operates in the social but also maps how subjects negotiate these conditions and how the process of relational engagement transforms subjects and potentially shifts social discourses too (Walkerdine *et al.*, 2001). As Gill (2008: 18) has suggested, the key challenge in theorising feminine agency 'has been to understand how … disciplinary power works, exploring the complex relation between culture and subjectivity in such a way as to render women [and girls] neither passive, docile subjects, nor the fictitious autonomous, freely choosing persons of liberal humanism'. Gill (2008) also calls for an 'intersectional' analysis capable of dissecting the complex classed and raced discourses through which discourses of 'compulsory' choice are taken up.[6]

In the following chapter, I will explore how various psychosocial approaches can help us further in thinking through the dualism of cultural dope vs the purposeful rational cogito, by uncovering the psychical instabilities and irrationalities underpinning the constitution of our subjectivities. I review Butler's theories as important in offering further tools for understanding the psychical complexities of subjectification and specifically in theorising re-signification of injurious norms, although I trouble the notion of discursive agency. The psychosocial approaches I explore highlight the ambivalent, contradictory subject positions on offer to girls that girls must psychically manage and negotiate in complex ways. I will also elaborate how new attention to 'affect', and particularly Deleuze and Guattari's thinking, is becoming increasingly influential in education. I outline how this approach offers new sociological/philosophical tools for mapping the intricacies of flow of affect and ruptures of normative capture, offering new ways of thinking about, researching and interpreting feminine subjectivity.

6 Towards a new discursive, psychosocial and affective theoretical–methodological approach

Introduction

This chapter explores the chain of theoretical-methodological resources that I draw upon to theorise and research feminine subjectivity through a poststructural (St. Pierre and Pillow, 2000) specifically psychosocial approach. I respond to the questions I posed in the previous chapter about girls' agency as 'choosers', but also to discursive determinism in Foucauldian approaches. Here, I explore Butler's theories of subjectification, discursive agency and re-signification, but ask questions about how we can develop the psychosocial implications of her approach. Next I explore a 'psychosocial' research tradition in the UK, which attempts to build on Foucauldian poststructural discourse analysis, with tools from psychoanalysis, including Lacanian theory (Walkerdine *et al.*, 2001). I explore how psychosocial trends are useful theoretically and methodologically in conducting and analysing empirical research.

In the final section, however, I question the pathologising force of psychoanalysis, and discuss a recent 'affective turn' in sociological and educational thinking. I explore the post-psychoanalytic poststructuralism derived from Deleuze and Guattari, which is increasingly influencing debates in education and social science, considering new tools for mapping affect and disruptions of 'molar' power formations (Jackson, 2010). Throughout I will illustrate applications of these various approaches methodologically, evaluating the methodological possibilities and limitations of the strains of thinking under review.

Subjectification, discursive re-signification and discursive agency: Butler and beyond

Judith Butler's work has been extremely important to researchers working on gender and sexuality in educational research. Butler expands Foucault's thinking to argue that subjectivity is discursively constituted through a 'heterosexual matrix' of norms that constrain our ability to understand, act out and 'do' our gendered and sexual identities. These ideas have been widely applied in education to think about the discursive organisation of gendered identity and power relations across age groups and levels of schooling and education from primary through secondary to higher education (Renold, 2005; Rasmussen, 2006; Davies, 2006; Nayak and Kehily, 2006; Youdell, 2006; Burke and Jackson, 2007).

As mentioned by Maxwell and Aggleton in the previous chapter, Deborah Youdell (2006; 2010) has done important work translating Butler's theories for an educational audience. She has identified subjectivation, performativity and intelligibility as key conceptual cornerstones to Butler's work. Discursive subjectivation is the theory that Butler develops drawing on Foucault that 'the person is subjectivated – s/he is at once rendered a subject and subjected to relations of power through discourse' (Youdell, 2010: 137). Subjectivation happens through patterns of incitement and repetition, or what Butler terms 'discursive performativity'. Butler also uses the Althusserian notion of 'interpellation' to outline the idea that discourse 'produces that which it names, [works] to enact its own referent, to name and to do, to name and to make' (Butler in Youdell, 2010: 135). Using this approach Youdell (2006) describes, for instance, how normative hetero-feminine subjects are constituted and regulated in school through gender binaries like the whore/virgin binary where some girls get constituted as sluts or 'slappers' but all girls are at risk of this subjectification. Performativity is tied as well to social norms or regimes of 'intelligibility' so power works through subjects being recognisable and intelligible within normative constraints – and those outside intelligibility tend to be punished (Davies in Youdell, 2010: 138).

Youdell (2010) suggests that this set of conceptual tools has been seen as pessimistic and fatalistic by not offering space for change and action (or agency). She goes on to elaborate Butler's theory of 'discursive agency' and 'performative politics' which means discourses are open to transformation through particular types of performative acts, pointing to Butler's suggestion that 'contexts are never fully determined in advance … the possibility for the speech act to take on a non-ordinary meaning, to function in contexts where it has not belonged, is precisely the political promise of the performative' (Butler in Youdell, 2010: 140).

Thus, Butler's theories offer possibilities of change through discursive mis-recognition and misfire, when interpellation is not secured in the intra-psychic exchange between subjects. This theory has offered space for thinking about how re-signification of signs or words happens in unpredictable moments where signs are reworked. Taking the classic example of the re-signification of the injurious norm 'queer', for instance, queer has been socially transformed through a process of reclaiming and inverting the very meaning of the sign from injury to celebration (Hey, 2006). Anoop Nayak and Mary Jane Kehily (2006: 461–462) have very usefully elaborated upon the nature of the performative acts of gender in schooling through a Butlerian analysis of observations and interview materials in schools, showing how girls can rework derogatory injurious terms like 'lesbian':

Sam:	We could be sitting together like now and the boys could say, 'Oh – yer lesbian' or summit, and you just take it in.
Carla:	Laugh it off.
Sam:	We just laugh it off.
Julie:	Me and Carla do.
Carla:	We'll just say, 'Oh yes!'
Anoop:	And they'll actually say that to you?

Samantha:	Mmm. And we'll just carry it on and say, 'Oh, are you coming up in the bush?' or summit, and like carry it on as a joke or summit.
Julie:	Me and Carla get called lesbians [by the boys] all the time but we just say, 'Oh yeah, we're proud of it!' and we just shrug it off.
Emma:	Yeah. Because you know you're not.
Samantha:	When you answer back, they can't say anything because like …
Carla:	Exactly! We say, 'Yes, we are …'
Nicky:	… [Name of a male student] We turn round and say, 'Oh, do you want a threesome' or something, and he'll go, 'Oh, I don't know' and they just like be quiet.

These authors analyse this narrative exchange as illustrating how the term 'lesbian' is turned from a sign of abuse against the girls, which represented being 'gay', 'frigid' and 'boring', into a sign of affirmation ('we're proud of it!'). The girls overturn or resignify the meaning of this word when they use lesbian as a sexually assertive style of femininity and reverse the implication of frigidity by asking the boys provocative questions about 'threesomes'. The authors argue that the girls':

> discursive enactment [of lesbian] opens up the sign of gender to a multiplicity of subject positions that simultaneously bespeak a heterosexual femininity, lesbianism, bisexual identifications and sexual practices with multiple partners. Each of these imaginary identifications is ambivalent, split and inscribed within the other, giving rise to 'hyperbole, dissonance, internal confusion and proliferation' (Butler, 1990, p. 31) … the initially derogatory remark 'lesbian' is subjected to a frisson that transforms its signification through discursive interplay, parody and subversion. That is to say, the production of these 'logical impossibilities' leads to the incitement of 'subversive matrices of gender disorder'.
>
> (ibid.: 462)

Butler's theory of discursive re-signification is crucial for my work and forms a vital dimension of my psychosocial analytical frame for thinking about how discursive contradiction and interplay can subvert the gender order. In Chapters 7 and 8 I will explore how certain injurious terms like 'bully', 'fat', 'slut', 'whore' and 'slag' subjectivate teen girls, but also explore how such girls rework and negotiate these slippery injurious signifiers, exploring which terms can stretch and be reworked, and which cannot.

My worry, however, is that the focus on 'discursive agency' even when deployed with great theoretical nuance can be subsumed back into 'common-sense' notions of agency in the readings of such accounts. This is not to detract from Butler's theories of subjectification, which offer crucial tools for revising structural, Marxist understandings of 'interpellation' with gendered and sexualised meanings. In my reading, Butler's psychoanalytic-informed approach is useful in disrupting the fixity of 'social fields' (Bourdieu) as well as the 'almighty symbolic' (Lacan). However, the nuances of her psychoanalytic repertoire are actually rarely taken up in their psychosocial complexity in educational research. Uses of Butler can remain tied to a form of discursive determinism in its deployment.

In my use of Butler I will elaborate the *psychosocial* dimensions of her theory for understanding subject formation and also psychical negotiation. Concepts like performativity are understood to be enacted via psychical, subjective negotiations like 'identification' and 'dis-identification' (of a subject with a discourse), 'recognition' (of a subject within a discourse) and 'abjection' (a process through which a subject is not recognised and rendered unviable via discourse) (Butler, 1997). I will elaborate the processes through which girls internalise and form a relationship to, and often 'precariously' live out, social norms (Butler, 2004b).

The psychoanalytic aspects of Butler have been usefully elaborated by a few educationalists, like Bronwyn Davies who augment early Foucauldian approaches to discursive positioning theory (see Davies and Harre, 1990) with the psychoanalytic dimensions of subjectification. Davies and colleagues (2001) outline, for instance, the psychical 'costs' of subjectification via discourse and language elaborating concepts of psychic ambiguity and (mis)recognition. Marnina Gonick (2003: 11) has also combined psychoanalytic theories of (dis)identification and recognition (Benjamin, 1998) in relation to 'citational norms' of femininity and masculinity, using Butler as part of her explorations of contradictory and ambivalent discourses of girlhood. For the most part, however, the psychosocial dimensions of Butler's approach and its methodological implications for educational research have not been elaborated in enough detail. For this reason, I seek to combine Butler's tools of analysis with other 'psychosocial' approaches.

Psychoanalysis and psychosocial research

Psychoanalysis has been increasingly drawn on in educational research to explore notions like the unconscious and the irrational, which mesh well with the poststructural and de-centering of the rational, knowing, conscious cogito of humanism. Psychoanalytic theory has highlighted processes of internal resistance, defensiveness and anxieties as well as reparative thinking which holds complex affective qualities that complicate educational thinking about teaching, learning and being (Britzman, 1998; Pitt, 2001; Bibby, 2010). In the UK a type of theoretical and methodological thinking now called psychosocial studies has grown out of discursive psychology (Frosh, 2003), which applies both discourse analysis and psychoanalytic concepts to develop new ways of analysing empirical data (Hollway and Jefferson, 2000; Frosh *et al.*, 2001).[1]

I am particularly indebted to the psychosocial approach developed by Valerie Walkerdine whose work has been exemplary in drawing upon and elaborating Foucauldian theory to focus on the negotiations of discourse via powerful empirical research on girls and women. Not satisfied with Foucault's rejection of psychoanalysis, she has worked to understand connections between Foucault and Lacan, making important contributions to educational, cultural, media and film studies. She has called some of her writing 'poststructural psychoanalysis' (Walkerdine, *et al.,* 2001). These theorisations were apparent in her early work with colleagues in *Changing the*

Subject (Henriques *et al.*, 1984) and later in *Growing up Girl: Psychosocial explorations of gender and class* (Walkerdine *et al.*, 2001; see also Walkerdine, 2007). Walkerdine and her various colleagues have sought to move beyond the structural constraints of Lacanian theory by substituting discourse for the symbolic order in Lacan to think about how discourses are historically constituted, specific and always gender-differentiated, but also subject to change.

Lacan argued: 'Repression creates gaps and longings and loss, creating (psychosexual) desire (desires for being exclusive object of mother's desires are jealousy in adult sexual relations)' (Lacan in Henriques *et al.*, 1984: 216). In this formulation desire is inevitably un-fulfill-able, subordinated to fantasy (ibid.: 216). But these authors began to try to trouble the split Lacanian subject, subjectified via language in deterministic, fatalistic ways. They trouble the reduction of desire to lack, and insist that 'discursive contradiction' might be a key mechanism through which subjects move and exceed lack. They also argue the role of the researcher is to 'outline' these complexes and the role of competing social discourses.

Henriques *et al.*'s (1984) work is valuable for this chapter because it questions both a rational, choosing agent and an over-determined, subjectified, trapped subject, instead suggesting a new vocabulary to try to understand how subjects *negotiate* discourse, that is, comply and resist through conscious and unconscious psychical processes informed by regimes of power and discursive contradictions. Henriques *et al.* (1984: 113) suggest 'Discourses are complex systems of regulated differences that are intricated in ongoing struggles involving power and social relations', noting their aim is to 'contribute to a more incisive analysis of the microscopic processes of power'. Henriques *et al.*'s theories raise a series of questions that move beyond Foucauldian discourse analysis. They wonder if the individual subject is:

> more than simply the sum total of all positions in discourses since birth; and how are various positions held together? What accounts for continuity and predictability in positionings? Can people's wishes and desires be encompassed in an account of discursive relations? How do we account for motivational dynamics, investments and emotional commitments to taking up specific subject positions? How do particular discourses set parameters through which desire is produced, regulated and manifest? What is the role of fantasy in these processes?
>
> (ibid.: 203–205, 220)

Wendy Hollway's (1984) chapter 'Gender difference and the production of subjectivity' in *Changing the Subject* is particularly salient as it outlines gender discourses and fantasies through which idealised femininity are constituted. She suggests we have to make sense of why men and women 'choose' (ibid.: 236) to position themselves via particular discourses of masculinity and femininity, via powerful fantasies of sexual control and submission, for instance, and how particular positionings may be in contradiction with one another (e.g. feminist discourses in contradiction with 'investments' in traditional femininity in ways that could set up new spaces of awareness).

Walkerdine's work has likewise outlined powerful fantasies of femininity, but largely in relation to education and classed subjectivities through important texts like *Schoolgirl Fictions* (1991: 97) where she has documented girls' preparation for adult heterosexual attachments through investments in fantasies of romantic rescue by powerful men (the prince), for instance, as part of en-cultured and classed ideals of femininity. Walkerdine's work has also showed the deeply contradictory discourses underpinning both working class and middle class femininity via a psychosocial lens in *Growing up Girl* (Walkerdine *et al.*, 2001). To take merely one powerful educational narrative in *Growing up Girl*, these authors discuss the case of a working class girl 'Sharon' who had an elaborate fantasy of having a career in law and becoming a judge, which was in some ways realisable, but also presents a contradictory account of having unprotected sex with her boyfriend, suggesting her mum says 'if it happens it happens', 'It's the chance that you take, in't it?' (ibid.: 207). The interviewer recounts how 'incredibly irritated' they were with Sharon who seems to be undermining her educational goals, and the authors suggest that at some 'largely unconscious level' Sharon was making sure she would never become a lawyer, suggesting this is a working class ambivalence as Sharon and her parents were 'secretly terrified' of her ambition (ibid.: 208).

I aim to build on this type of powerful psychosocial analysis of fantasy and unconscious dynamics to understand contradictory discourses of idealised femininity in my data chapters. I will explore how and why girls 'invest' in both repressive and problematic discourses of femininity and how and through which processes, oppressive discourses can also be resisted. The psychosocial methodological approach is oriented toward getting to grips with the complexities of empirical data and narrative accounts, and is also particularly helpful in moving beyond the surface claims of narrative and 'voice', which can ground sociological/educational discussions of 'agency', discussed in the previous chapter. It helps us conceptualise and highlight the gritty psychical and intersubjective nuances through which discursive positions are enlivened in specific psycho-social spaces found in research encounters. Hollway's later work with Jefferson (2000), in their methodological text on free association and narrative methods in qualitative research, maintains researchers cannot rely on un-theorised assumptions that subjects are 'telling it like it is'. They suggest the psychosocial approach helps to challenge:

> What we might call the 'transparent self problem' ... [and] a 'transparent account problem' ... neither selves nor accounts are transparent ... Treating people's own accounts as unproblematic flies in the face of what is known about people's less clear-cut, more confused and contradictory relationship to knowing and telling about themselves. In everyday informal dealings with each other, we do not take each other's accounts at face value, unless we are totally naïve; we question, disagree, bring in counter-examples, interpret, notice hidden agendas. Research is only a more formalized and systematic way of knowing about people, but in the process it seems to have lost much of the subtlety and complexity that we use, often as a matter of course in everyday knowing. We need to bring some of this everyday subtlety into the research process.
>
> (Hollway and Jefferson, 2000: 3)

Walkerdine *et al.* (2001: 106) suggest similarly that as part of analysing their data they needed to get beyond 'the "face" value account [through] a method that would allow us to identify the significant pieces of narrative as well as taking into account any avoidances or omissions'. This had to go beyond:

> discursive and post-structuralist approaches that offered no way of understanding how the subjects lived the contradictions of positioning, the demands of imposed fictions of the exigencies of everyday life ... the challenge for those who talk about gender and class is being aware of the emotional dynamics within their own lives and finding some way of accounting for themselves, for their own subject position.
>
> (ibid.: 106–107)

Indeed, they suggest psychoanalytic theory is the most useful as a tool to analyse the desire for objectivity by the researcher as 'the production of distance as a defence ... against ... intrusive feelings about the research process, the subject, the relation between the two, including issues of transference and countertransference' (ibid.: 63).

Challenging the desire for conscious and rational research projects, subjects and data, and taking account of 'both the psychic and the social processes' through which research is forged has been the great contribution of the psychosocial methodology focused on 'subjectivity' (that of participants and researchers) developed by Walkerdine and colleagues (Walkerdine *et al.*, 2001: 87, 106). I will draw upon the range of innovations presented by this psychosocial theoretical and methodological framework to think about psychical complexity, defensiveness, the status and meaning fantasy, and other psychosocial dimensions of interpretation throughout my data analysis chapters.

Yet I am caught between my own attachment to psychoanalytic ideas about subjectivity as forged through lack and the idea that the social and embodied experience also far exceeds this 'lack'. I am also caught between understandings that discourse is the medium for processes of regulation and re-signification, and the realisation that experience exceeds discourse and discourses shift and mutate. I therefore want to hang on to the tools of subjectification offered by Butler and psychosocial approaches informed by Lacan, but also go beyond them. I will explore next how Deleuze and Guattari have offered alternative but reconcilable frameworks and vocabularies for understanding the body, subjectivity and power and possibilities for disruptions of norms. While their work is set against psychoanalysis, it is also informed by it. They offer useful ways of moving beyond an understanding of subjectivity as trapped through a 'cultural freeze frame' of subjectification offering tools to see 'movement and qualitative transformation' (Massumi, 2002: 3). They also help us re-think desire beyond simply being structured via lack and longing as I elaborate below.

Deleuze and Guattari and the 'affective' turn

> With the ethico-politics of Deleuze, a distinction shatters … the disengagement of the beautiful soul (who celebrates an incorporeal counter-effectuation which doubles no state of things) and the spontaneous praxis defended by the dialectical donkey (who works only on the actual) are dismissed with one and the same gesture.
>
> (Bergen, 2010: 39)

Deleuze and Guattari's work has typically been viewed as 'high' theory, and as a set of ideas that work in an abstract way but which have little relevance to 'doing research'. As such there has tended to be a focus on textual modes of analysis, with the 'practical' dimensions of Deleuze's philosophy and approach to the empirical largely neglected. In education this has resulted in some philosophical engagements with Deleuze (either with or without Guattari) that do not take up the empirical implications of his and joint work (e.g. Peters, 2004; Semetsky, 2004). Deleuzian ideas have also been widely explored in social, cultural and feminist theory (see the books published in the Deleuze Connections series) and in the fields of art, film and media studies (see for example O'Sullivan, 2006; Pisters, 2003). Deleuze and Guttari are viewed as offering significant resources for thinking that is 'post-signification', that is which attempts to address the impasses of discursive determinism through what are termed 'post-humanist' theories of materiality, embodiment and affect (Alaimo and Hekman, 2006). The theories are post-human because they foreground the non-human and often non-intentional nature of force relations between bodies and things. Clough and Halley (2007: 2) have suggested we are witnessing an 'affective turn' in the social sciences where 'a new configuration of bodies, technology, and matter' require new modes of thinking. Deleuze and Guattari have been central in this 'affective turn'.

Recently, however, Deleuzian-inspired methodological thinking in the social sciences and education has been steadily growing (see, for example, Hickey-Moody and Malins, 2007; Olsson, 2007). There is growing recognition that Deleuze and Guattari's 'geophilosophy', in *Anti-Oedipus* (1984) and *A Thousand Plateaus* (1987), has offered new conceptual, ethical, and methodological tools for mapping tactics of domination (what they call capture/territorialisation) and for understanding how energetic forces (affect) might break off from normative regimes (lines of flight) in education and beyond (Kaufman and Heller, 1998; St. Pierre and Pillow, 2000; Bonta and Protevi, 2004). Deleuze and Guattari's influence in shaping educational and social science research practice through offering methodological tools is growing at a rapid pace as is evident in a range of journal articles, special issues and edited collections (Mazzei and McCoy, 2010; Masny and Cole, 2011; Coleman and Ringrose, 2012). A 2010 issue of *Qualitative Studies in Education* called 'Thinking with Deleuze in qualitative research' highlighted the complex issues involved in 'operationalising' the concepts, at the same time, however, suggesting that 'the difficult theories of Deleuze are now becoming the easy part, whereas the handcraft and inventive creative process of doing analysis becomes what is difficult' (Mazzei and McCoy, 2010: 505).

In my own work I have drawn on Deleuze, particularly his joint writing with Guattari. They called their theory a form of 'transcendental empiricism' because it seeks to move beyond pre-existing possibilities of interpretation. The quote with which I began this section gestures towards their unique contribution. Deleuze and Guattari rail against philosophical abstraction for its own sake – the disembodied philosopher (beautiful soul) who has no effect (Deleuze and Parnet, 2002). But they are just as eager to disrupt the fixations of the 'dialectical donkey' (empiricist) who only works on the 'actual' – a not so subtle dig at the forms of banal empiricism that can dog some social science research intent on uncovering 'the real'. I will go through the implications of their approach for doing feminist-grounded empirical (specifically qualitative) research and analysis as I proceed.

The critique of psychoanalysis

First, Deleuze and Guattari attack structural psychoanalysis and its 'negative' rules for understanding and interpreting the symbolic organisation of desire as lack. They recast the meanings and possibilities of human desire, complicating the psychoanalytic theory of lack via symbolic laws organised around the master signifier the 'phallus' (Lacan, 1977) toward a corporeal theory of action and give us tools as researchers to map 'cartographies' of flows and particles of energy that disrupt repressive regimes (Reynolds, 1998). According to Deleuze and Guattari (1984, 1987) capitalism has produced neurotic and paranoid desire, effecting the greatest repression of desiring-production in history by re-territorialising anything sacred, ritual and traditional and by undercutting anything that represses the mythologies of the autonomous individual. A lengthy attack on Freud's developmental theory of Oedipus forms the basis of Deleuze and Guattari's first joint book, *Anti-Oedipus* (1984), where they rail against assumptions about normal, healthy psychosexual development that underpin Freudian psychoanalysis, offering alternative theorisations of desire.[2] Deleuze and Guattari argue that psychoanalysis is taking part in the work of bourgeois repression at its most far-reaching level 'completing the task begun by nineteenth century psychology, namely, to develop a moralised familial discourse of mental pathology, linking madness to the "half-real, half-imaginary" dialectic of the family' (1984: 54). They argue the Oedipal myth and interpretation stops us understanding the flows and particles of energy or affect – it also channels desire shutting down desiring-production. For them, life energy is continually channelled and blocked through 'the great molar powers of family (oedipalisation), career (capitalism) and conjugality (heterosexualisation)' (Deleuze and Guattari, 1987: 257).

This part of their philosophy is useful for thinking about the trapping of libido through 'molar' gender norms, and how girls and women's libido in particular is channelled through the oedipal bondage of signifiers, which turns the feminine into lack (of the phallus) and which works to negate and repress women's desire/aggression/ anger. If we use Lacanian, Foucauldian and Butlerian thematics to describe this regulation, 'oedipalisation' is the ushering into the normative signifying discourses, structured through a dualising sex-gender system. Heteronormative femininity is merely one discourse regulating the flow of desire in capitalist regimes of production, into commodified versions of gendered subjectivity. I use Deleuze and Guattari's anti-psychoanalytic critique of Bourgeois, capitalist and heterosexualised repression to think about how affect gets channelled in the lives of teen girls in normative and regulative, yet not always predictable, ways.

Schizoanalysis as alternative method of analysis

Second as an alternative to psychoanalysis, Deleuze and Guattari develop what they call 'schizoanalysis' – a method of seeing and mapping – to deconstruct the oedipal myths and to 'blow apart' effects of 'dualism machines', like the binary between sanity/pathology. As a directly reactive notion to psychoanalysis, schizoanalysis is meant to work at several levels. Deleuze and Guattari suggest that the principal 'negative task' of schizoanalysis is the overthrow of psychoanalysis (which reproduces binary logics, normative strata and totalising theory). The two positive tasks of schizoanalysis are first to discover desiring machines that are dammed up by the forces of Oedipus and society 'learning what a subject's desiring machines are, how they work, with what syntheses, what bursts of energy in the machine, what constituent misfires, with what flows, what chains and what becomings in each case' (1984: 338). The second is to find lines of flight from a given stratum which is to map de-territorialisations and locate positive desire-production, operative as flow and multiplicity that ruptures a given stratum.

Deleuze and Guattari argue that desire is social not familial and the best guide to social desire is the schizoid, multiple and contradictory id rather than neurotic, ego-bound, and unitary, logics of the self. Here we can see that they are not completely eschewing psychoanalysis but seeking to re-work a theory of desire for understanding how to think and become otherwise. For example, they put forward the notion that men should attempt to think outside the normative molar in order to grasp the experience of the 'minority' (the less powerful) by 'becoming woman' or 'becoming animal'. Feminists like Elizabeth Grosz (1994: 163) have, however, derided schizoanalysis as Deleuze and Guattari:

> invest[ing] in a romantic elevation of psychosis, schizophrenia, becoming, which on one hand ignores the very real torment of suffering individuals and, on the other hand, positions it an un-livable ideal for others. Moreover in making becoming woman the privileged site of all becomings, Deleuze and Guattari confirm a long historical association between feminine and madness which ignores the sexually specific forms that madness takes.

While these are important cautions, I understand schizoanalysis more as a way to draw attention to the contradictory, schizoid conditions that typically surround us in conditions of 'late capitalist modernity' (Braidotti, 2006), but which we are demanded to erase, through calls to inhabit unambiguous, 'unitary', non-contradictory subjectivity (Bauman, 2001). The Deleuzian approach highlights painful contradiction in the social, deflecting criticism away from individual pathologisation of the inability to conform to impossible social conditions (particularly those of freedom, choice and achievement rife under the regulative, constrictive domain of neo-liberalism). For social scientists schizoanalysis is therefore an important methodology for grasping schizoid social conditions, directing our attention to social flows and forces, for instance the schizoid conditions informing new norms of teen femininity (Renold and Ringrose, 2011).

I want to use schizoanalysis as a methodological tool to challenge the pathologisation of the feminine binaries that get drawn in the social, for instance around the three major 'luminosities' (McRobbie, 2008) of girlhood I've been mapping: the academically successful vs failing girl, the nice vs the mean and/or aggressive girl, and the virginal innocent vs the over-sexualised slutty girl. These are contradictory discourses that specific girls have to manage in particular ways. So it is *not* the girl who is the pathological individual subject (Walkerdine, 1991); rather contradictory social conditions and competing demands of femininity create incompatible and therefore schizoid social conditions through which subjectivity is to be forged (Renold and Ringrose, 2011). Schizoanalysis as a method also goes beyond a Lacanian focus on binaries and lack and contends we need to stop merely psychologising and/or psychoanalysing these issues and actually map embodied responses that illustrate disruptions of normative power relations. It is this resistance to psychologising trends that individualise subjectivity that I find particularly important and refreshing in their approach. Thus while Deleuze and Guattari's 'becoming woman' may well be a flawed, simplistic example of their own desires for revolutionary immanence (see also critiques from Braidotti, 1994; Ahmed, 1999), it is actually possible to use their tools of analysis to map 'the sexually specific forms that madness takes' (Grosz, 1994: 163) or how feminine madness is produced as a mode of molar (dominant) capture in the social, which gets read onto particular girl bodies. It is just this type of analysis I want to provide – about the imposed social impossibility and schizoid nature of girls 'becoming woman' that I will apply in my data analysis chapters.

Rethinking power: affective assemblages

Third, in thinking about mapping desire, it is also important to note that Deleuze and Guattari slip in their work between notions of desire or desiring machines in *Anti-Oedipus* to the notion of affect in later works to move away from psychoanalytic notions of interior personal desire as lack to consider the productive flows of desire. Affect is more the flows out of and between bodies through points of connection. Brian Massumi's (1987: xvi) definition of affect in his introduction to *A Thousand Plateaus* describes how 'affect is not a personal feeling. Feelings are personal and biographical, emotions are social, and affects are pre-personal'. Affect thus presents an alternative way of thinking of libidinal flows of energy (Cole, 2011) and differentiating these from the normative patterns of 'emotion' that capture and code (structure) affect and channel libidinal flows. I retain the notion of desire as well as affect, to think about how human wants (unconscious and willful) can underpin affect, but affects flow through and beyond the human body via non-human formations that are non-individual and non-intentional as well.

Affect is not, however, some neutral form of unmediated 'flow'. Indeed Deleuze and Guattari (1987: 284) insist we examine how affect is charged up and operates as a set of force relations:

> we know nothing of a body until we know what it can do, in other words, what its affects are, how they can or cannot enter into composition with other affects, with the affects of another body, either to destroy that body or be destroyed by it, either to exchange actions and passions with it or to join with it in composing a more powerful body.

Thus 'affect is not a personal feeling, nor is it a characteristic, it is the *effectuation of a power*' (ibid.: 265, my italics). We see a shift from ontology of being and fixity to ontology of 'effectuation' and affective processes in constant motion. Massumi again describes affect as 'an ability to affect and be affected ... a pre-personal intensity ... implying an augmentation or diminution of that body's capacity to act' (in Gilbert, 2004: 3). The 'affective' dimension thus presents a way of analysing power relations within and between bodies and assemblages, and mapping 'flows of energy' and desire (Cole, 2011).

What social scientists can do with this approach methodologically is to think about bodily capacities to affect and be affected (at various scales and intensities) and map these (Coleman, 2008). Deleuze and Guattari offer some different conceptual vocabularies to understand bodily relations and flows of affect pointing to different economies of scale and social organisation. Bodies plug into and out of various scales of what they call 'machinic assemblages' or complex social configurations through which energy flows and is directed (Malins, 2004). 'Assemblages' is a useful way to think about social entities as 'wholes whose properties emerge from the interactions between the parts' (De Landa in Tamboukou, 2010: 685). Assemblages are 'characterised by relations of exteriority ... [that] imply that a component part of the assemblage may be detached from it and plugged into a different assemblage in which its interactions are different' (ibid.: 10). Through assemblage theory, the human body is also a 'machinic assemblage', which interacts with and has various capacities to affect other bodies and other scales of assemblages: 'A body's function or potential or "meaning" becomes entirely dependent on which other bodies or machines it forms an assemblage with' (Malins, 2004: 85). In previous work I have brought the concepts of affect and assemblage together to help think about how peer groups in schools and online social networks are various forms of 'affective assemblages' (Ringrose, 2010b). I will use this concept to think about teen peer groups as assemblages constituted through interactions among the various parts, with various affective capacities.

What I have also argued, following others, is that we need to recognise the ethico-political nature of Delueze and Guattari's approach. Assemblages never simply operate as a free flow of energy or desire, but are cut through with relations of power. According to Bonta and Protevi (2004: 10), Deleuze and Guattari's work allows for the 'investigation of "bodies politic" material systems of "assemblages"' which have ethical axes: that is we need to map 'the life-affirming or life destroying character of the assemblage'. Deleuze and Guattari (1987: 444) ask: 'Do assemblages have affinity with the state or with the nomadic war machine?' By this they mean, what do assemblages enable or disenable bodies to do and how does this align with or disrupt dominant (molar) power formations?

Power: space and matter

Fourth, Deleuze and Guattari develop further 'geo-philosophical' notions of striated and smooth space and molar and molecular matter to analyse the ease or constrictions of flows of energy in the social. As Maria Tamboukou explains (2008: 360) 'striated spaces are hierarchical, rule-intensive, strictly bounded and confining, whereas smooth spaces are open dynamic and allow for transformation to occur'. Deleuze and Guattari call for breaking down 'molar aggregates' which are normative constructions of sameness of being. Following the micro-sociology of Gabriel Tarde they suggest we need to explore the molecular level of movement and becomings – formations of desire in the social (Deleuze and Guattari: 1987: 340). I will use these tools to think about how school space and peer groups are cut through by commodifying dynamics organised through gendered and sexualised norms and idealisations that 'striate' the space, through 'molar' (normative) encodings of identity (ideals of 'sexy' girl and 'player' boy, for instance). In a recent article in *Qualitative Studies in Education*, Alecia Youngblood Jackson (2010: 584–585) applies this form of spatial analysis of matter to analyse an extract from ethnographic field notes about a girl Jesse:

> You step out of your car and begin to walk slowly up the gentle hill toward the school, comfortable in your own skin. Rather than a backpack, you carry a black Adidas gym bag slung on your shoulder. You are petite and stocky like a gymnast, and the gym bag bounces around well below your hips, almost to your knees. You wear black baggy sweatpants, a black tank top, and flip-flops. You ought to be wearing your cheerleading uniform today; there is a pep rally this afternoon and a basketball game tonight. The expectation is that, on game days, you overcode your body with molar constraints: you parade around school in your short skirt for the whole day, remove your nose ring, tame your wildly layered hair, and decorate the teams' lockers with ribbons and candy, but you do not do that. Just as molarity is a mode of desire, your leaving molarity behind is a desire. You direct your molecular freedom toward working that tension between molar/bodily limitations of cheerleading and supermolecularity, you counteractualize.
>
> You edge around the front of the school and reach the basketball gymnasium; you have a brief cheerleading practice this morning. You grasp the door handle, roll your eyes, and yank open the door. You know what is about to happen.
>
> You enter The Empire of Like, 7 occupied by molarized bodies and a bundle of complex forces of rules, laws, traditions that form those bodies into docile substances. There stand decades-old cheerleaders, decked out bow-to-tie in red-and-black school spirit: tight ponytails bound by curly ribbons, halter-tops, 10-inch pleated skirts, skin tanned from UV sun beds. They are heiresses of habitual patterns and normalities of femininity and sexuality. They dress to entertain;

they move to seduce. Molarity is a desire; fitting-in is a desire. They wear the uniform with pleasure, hyperaware of its sexiness and power. They enter into the social contract of molar co-existence, they actualize.

In this analysis we can see how molarity is used in a way similar to normativity. There is an attempt to explain how Jesse is somehow disrupting or troubling the 'molarity' of 'fitting in as a desire', with something else that her body enacts through its specific 'supermolecularity' or micro-movements in space that 'counteractualise'. For example, she enacts a subversive desire away from normative sexy feminine cheerleading dress with baggy sweatpants. What is relevant here is accounting for the molecularity of movement where we see small movements not mass revolution, where Jesse 'does' cheerleader a bit differently.

Here Deleuze and Guattari's theories move us beyond sociological traps of mimesis where we witness the social simply reproducing itself, in for instance structural accounts like Bourdieu's habitus. Mimesis is never straightforward copies but also production according to Deleuze: newness and difference may always enter into repetitions (Deleuze, 1986). As Deleuze and Guattari (1987: 12) have insisted:

> Mimicry is a very bad concept, since it relies on binary logic to describe phenomena of an entirely different order. The crocodile does not reproduce a tree trunk, any more than the chameleon reproduces the colours of its surroundings.

We need to map the specificity of becomings, which I will do in my analysis of girls' subjective performances of self.

As Tamboukou (2008: 360) articulates similarly 'we constantly move between deterritorialisation – freeing ourselves from the restrictions and boundaries of controlled, striated spaces – and reterritorialisation – repositioning ourselves within new regimes of striated spaces'. The notion of territorialisation is also spatial, describing when energy is captured and striated in specific space/time contexts. Leisha Jones (2011: 396) considers how territories are harnessed by girls suggesting we need to analyse different rythms of 'rhizomatic' activity through which they code and decode these territories (she uses the example of the exclusionary girl group 'the Plastics' in the *Mean Girls* movie). She says the 'territory of one girl body makes possible the territory of another' as girls work to survive the peer groups at school (ibid.: 394). I will apply this mode of analysis in my data chapters looking for moments of de-territorialisation when energy might escape or *momentarily* move outside normative strata, and re-territorialisation, which describes processes of recuperation of those ruptures. I also map 'lines of flight' or de-territorialisations or proliferations and excess that do not stop 'but branch[es] out and produce[s] multiple series and rhizomic connections' (Deleuze and Guattari, 1987: 15). Lines of flight break off from lines of subjection. They are rhizomatic 'becomings', 'tiny connections' and 'movements' which are operative at the minute or molecular level. It is this very small, micro form of 'imperceptibility' which we can map (Beddoes, n.d.).

Importantly, lines of flight are not magical escapes as implied by some critics. Butler (2004a) critiques Deleuze's philosophy as imbued with manic desires to flee existing matrixes of power: 'I feared that he was proposing a manic defense against negativity' (Butler, 2004a: 198). Deleuze and Guattari are actually quite clear, however, that some lines of flight are totally destructive as when they describe drug addiction, for instance: 'the creative line, or line of flight immediately turns into a line of death and abolition' (1987: 314). They are also explicit about the need to map whether lines of flight are destructive or productive (or both) and to consider what they enable or affect in specific space/time configurations.

In my work alone (Ringrose, 2006b) and with Emma Renold (Renold and Ringrose 2008, 2011; Ringrose and Renold, 2011) we have investigated the status of lines of flight from hetero-normative strata and territorialisations and the complexities of interacting assemblages. We argue that Deleuze and Guattari's rejection of the normative drive of psychological theories that pathologise girls and women is productive, and that their theories of affect and assemblages help us map striations, blockages and flows of energy happening in and around the spaces of schooling. I will elaborate the use of these tools further in the following chapters, mapping the nuance of girls' affective relations and capacities (or not) to trouble the boundaries of norms of being and doing 'girl' with new forms of 'becoming'.

Conclusion

In this chapter I have explored various psychosocial tools of analysis ranging from Butler through Walkerdine and psychosocial researchers to the work of Deleuze and Guattari. I am left with some questions about the possible uses of the tools of Deleuze and Guattari for *feminist* theory and research. Deleuze and Guattari have (in)famously argued that:

> Schizoanalysis is the variable analysis of the sexes in a subject beyond the anthropomorphic representation that society imposes on this subject, and with which it represents its own sexuality. The schizoanalytic slogan of the desiring-revolution will be first of all: to each its own sexes.
>
> (1984: 325)

Attias (1998: 103), like feminist critics Grosz and Butler, perceives Deleuze and Guattari's schizoanalysis as problematic if they 'wish to argue that every possible desire (including the desire for money or for power or for the phallus) challenges the dominant system'. I would assert, however, that what Deleuze and Guatarri offer is some new ways of perceiving desire and affective relations so we may find evidence of resistance (not necessarily conscious or rational) to unitary, molar identity formations as well as to what they call the 'micro-facisms' of everyday life, in both likely and unlikely places.

I have suggested that Deleuzo–Guattarian concepts are usefully brought into dialogue with other psychosocial approaches. I want to use this plurality of tools to map and potentially intervene into subjectifying processes and life-destroying and coercive 'dualism machines' that capture bodies and shape affects in young people's lives. One of the key organising principles of Deleuze and Guattari's approach is to ask the question 'What can a body do?' This question invites us to restage questions of agency to think at a different ontological level about how the body (subject/object) can act/move or not. As a social researcher working with young people and particularly girls, this approach helps me to ask: What can the sexed body of the girl do to disrupt normative power relations? How do we perceive and map such 'doings'? What is a line of flight? When are lines of subjectification recuperative (or re-territorialising) of affect? When do they exceed the modalities of capture, indicating an opening up of energy/desire? By allowing one to pose such questions the Deleuzo–Guattarian approach helps us to challenge and re-think the boundaries of research encounters and analysis, providing new tools to map what living as a girl and 'becoming woman' looks like in particular time/space parameters.

My hope is that this is where the immanent motion of Deleuze and Guattari's philosophy comes into further play in the following chapters. As researcher/educators we have to continue to initiate lines of flight in our *thinking* which, as the Deleuzian feminist scholar Braidotti (2008) suggests, means staging 'experiments in thought'. Deleuze argues for a revolutionary spirit of intervention in thinking and philosophy:

> What we most lack is a belief in the world. We've quite lost the world. It's been taken from us. If you believe in the world you precipitate events, however inconspicuous, that elude control, you engender new space-times, however small their surface or volume …
>
> (Deleuze and Negri, 1990: 176)

If we conceive of the research process itself as a space-time continuum where bodies and forces intersect, creating new possibilities for thinking and doing, then we are more open to experimenting with different forms of and combinations of tools for doing social science research and analysis. This is not unhinged from power in some naïve interpretivist hermeneutic that falls into cultural relativity. As Hickey-Moody and Malins (2007: 18) argue, 'Deleuze's philosophy makes socio-political empiricism an imperative, because the assemblages that social researchers and practitioners form with the world necessarily have implications for bodies and their capacities'. Within this framework, if we find moments where the research-space-time opens up new possibilities of understanding the transforming nature of gendered and sexualised desire and bodies then we are actually making molecular interventions in our own thinking with immanent possibilities of becoming. This is the philosophy and practice of transcendental empiricism in motion.

7 Sexual regulation and embodied resistance

Teen girls entering into and negotiating competitive heterosexualised, postfeminist femininity

This chapter sets the theoretical terrain and methodological strategies mapped in the previous chapters into motion, exploring how girls are navigating contradictory postfeminist discourses of girlhood. In contrast to the mythologies of 'successful' schoolgirls who have magically escaped their feminine bodies (Kindlon, 2006), I will explore a competitive 'heterosexualised matrix' (Butler, 1997) of power relations constituting school-based teen girls' relationships. I illustrate the primary importance of the sexualised feminine body in friendship groups, documenting some of the conflicts that are staged in managing transitions into heterosexual dating cultures at school.

I map the experiences of a girl friendship group of tween to teen 12–14 year olds who reflect on their transitions to secondary school, drawing on data from an empirical study of 'ordinary' working class girls in a low achieving secondary school in South Wales. This group are managing routine anxieties around educational performance, but the central locus of their concerns is upon the social hierarchies in the peer network. I explore issues facing differently classed and raced girls who face challenges in relation to navigating the popularity hierarchies organised around the heterosexualised playing field at school (Currie *et al.*, 2007).

I will elaborate my psychosocial approach to re-theorise girls' relational cultures, speaking to the developmental psychological literature that suggests girls are relationally orientated, which means they have trouble managing direct conflict, as reviewed in Chapter 3 (Gilligan and Brown, 1992; Crick and Rose, 2000). I aim to contribute to the sociology and education literatures which have explored girls' friendship cultures (McRobbie and Nava, 1984; Hey, 1997, 2005; Aapola *et al.*, 2005) and issues of sexual regulation and reputation (Cowie and Lees, 1981; Holland *et al.*, 1992; Kitzenger, 1995; Kehily, 2002, 2008). School peer cultures are part of the 'informal curriculum' of schooling and crucial to understanding the everyday lived educational contexts and experience of young people (Stromquist, 2007).

My input will be to *explicitly* locate the roots of much of the relational difficulties and aggression between girls as linked to having to manage a compulsory 'heterosexualised matrix' (as theorised by Butler and outlined in Chapter 6) at school and in teen friendship and relationship cultures (Renold, 2005; Nayak and Kehily, 2008; Youdell, 2006; Ringrose and Renold, 2010; Kehily *et al.*, 2002). I suggest that a great deal of conflict among girls relates to entering into and navigating intensifying forms of compulsory heterosexuality, and the discursive incitement to shift from primary relationships with girls to a heterosexual orientation toward and higher valuing of relationships with boys. Linking together research on girls' sexuality and girls' aggression, I illustrate how the most pressing and affectively charged conflicts between girls at school relate to sexualised status, identity and competition, where girls sexually regulate and shame one another (Tolman, 2002; Lamb, 2002). These data also illustrate classed and raced positionings of the girls, showing how they navigate peer sexual cultures and indicate points when sexually regulative discourses break down. My psychosocial analysis foregrounds ruptures and fantasies where something different emerges as 'lines of flight' from normative, developmental heteronormative femininity and the heterosexual matrix (Driscoll, 2002; Deleuze and Guattari, 1987; Renold and Ringrose, 2008).

Methodological design and fieldwork

This chapter outlines the findings from a Social Sciences and Humanities Research Council of Canada funded qualitative small-scale study in 2004/2005, 'Girls and the subject of aggression and bullying'. The study mapped out international media, policy and research contexts around issues of femininity and sexualised aggression and collected data in Wales, UK, through a series of in-depth focus and individual interviews with a mixed ethnicity friendship group of girls: Faiza (14) and Safa (12) who were sisters, both Iraqi-Welsh; Lucy (13), Vietnamese-Welsh; Elizabeth (13), White-Welsh; and Gwyneth (13), White-English. Faiza, Lucy, Elizabeth and Gwyneth were all in Year 9, and Safa was in Year 8. I also refer to an interview with Gwyneth's mother, Sue.

In a research climate where it is increasingly difficult to gain access to schools, particularly for research on sensitive issues like aggression, I opted to do community-based research on this issue. In the autumn of 2004 I contacted a community centre in Portsview,[1] a highly ethnically diverse and working class area of the city. I first interviewed the director of the community centre about the issues facing the young people in the area. I was introduced to several members of staff, including Sue, whose daughter attended Herbert Secondary. Sue told me her house operated as a sort of 'home base' for her daughter's friends, who spent a great deal of time hanging out there; she also said the group would be interested to speak to me about issues of aggression and bullying. From here I was able to establish a relationship with Sue's daughter, Gwyneth, and her friendship group. I conducted a focus group interview with the girls, individual interviews with each girl and with Sue, and then a follow-up focus group interview with the girls. The focus group interviews explored their experiences of schooling, friendships, bullying, fighting, boys, intimacy, etc. Individual, in-depth interviews with each participant explored these topics and the issues that had emerged in greater detail. These multiple interviews over time generated rich, narrative-based accounts about the girls' experiences of friendship, conflict and aggression (Seidman, 1998).

My methodology drew on work in cultural and youth studies, which have developed strategies for working with young people outside of the regulative institutional context of schools. I drew on the successful snowball sampling methods of feminist researchers studying girls and young women in various non-school settings (McRobbie and Garber, 1976; Brown, 1998; Pini, 2001). Researchers working with young people in alternative contexts like youth clubs, community centres, homes and bedrooms each have access to different types of data than might be possible to gather through work in the institutional contexts of schools (Cullen, 2010). This is a significant aspect of my community- and home-based study, since my discussions with the girls were able to tap into the social dynamics of their school life and friendship group, possibly to a greater degree than research within school walls. Interviews were in Sue's lounge, facilitating an entirely different embodied, psychosocial dynamic between the researcher and the researched.[2]

The school

Although the interviews were not conducted at the school, the geographical and cultural dynamics at work in the school and neighbourhood were crucial to this project which was interested in the classed and raced experience of girlhood in relation to experiences at school. The ESTYN[3] report describes Herbert Secondary as an '11–19, mixed, community school'. Herbert is 'economically disadvantaged with 44% of students entitled to receive free school meals, 63% of students from "minority" ethnic backgrounds, 56% of students with English as a second language, and 88% of pupils with levels of reading below their chronological age upon entry'. Herbert is well below national averages for National Curriculum and GCSE results.

The school was experiencing problems over the catchment area, which was divided between a wealthier middle class area and a much more working class and ethnically diverse area. These two areas were literally bisected by a major thoroughfare, and the working class area had become increasingly 'ghettoised' since the recent completion of a major sports stadium near the school. The school was increasingly losing students from the wealthier 'side of the tracks'. I became aware of the problems in the area and school through the educational research culture at my university. Anecdotal stories that Herbert had 'the highest teen pregnancy rate in Europe' circulated among the postgraduate students and faculty, who also reported it was 'rough' and 'had a lot of bullying'.[4] These stories suggest Herbert held a place of urban legend as a dangerous or what Lucey and Reay (2003) call a 'demonised school'. In a context of 'failing schools', a standards agenda and school performance discourses, issues of reputation about the student body attain increasing importance and schools that are viewed as providing inadequate education and/or protection for students are subject to increasingly public and governmental scrutiny (Reay, 2004).

The schools' positioning vis-à-vis discourses of perceived performance, economic and cultural diversity of students and 'bullying' cultures is important as it fuelled parental anxieties and responses to the peer social network at the school and also fuelled a discourse of parental 'choice' (Vincent and Ball, 2006) where middle class parents were faced with dilemmas over whether to send their children to the school or not, as I explore. I will illustrate, for instance, how dynamics of parental 'choice' are thoroughly informed by perceptions about the cultures of masculinity, femininity and sexuality in the school. Thus, what is typically regarded as a banal issue of girls' name-calling and 'falling out' are actually central to discourses of school performance, something that should be articulated to raise the visibility of sexualised competition and hierarchy in order to develop more effective strategies for addressing these issues.

Being 'known': the dilemmas of perfect and 'nice' vs horrible and 'mean' femininity

These girls like most others at school had common sets of worries about exam performance and the problem of friends being displaced through ability setting at school. Faiza discussed the issue of Lucy being moved down a set which disrupted the friendship network, while Lucy talked about how much pressure she felt to perform given she dreamt of becoming a lawyer (and I will return to their aspirational fantasies later in this chapter). However, I want to stress from the outset that the girls did not explain their group identity in terms of academic achievement; rather what was important to them was how they were locatable in the school hierarchal assemblage in terms of visual currency of being recognisable and 'known' to others. Being 'known' and popular on the basis of appearance and sex appeal was crucial and mapped directly onto popular cultural formations of femininity. For instance, the girls referred to themselves explicitly as the 'Spice Girls' (see also Reay, 2001) in an attempt to position themselves as being known and popular and embodying desirable forms of femininity:

Faiza: It's like we're the Spice Girls, there's a sporty one, there's a fashionable one, there's a girl one, there's a baby, it's like that. There are groups in school that everybody knows about. We are not the popularest of groups but we are not unknown. Like say eighty-five per cent of Year 9 and below know us.

At this age, the girls were also navigating complex ideals of perfect age-appropriate, good girlhood, set against the partial realisation that these were actually impossible ideals. Asked to describe both their friend group and their idea of an ideal girl, these were some of the responses:

Gwyneth: Not like stuck up or nothing. Not like always boasting about what she has bought and stuff like that. Funny. Kind.
Elizabeth: They'd be pretty and they'd be blond [Elizabeth is blond]. And they'd be like fun and playful and nice and ... hang around you all of the time like Gwyneth, except the blond thing ...
Faiza: Sporty, pretty, funny, intelligent, friendly, kind and fits it ... gets along with everybody, not just in one group, she is like in everybody's group.
Jessica: Do you know any girls like that?
Faiza: No.

This passage is important for highlighting 'an ideal type of what it is to be a girl' (Paechter, 2006: 366). Idealised femininity is described here as being modest, funny, kind, pretty, blond, playful, nice, intelligent, fitting in, and getting along with everybody. Valerie Walkerdine (e.g. Walkerdine, 1984, 1991) has argued for over two decades that femininity and girlhood has historically been organised around a series of binary oppositions: a feminine/masculine binary, but also a good/bad binary of femininity. This formation illustrates in detail how ideal femininity is constructed in opposition to qualities of masculinity, like physical, direct and rational. Ideal femininity is also set against deviant, otherised bad qualities such as: conceited, vain, cruel, ugly, dark, serious, mean, conniving, stupid, and doesn't get along with anybody.

Lynn Mikel Brown (1998: 100) has written extensively about how demands for perfect femininity and expectation for conflict-free relationships among girls cuts off the possibility of the open expression of anger as acceptable. Indeed, the girls debated how boys can 'punch each other' but girl have to talk about how they 'feel' – a feminine demand for relational connection that can lead to problems:

Lucy: Yeah but boys treat each other mean as well just in another way, like they punch each other or like.

Faiza: No, boys don't let their feelings out, they don't talk about personal stuff and girls will and that's how the whole stirring happens.

Elizabeth: Yeah because girls think, 'O I can trust him because most of my friends, tell them a secret and they like might slip it out'.

Faiza: Or betray them, they're say something else.

Lucy: And then get girls upset because they think, 'O they're betraying me' and stuff like that but boys will just punch.

Faiza: Yeah but boys won't even, and they won't even mention anything about their personal life anyway.

Jessica: So what do you think about this whole thing, that you're saying about, girls will say they're, you're betraying me or whatever?

Lucy: Girls will just tell someone straight how they feel but like boys won't.

Faiza: Who? You can't keep your secrets to yourself because no girl keeps their secrets to themselves, so like tells someone and then that's how they betray each other, stop talking about me!

There are two conflicting views here, between Lucy who suggests girls will say what they feel and boys won't and Faiza who insists that girls can't keep secrets and betray one another. The affect is described in rich ways as the problem of feelings 'stirring around' and then the issue of escape or information 'slipping out' when they are discussing personal details of friendship with one another. This invokes an 'affective economy' at play where personalised information can be used as 'currency' in friendship groups (Ringrose, 2010a: 598; see also Brown, 1998; Hey, 1997; Currie *et al.*, 2009). Faiza also talks about how girls can't 'keep secrets to themselves' implying leaky relations between girls and ends by addressing the room at large with 'stop talking about me!'

There was some resignation at the impossibility of the demands of femininity hanging between the polarised domains of nice and horrible, something that was discussed in relation to the ultimate metaphor of feminine pathology – being 'two-faced':

Lucy:	I think that girls can be really nice and then they can be really like horrible.
Faiza:	All girls are two-faced.
Lucy:	Yeah, everyone is, do you get what I mean, like everyone slags someone off behind their …
Elizabeth:	You know Jenny and that, they all slag each other off behind their backs.
Lucy:	I know, and then they're best friends …
Faiza:	I don't know, everyone's two-faced because like if someone says, oh I'm not two-faced.
Jessica:	What do you mean two-faced?
Faiza:	Like everyone slags someone off in their lives, do you get what I mean? Everyone like slags someone off before.
Lucy:	Yeah but what's that got to do with girls being strong and sticking up for themselves?
Gwyneth:	Because girls are mean.

The expectations around ideal femininity as 'nice' (Paechter, 2006: 368) set up femininity as a site of perpetual failure. The ideal of femininity as non-competitive and nurturing comes into harsh contradiction with the realities of heterosexualised and other axes of competition, organising contemporary neo-liberal performance-based schooling culture. The girls reproduce the very convictions about pathological mean-ness or 'slag-ness' as endemic to femininity that I outlined in Chapter 3. The strength of the discursive positions of girls as 'two-faced' (a metaphor for a split and potentially destructive subject) and the notion that all girls are susceptible to this pathology makes girl a subject to a position that is a site of risk. You have to identify with it, but can never comfortably inhabit it. Lucy, however, challenges Faiza's conviction about being two-faced and 'slagging' others off, asking 'what's that got to do with girls being strong and sticking up for themselves?' Lucy is refusing universalising narratives about girls' pathological nature raising the issue that girls should be allowed the space to stick up for themselves and be 'strong' that is to question injustices and competition between girls, invariably discussed as a problem that related to sexual conflicts 'over boys'.

Bitching over boys: negotiating 'reputation' and the signifier 'slut'

Faiza:	Girls, they argue, they like bitch about each other.
Jessica:	So tell me what kind of things happen?
Faiza:	They argue about boys, they argue about looks. Like if you just look at them.
Jessica:	What do you mean, do you argue over boys?

Faiza:	No it's stupid.
Lucy:	Those two had an argument over a boy about a week ago.
Jessica:	Which?
Faiza:	Gwyneth.
Jessica:	Okay, tell me … One at a time.
Lucy:	There's this boy called Sam Laney and there were these three days Gwyneth was off school because she had like a flu or something and within those three days, he, this boy would go to Elizabeth, start hugging her, start like … touching her and everything and Gwyneth had found out about it, she wasn't very pleased because Gwyneth and Elizabeth both fancy him, yeah … and then Gwyneth thought, okay a bit unfair that, she gets all the fun with him or something, so then they stopped talking for like a day and then.
Gwyneth:	It wasn't even a day, it was like an evening …
Faiza:	Well then at the end of the day, the boy comes and tells Elizabeth that he doesn't like her and goes out with Amy.
Jessica:	So he's going out with someone else now?
Lucy:	Remember telling Kelly he didn't like Elizabeth?
Gwyneth:	No, yeah. He said he didn't like Elizabeth because she was a frigid.
Faiza:	That means that she don't do something.
Jessica:	And Amy does?
Faiza:	Yeah.
Lucy:	She was, you know in primary school, guess what she did?
Faiza:	In primary school she used to go out with boys younger and do things with them … some of like our friends … she does like hang around, her reputation is known as the person who, who go around, let boys do anything to her because that's the kind of why boys go with her but that's not like everybody, not everybody in the year thinks that …
Jessica:	Like what do you mean will do anything?
Faiza:	Not anything and it's not like she doesn't, she doesn't mean to attract the boys, like it was on sports day that she was wearing that yellow skirt.
Lucy:	No.
Faiza:	She's kind of slut if you think of, in my perspective, it's not like she's fat and she's like, she looks horrible, she has got a nice figure but like she shouldn't do it, she shouldn't show it off to everyone.
Elizabeth:	She wears skirts about that big [puts hand at top of thigh].
Faiza:	Because having a reputation isn't a good thing, it's a bad thing because will go, Oh don't go out with her, she'll go out for a week and then.
Safa:	No but go out with them because she'll do anything with her and stuff like that.
Faiza:	In other words the boys are taking advantage because they, they, the only reason they start going out with her is because they think she'll do stuff with them but like, she is quite nice, ain't it, do you know what I mean, she is a really nice girl.
Safa:	She is a really nice person but like …

As has been documented at length by feminist scholars of girlhood (Kehily, 2002; Currie *et al.*, 2009), girls seem to have to manage an impossible set of demands to be attractive but not inappropriately sexual, and the long-standing signifier of sexual regulation used to discipline girls' reputation at school is 'slut'. Open sexualised performances and attention seeking were not easily tolerated. If one girl was thought to set herself apart from the others or to, as Rachel Simmons (2003) has put it, think 'she's all that', she was met with harsh reprisal. We can see the complex negotiation of heterosexuality among the girls as they describe the conflict that broke out between Gwyneth and Elizabeth over the attention of a boy. A resolution is partially available between Gwyneth and Elizabeth because the boy rejects Elizabeth as 'frigid' in favour of another girl Amy who is dismissed as popular with boys because she will 'do anything' with them. I was interested to pursue this term 'slut' further:

Jessica:	So who called her a slut? Is that a word you would use for other girls too in the school?
	[Loud conversation …]
Lucy:	Shut up! Not me! Gwyneth Robertson, slut!
Jessica:	Why are they joking about this with you?
Gwyneth:	Because they're horrible! Just because I've gone out with all of them … I haven't. I haven't really!
Lucy:	She's been around!
Gwyneth:	But I don't do things with people I go with out with, like Amy.
Faiza:	No, no, it's just a joke when we say she's a slut.
Gwyneth:	So you have to cross it out now, you have to cross it out now!
Elizabeth:	No she doesn't do anything.
Jessica:	So how … does she flirt?
Faiza:	… she's [Gwyneth] nice to be friends to but she's not flirting, she's just being nice … But they [boys] might take it the wrong way, they might get the wrong end of the stick.

Again, the girls discursively constitute and negotiate the subject position of 'slut'. Slut constitutes a discursive nodal point (Laclau and Mouffe, 1985) of fixation in the discourses of adolescent girlhood or what I have termed a sticky signifier that glues bad affects onto girls bodies (Kofoed and Ringrose, 2012). These girls are in the early stages of a complex identificatory gendered process navigating sexualised culture where they have to take up a position around what form of girl and sexuality they will perform. Slut is the signifier for the bad and excessive sexuality when girls get this balance wrong. Currie *et al.* in their study of girl power explored how relationships with boys can confer status and popularity onto girls, but suggest it is a high-risk game where those viewed as 'slutty' are excluded by other girls (2007: 29). This is a practice of 'slut shaming', a notion that has recently been popularised to explore the dynamic of sexual regulation where a girl's reputation can be invoked and scrutinised to discipline her through codes of sexual conduct (Albury *et al.*, 2011). Psychosocially slut-shaming appears to express a dynamic where jealousy gets sublimated into a socially acceptable form of social critique of girls' sexual expression (Ringrose and Renold, 2012).

The girls play around with what slut is and what it can mean as it travels across different bodies and moves around the room. In the first extract they position Amy as a slut because she'll 'do anything'. She is positioned as both sexually aggressive and a passive container for boys' lust. In the second extract someone suggests Lucy is a slut then she deflects the label onto Gwyneth, who then defends her status by distinguishing herself from Amy, saying she doesn't 'do things', which Elizabeth confirms. Slut is ambiguous because it holds the connotation of being known, sexy and desirable but also excessive, dirty and wrong. It ends up 'sticking' on Amy, who becomes the projective receptacle for inappropriate sexual excess. Faiza then works to position Gwyneth as an innocent, unintended victim of male advances, saying it is her niceness that boys take the 'wrong way'. It is interesting that Faiza and her sister Safa who are Iraqi led the discussion about girls who will 'do anything' and boys 'taking advantage' of such girls, which serves to position boys as sexually powerful and girls as sexual victims and to also defensively regulate those girls perceived to 'show it off to everyone' as a 'slut'. Through this exercise they sexually regulate femininity but also try to resist the imperative to display a form of sexually compliant girl.

The embodied subtext to this conversation is important. The five girls are squeezed onto a small sofa and the floor of the lounge, with me hugging a corner of the couch in front of the tape recorder. Their bodies are pressed close upon one another, cuddling, touching, pushing, poking, and jostling one another as part of their pleasure in articulating the signifier 'slut', of navigating being recognised as 'known' by the boys, as having the collective authority to mark out boundaries and discipline the acceptable and unacceptable in displays and performances of feminine sexuality. The allure of sexual prowess was both revered and resisted:

Lucy:	Lauren Taylor, she's known as the, wow the stunning one in our year.
Faiza:	She's butt ugly, she's butt ugly though.
Lucy:	Stunning to boys, stunning to boys …
Jessica:	Why is that?
Lucy:	The reason because she lets people do the things to her. She's not really ugly or nothing but she's not the prettiest.
Elizabeth:	No, she's not pretty at all. She's got a nice figure, that's why boys like her.
Lucy:	And because she lets them do it, in like flirt with them and stuff, which I don't do.
Faiza:	She's got a stunning figure, that's why boys like her and she lets boys, even though she's got a boyfriend, she comes up to her, she lets boys come up to her and touch her bum even though she goes out with a boy.
Lucy:	And he's quite tough so he could beat up any.
Faiza:	And I told her once 'why don't you stop it?' She goes, 'I have no choice'. Obviously you have a choice.
Jessica:	What do you think she means?
Faiza:	I think she likes it but like if she didn't want them to do it, she could just like turn around and go like stop because what she does, is 'Oh stop that' (high effeminate voice), ar, ar, ar … and you've got to say 'STOP!' by the way.
Safa:	She should.

In the relationality between the girls so privileged as a form of ideal femininity, there is a boundary drawn between girlish femininity (sexual innocence) – which is a primary identification or allegiance with girls – and allowing attractiveness to boys (sexual maturity) to take precedence in the peer network. The girls comment on Lauren's body as stunning, that is able to 'stun' and therefore seduce boys. Faiza takes up this discourse, but reads intentionality onto the girl, who 'lets' the boys 'do it', which is read simultaneously as passivity and weakness and collusion and sexual aggression. Again, Faiza and her sister Safa are the most vocal in saying Lauren should stop the touching. They were the only two members of the group whose parents would not let them date boys, an issue likely related to their Muslim background. This corresponds in interesting ways to Debbie Weekes' (2002: 256) research, which suggested that black teen girls who were marginalised from dating cultures and from ideals of white, feminine desirability, worked to sexualise 'popular' white girls as 'blowers' (i.e. would give boys blow jobs), constructing their own image of respectable, clean, monogamous, non-sexual femininity. Girls' sexual cultures are inflected through ethnic, racial and cultural dynamics, which mediates their individual investment in sexual discourses and their collective negotiation of acceptable behaviour among friends. Faiza mocks Lauren, mimicking an effeminate version of 'Oh stop it', contrasted with her shouting 'STOP!' which ruptures the performance of femininity. I will return to Faiza's rupturing of normative heterosexualised discourses of femininity again, later in this chapter.

Sexual competition and the politics of 'bad' fighting

As I have been discussing, my data like others' (Hey, 1997; Kehily, 2002; Renold, 2005) repeatedly indicated that sexual regulation of femininity was central to the fabric of girls' friendships, as girls constituted their own version of ideal 'girl' against others. I want to emphasise that sexual regulation of other girls provides the *primary* means through which girls are socially sanctioned to express their assertiveness, aggression and rage (against other girls), usually against a particular member of their affective networks (friendships) at school. When jealousy and competition emerge they are legitimately allowed to discipline other girls' sexual subjectivity, a dynamic that works to bring some of the friendship group closer together while other girls are projected onto as objects of hatred, shame and/or disgust:

Jessica:	Okay, do you ever get in fights? Do you ever get in like bad fights?
Faiza:	Bad fight is making you fight your other friends on your side, so your best friend doesn't get anyone on their side.
Jessica:	Has it ever happened?
Faiza:	Katie.
Gwyneth:	No Katie had like Natasha.
Faiza:	Yeah I know but she was trying to get people to go on her side, so she started hanging around with Natasha, who she always use to talk about, she started to hang around with Amy Turner who she use to talk

about … she didn't go to school for four months and surprised like the council or the school really didn't do anything about it. The reason is she left school, according to her, was because her best friend goes to St David's.

Gwyneth: Yeah, well why did she leave school? If her best friend goes to St David's, when she goes to Chapel Hill now, shouldn't she have gone to St David's?

Jessica: So how do you feel about this girl now?

Gwyneth: I hate her.

Faiza: The things she did, at one stage she was dressing up in skirts the length of her knickers and we talked, dressed like that, with like nothing there and she would be all really weird, in other words, she made herself small … It was like, Oh she walked past a boy and she goes, Oh he fancies me or.

Lucy: Not you, because I'm prettier than you.

Faiza: When in fact she was the ugliest girl in our year.

Lucy: But you don't exactly want to hear that you're ugly.

Jessica: So if she left …

Faiza: She left the group for the good of herself and for the good of us.

Jessica: But you think you would say in your own mind maybe that you won or …

Lucy: Not won.

Faiza: Won what, the fight, yeah, why not? She would, why … What did she say to you?

Elizabeth: Because she said that, when … me and Luke were boyfriend girlfriend, she said that she would kiss Luke even though I was going out with him and I was meant to be one of her closest friends and then I asked her to her face is that true that you said that? She said no, that she never said anything like that.

Lucy: She admitted to little Gwyneth she said it.

Faiza: She's two-faced, a two-faced little pig.

Jessica: What happened?

Faiza: They have a picture together (pointing to Elizabeth).

Jessica: So you were friends with her also?

Elizabeth: Yeah we all were.

Faiza: Yeah but you [Elizabeth and Gwyneth] got close to her in Year 8.

Elizabeth: Yeah like me, Gwyneth and Katie.

Faiza: In Year 8 them three got really close to each other, really close, they'd leave us two out, you always.

Gwyneth: I didn't say that, I didn't know you felt like that!

This dialogue explains the girls getting into a fight with Katie during the previous Year 8. This event was significant and took up a lot of discussion in focus group and individual interviews. Katie is described as an 'ex' member of their friendship group, criticised for being too full of herself, which they say made herself 'small' but also at other points made the others feel 'small'. This descriptor is affectively interesting as a way of signalling a reduction in one's status, power and positivity.

In Currie *et al.*'s (2007: 146) study they found that aggression and competition with other girls made some girls more popular and attractive to boys and Duncan (2006) had similar findings. But I want to highlight here the aggressive fall-out and destructive sexual regulation of Katie by the friendship group. Gwyneth declares 'I hate her', and Faiza describes the inappropriate dress and mannerisms that justify this hatred. While Lucy hesitates to say they 'won' this fight, Faiza, the most condemning of Katie, agrees unequivocally to my provocative interpretation, calling Katie a 'two-faced little pig'. We see again the binaries that separate slut, bitch, two-faced, pig and 'horrible' from good, loyal, rational and appropriately (non-)sexual within the terms established in the micro-dimensions of the group.

Katie is also described as lacking boundaries and saying she would kiss the other girls' boyfriends and lie about it afterwards. The group respond protectively against Katie's perceived violation of the group, including liking Luke whom Elizabeth liked. It also emerged that Faiza felt threatened when Elizabeth and Gwyneth grew close to Katie in Year 8 and left Lucy and her out. Deception, lying, secrets and betrayal about sexual status are all discursively organised further discussion of what actually started the fight with Katie:

Faiza: Remember how this all started when you went to Daffyd Park and she said that she'd gone with someone, that's how it all started. What happened was Elizabeth hadn't like snogged anyone …

Jessica: Where's that [Daffyd Park]?

Faiza: It's like this 'adventure' weekend we went to … Like a rock climbing kind of, and we went there and we were staying in a room with like older girls fifteen now and they were a bit younger then and there was like me, Katie, Elizabeth in there and then the girls were saying 'have you liked snogged anyone?' They got to Elizabeth and she said 'no', and they said, 'oh don't worry about it like, it's better if you admit it, it's like we're not going to tease you and stuff like that,' so Elizabeth says like, 'alright,' and then got to Katie …

Lucy: No, hold on but before, they went to Elizabeth, she said no, they said that was okay and then the rest girls after Elizabeth all said 'yeah,' and then they got to Katie last … and then they goes 'have you?' and she goes, 'yeah when I was in Cornwall I snogged this boy' …

Gwyneth: She never told us that. She went 'yeah I didn't want to tell you.'

Lucy: And then we got her by her … we kind of … 'you never said that' to her and she goes, 'I never wanted to tell' like and then she was like, she started teasing Elizabeth but like, but like not really saying it out loud but she was saying just because I have … and looked at Elizabeth, stuff like that. It's not like very fair because Elizabeth should wait until she wants to with someone who she really likes. And then Katie started making fun of it even though she hasn't done it. Katie liked lied about it, init. And then made Elizabeth feel like stupid because she hadn't done it, and then I was sleeping over her house one time after that and I goes, 'so why did you like say' …

Faiza: Like we said, 'oh why, why did you tell them?' She goes 'because I didn't want to be the only one' and we said 'yeah but Elizabeth said she didn't', she goes 'yeah but I didn't hear anything'. 'Yeah but you were like teasing her about it' she goes 'okay, calm down, stop hassling me about it, silly me'. And then, so me and Elizabeth then like closed down and said 'oh it's kind of rude' about what she said like you and then it started from there.

What is being negotiated here is the sexual 'knowingness' and 'expertise' (Bragg and Buckingham, 2009: 132) vs good girl, childish innocence and inexperience. Katie is said to have lied about snogging a boy to elevate herself with a group of older girls, thereby shaming Elizabeth as sexually inexperienced (having already been said to have been called 'frigid' by a boy Sam in the discussion earlier). This tension over who is more desirable in relation to sexual experience (or lack thereof) is said to have started the momentum leading up to the 'bigger' fight:

Jessica: So I just want to try and understand how it first happened that you got into this disagreement.
Elizabeth: She thought she was better than us.
Gwyneth: One time she was walking down the, and she was talking about how many boys fancied her and everything.
Elizabeth: And then like, 'Oh who fancies you? No one, Oh well I guess they all fancy me then …'
Gwyneth: Like she would say really horrible stuff to me and Elizabeth like, make us feel all small and that and like, then one day we were talking we realised she'd been saying it to both of us … because we thought she had just like to one of us like, so we thought we'll talk to her about her and then she went … and told her mum.
Jessica: So when you talked to her at school what happened?
Elizabeth: We got her by herself like because we didn't want to say it in front of everyone …
Gwyneth: Yeah and we really didn't want to embarrass her because we wanted to, like see if she had an explanation of about what's been saying, like if she was upset about something … she was like denied it all …

Again it is apparent that the conflict revolves entirely around heterosexual prowess and Katie thinking she 'was better than us'. Gwyneth and Elizabeth describe confronting Katie at school, and how Katie told her mum. While this episode may appear as banal, everyday and un-noteworthy to teachers, parents and researchers in close contact with girls, the episode took on great significance for the girls, when Katie's mother called the school about the incident and the girls were sanctioned through an anti-bully provision. Katie's mum then took her off school for several weeks, finally transferring her to another school.

The gendered, sexualised, classed and race discourse of 'bullying'

I want to unpack this episode further through the discussions in individual interviews. By examining the episode in greater detail I will illustrate how bullying intervention at school can miss the complex power relations of gender, sexualised and classed culture, and parenting and school choice, which shapes the unfolding of the interpersonal dynamics between the girls.

In my interview with Gwyneth's mother, Sue, the politics of this episode became clearer, since Sue related that Katie's best friend Hannah was also pulled out of Herbert by her parents only two weeks into the Year 7 school year, after a different conflict among the girls at school, and placed at St David's, a Welsh religious school. Sue felt this backdrop of events greatly influenced the dynamics between the girls. Gwyneth related in her individual interview that during the first two weeks of school when Hannah was there, Katie and Hannah sat together in form class and left Gwyneth to sit by herself. When Hannah suddenly left, Katie asked to sit with Gwyneth:

Gwyneth: Katie came up and said 'Oh, can I sit with you?' And I felt a bit sorry for her but then at first I thought 'Oh', she did that to me so for a couple of lessons, a couple of mornings I made her sit by herself like said she couldn't sit with us, but then I said come and sit with us because I felt horrible making her sit by herself. And um ... so she came and sat and everything and um ... that was when we started being friends and everything. So we were friends then, but she [Katie] used to make comments and stuff, because I had like, boyfriends and she didn't to start off with. And she would say ... 'How many people have you been out with like ever?' and I goes 'I don't know.' And she goes 'Oh well I've never been out with just as many people as you, I don't say yes all the time.' I would say yes, because I felt rude like saying no, might like embarrass them if I say no to them, if they ask me out kind of thing. So she like made out that I was like a slut only she was. And then she like was really horrible and told a secret of Elizabeth's to like boys and it was like a really personal secret ... And we were angry with her. And then, it probably would have blown over, it probably would have been just a little fight and we wouldn't have talked for a few days and then make friends, that kind of thing. But then her mum got involved and like rang up the school and said that we were bullying her. But Katie said no they are not bullying me because I did something horrible ... It's like I can see why they'd be angry and mean and stuff like that ... but her mother said no, like rang in and we all got in trouble and we got told that we were bullying her but they didn't even hardly listen to our side of the story. They just believed her mum and stuff. But then when we told them what happened they said oh. Ok you weren't bullying her and everything, but just like be friends. But then ... She just left the school.

The original conflict being described is Katie and Hannah's exclusion of Gwyneth from their friendship group, and the shift that happened when Hannah left. Gwyneth says Katie implies she is a 'slut', which she deflects back onto Katie. Katie's betrayal of Elizabeth's secret (of not having snogged any boys) is also mentioned. The sexual rivalry culminates in slut-shaming on the one hand and 'frigid'-shaming on the other, forming the central power relations through which friendship is to be staked or refused.

We are also told in this extract that Katie's mum rang up the school, which then got involved. Gwyneth recounts being told by a teacher that they *were* bullying Katie then they were told they *were not*. How much this memory corresponds to the 'actual' events is not as important in the context of narrative-based and psychosocial research methodologies, where the story is to be analysed for what it means to the narrator but also the researcher (Andrews *et al.*, 2001; Walkerdine *et al.*, 2001). Here, Gwyneth's narrative illustrates the overall ineffectualness of the concept of bullying. The teacher is reported to have said 'just be friends', during the disciplinary meeting with the girls, a sentiment that trivialises and obscures the competitive heterosexualised affective economy at the school and deflects responsibility for coping with conflict back onto girls. Brown (1998: 100) has discussed how middle class girls enact a public/private split where they will not express overt anger in public, whereas working class girls refuse this split, thereby being viewed as disruptive and difficult. Carolyn Jackson (2006) has also written about working class laddette girls that get constituted as vicious and are more harshly judged for any direct aggression or violence (see also Reay, 2001). This dynamic seems partly at work here since the direct challenge of Katie at school is treated as an instance of bullying because it goes against codes of repressive, indirectly highly competitive and 'mean' normalised femininity. The hopelessness of the bullying discourse to address any of this is apparent in Elizabeth's humorous rendition of how the head of year tried to 'sort' the conflict:

Elizabeth: So then we tried to sort it out with one of the teachers at the school, the head of year and um … so we like sorted it out and Katie decided she wanted to move schools.

Jessica: How did you sort it out?

Elizabeth: Miss would be like 'ok, so what do you think about this?' and um … you know Miss would be to Katie 'so what do you think about this, they say you are making them feel a bit upset all the time' and she'd be like, 'ok, maybe I did do it but I don't realise I'm doing it'. It was like 'ok then, why didn't you say it before?' And she was like 'I was saying it before'. It was like 'no you weren't' and then she'd be like 'now you're just accusing me again'. We'd be like 'no we're not' and then she decided 'ok, I think I'm going to move schools and try to be with Hannah because I've been unhappy here ever since Year 7, since Hannah went'. And then … that kind of makes you feel like you have been used, like she hasn't liked school since Hannah went. She never even knew school when Hannah was here, Hannah stayed for two weeks. So, so it makes you feel like oh she was just being with us because Hannah wasn't here and we haven't shown her a good time or anything. Which I think we did because we would go out to the cinema, sleep over each other's houses, whatever … So she just moved school.

The 'sorting it out' here describes a literal back and forth sorting through the details between the girls that gets nowhere. This is because the categories of victim and perpetrator that organise bully discourses (Ringrose, 2008b) are totally inadequate for addressing the complex sexualised, affective nature of the fight. Elizabeth also implies that Katie rejected the group as not good enough, and for choosing them out of desperation, once Hannah left the school, something that tied into a classed discourse where the girls construct Katie as thinking she was 'too good' for them. Elizabeth went on to describe how both material and sexual competition and jealousy underpinned the conflicts:

Elizabeth: She'd be like 'oh, oh my god do you know what, like Luke said yesterday that he fancied me and so did Danny and Ryan'. I'm like 'ok Katie, it's not exactly like you scored or anything'. She'd be like 'oh yeah, does anybody fancy you? No? No. Ok then maybe next time'. And it's like 'Katie I don't really care if I don't have a boyfriend'. 'I didn't say you cared if you had a boyfriend' like. And she would wear make-up to school as well and she would flirt with the boys. I don't see what they saw in her, she was kind of annoying but now I like her better, now being apart … even if she doesn't go to the same school and she doesn't talk to me on MSN.

Elizabeth recounts being shamed as un-fancied by Katie, and retaliates by sanctioning Katie's wearing of make-up to school, and her flirting with boys, called 'annoying'. She also said Katie was a 'spoiled only child' because her mum got her 'a pair of fifty quid jeans every week … or a top from Top Shop'. Indeed, this issue of material goods emerged repeatedly in the interviews:

Elizabeth: She just started acting weird like, started being big headed and 'Oh, I've got this new pair of jeans, got any new clothes? No, oh, it's ok maybe you'll get them next week.' 'No, I'm not allowed any new clothes.' 'Oh, ok then. I'm getting another pair of jeans next week.' 'Oh good for you.' 'I know isn't it?' And 'ok then yeah,' and she would just try and make you, I'm not sure if she knew she was doing it but you would start feeling small whenever you were around her. I mean she wasn't exactly pretty or anything but, quite a few people fancied her, but that was all the Mosher people, who have now turned Townie. Then um … she started acting really weird and then, like we just thought ok, let's not make it into a big thing, let's just talk to her about it, so we just took her into a corner by ourselves, me and Gwyneth, we said um … 'I don't know if you have noticed but you are trying to, you are like making us feel small.' And she was like 'oh my god, no I never.' And she just denied everything that we said and she was like 'maybe I did it but I didn't know I was doing it and I don't think I did it.' And we were like 'Katie if you just say like sorry and just try and not act like it anymore we can just get on.' 'Yeah, well I'm not going to say sorry for something I didn't do, and you are just accusing me of things here that I haven't done.'

Elizabeth rationalises her anger over material goods, and Katie's popularity by calling Katie 'big-headed' and saying she makes her and the others feel 'small'. She seeks to minimise Katie's prettiness or desirability saying those who 'fancied' her were really 'Moshers' who had turned 'Townie' (not really middle class) and went on further:

Elizabeth: I don't know why people fancy her? She's not pretty, she's kind of, she's not exactly ugly or anything but, she's like funny but when you get to know her she gets a bit annoying and has these weird habits. Like she chews her hair and she always goes like, she always crinkles her forehead, just really annoying habits. I know we shouldn't be like getting annoyed about them, she should and whatever, oh and she had really bad breath. Really bad breath which in the end you just want to go 'shut up you stink'. So I kind of went like, she just kept talking and then, so I just went 'oh Katie your breath really stinks' and she had tic-tac and chewing gums and everything to cover it up. But that didn't work or anything. So I just thought oh there's no need to break friends or anything because of her breath, we just kind of be friends. And just started getting really annoying and making us feel small.

It is perhaps not surprising that Elizabeth invokes a very strong and cruel reaction given Katie's apparent teasing of Elizabeth about lack of sexual experience with (and therefore implied un-desirability to) boys. Elizabeth responds citing Katie's 'annoying', 'bad' habits, including her 'bad breath', which seems to be a way Elizabeth desires to explain Katie's funnelling of bad competitive energy, which Elizabeth feels was working to diminish her stature at school (makes Elizabeth small). Faiza expresses a similarly powerful narrative of embodied disgust at Katie and her mother:

Faiza: Well Katie was saying how she was better than the girls ... how she thinks boys like her better than us. When boys are speaking about it behind her back but we just didn't want to say anything to hurt her ... And she had this thing, like when she didn't get her way, she'd pinch people with, oooh disgusting nails about that long, painted black ...
Jessica: And what happened at school?
Faiza: I personally thought that we had sorted it. We all gave each other hugs, we walked home the same way and then suddenly she didn't come to school any more. Why? First of all she was ill, but she wasn't because we'd

see her in town … all of a sudden she'd want to change school … Katie's mind switched and wanted to go to St David's to go with her best friend, Hannah. She'd stopped phoning us, she didn't have an explanation and then … she'd be so scared to say it to our faces, she'd go on MSN oh, you stupid cow na, na, na … If she had guts, she would say it to my face. And … every time she was around me she would be like 'oh god, I'd never want to start a fight with you'.

Jessica: Really?

Faiza: She said to us that her mum made her change school … Make up your mind mum. She took her daughter off school for three months, so she can find her another school … Her mum would have been arrested, put in jail for not letting her daughter to go to school. But now she is in Chapel Hill, she is probably happy now. She didn't get accepted in St David's.

Jessica: It seems like it was … a difficult situation.

Faiza: She brought it onto herself. She talked about Gwyneth to me, she talked about me to Gwyneth, she talked about Lucy to Lizzy, she talked about Lizzy to Lucy, how stupid is that? If you are going to talk to someone, about someone else, it would be someone … we weren't best friends with. Then at last, she just left. And that had to be the happiest bit of Herbert for us four girls. She made us go through all that trouble of coming into a classroom and the teacher locking us in and we had to sort it out and then she left. Good.

What is important here is the heightened anxiety Faiza has about being seen as a violent bully. The school episode seems to have escalated Faiza's defensiveness and anger, as she calls Katie disgusting and stupid. Katie's relationship with her mother, which Elizabeth called 'horrible', was returned to by Faiza, who chides the mother for allowing Katie to change her mind. Faiza responds very defensively to having been positioned as a menacing bully by Katie and her mum who are recounted as being 'scared' of Faiza. The racialised dimension of this exchange, with Faiza a Muslim, Iraqi subject are important. The residual effects of being positioned as a bully are quite poignant as Faiza recounts angry exchanges with Katie over MSN, and fantasises about Katie's mum being put in jail for taking Katie out of school – a form of revenge for the girls having been 'locked' in a classroom to discuss the fight with the teachers.

Parental invocations of bullying

The parental/mother aspect of this account is also important. All the girls complained about Katie's mum being 'horrible' and 'blowing everything out of proportion'. And it appeared the conflict also spread out to the mums as Katie's mum was recounted as 'ignoring' Elizabeth's mum and 'running away from' Lucy's even though they 'used to be friends'. Gwyneth's mother Sue related how disruptive the parental fear over Herbert's being over-run by immigrants was:

Sue: I suppose what became clear to me in the infants school was this fear that
a lot of the parents that I knew had about their children going to Herbert's
... There were all these different strategies people had got to stop that from
happening. So, one thing you can do is go to a Welsh school ... And I
remember somebody explicitly saying to me you know that it was a good
way of avoiding having to go to a school with so many black people in it
... I found it quite disturbing but ... probably eight or nine people had left
in various ways ... and in the group that Gwyneth ... went to school with,
within a couple of weeks, another one of them had gone ... there was a lot
of anxiety ... and this [Hannah's] mother kept phoning up and worrying
about it all the time ... she was really, really anxious, you know she was up
half the night before her daughter went and then after two weeks ... the first
time her daughter felt upset about something, and who goes to school and
doesn't have worries, the daughter left but without telling anybody in the
school, even her best friend ... They had kept a place open in St David's. So
nobody was told about that, so that felt like this extremely disruptive thing
for this group of friends ... the girl who left after the two weeks was her
[Katie's] best friend, and they had been best friends all the way up through
school. So it seemed to me that some of what was going on for Katie ... that
thing of trying to find another best friend and ... there being difficulties
with that.

Sue's story about parental anxieties over Herbert Secondary offers important
social and cultural context to a racialised politics of parental choice (Ball and
Vincent, 1998; Levine-Rasky and Ringrose, 2009) that fed into Hannah then
Katie's mother's anxieties over Herbert Secondary and the pulling of their daughters
from the school:

Sue: Katie's mother ... was committed, you know she was one of the people who
was clear that her daughter was going to Herbert's but nevertheless it was a
difficult situation for her because she felt very hurt by what happened but
it also felt like it sort of destabilised something, it made the situation filled
with much more anxiety ... because it was almost like there was this fault line
about this school, whether you stay in the school or don't and so it played
into the anxieties that were around there for her parents ... I mean it felt with
that situation, there was very much this fear about the word bullying and
about whether bullying had gone on and I think there as some unfortunate
stuff happened at the end but my observation of it up until then wasn't that,
it wasn't bullying, it was girls falling out with each other and that Katie was
in there as much as anybody else was. But we couldn't support the girls to
a resolution partly because, due to that background, Katie went, she just
vanished ...

In this context of parental fear, one of the effects of the bully discourses is they offer
a space for Katie's mother to manipulate the boundaries of school allocation, securing

a place for Katie at one of the most successful comprehensive in the city, in the wake of this 'episode'. The inability of the anti-bullying policy and practices to address the heterosexualised conflict at play among girls led to Katie simply 'vanishing', an event with many residual effects as I've explored.

Negotiating the abstract 'bully' discourses and its (in)effects: Beyond the feminine as pathological

Despite these everyday conflicts at school, it was interesting that the girls continued to discuss bullying as an abstract concept they had never seen or experienced; rather, it was understood as something 'out there':

Elizabeth: Girls bully more, like I've never seen a girl bully or anything or being bullied or bullied anyone. But I have read about it in magazines and stuff, it seems that girls bully more, like boys they'll just break friends ... Like there was a chain letter on MSN and it was like ... a girl had been bullied so much ... she just committed suicide, which I think honestly happens a lot with girls, they bully so much people tend to do things like, harsh things, like cut themselves or they might hang themselves or commit suicide like. But, I don't get why people do it because, just because someone might be different, it doesn't mean you have to bully them or anything, you could just not talk to them, or not be friends, or, well you could just not talk to them.

What is interesting is Elizabeth positions herself as never having seen bullying (despite having been involved in a significant anti-bullying intervention at school), and invokes extreme bullying events like suicide and a discourse of tolerating 'difference'. Meanwhile, this is completely removed from the narcissism of minor differences (utter hatred of Katie's bad breath and disgusting long nails) that the group collectively and individually invoke in their discussion of the 'irritating' nature of Katie (Britzman, 1998).

It would also seem that the girls internalised the demand paramount in anti-bully discourse to always resolve conflict and to not be seen to be a 'problem girl' (Osler *et al.*, 2002; Lloyd, 2005):

Jessica: ... do you think you have learned anything from this or ...?
Gwyneth: Probably it's probably best to like, not to say it in front of people because it might make them feel that people are ganging up on like the person you are talking to, just get them by themselves and say it. We did kind of do that, me and Elizabeth got her by herself and everyone thought we were going to like argue so they all crowded around kind of thing, like all our friends, like oh what's going to happen but it kind of made it worse. It probably made her feel like she was being ganged up on. We learned to like talk to them quietly by themselves. Ask what she thinks before like we have a go at her.

The need to keep incidents totally secret from the school and parents indicates the shame and stress of negotiating the type of public spectacle incited through the school's bully discourses. Affective effects thus include 'learning' covertness as a tactic to avoid public humiliation. There is an internalisation of a middle class ethic of repressive and indirect feminine ideals of relationality, since to be positioned as a girl bully transgresses the normative conditions of femininity. Lucy also, however, called into question the label of bullying put onto the situation by the school:

Lucy: Some people would call that bullying. I wouldn't because maybe bullying, sometimes it can be like physical and we didn't do anything to her. Sometimes we'd just like say it but we didn't shout at her, we didn't gang up on her, we tried to talk it out calmly, like properly and then, but then that didn't work, so we just stopped. So some people would call it bullying but I wouldn't. Bullying, sometimes it can be someone's opinion, not like something that is true … we didn't bully her.

Lucy presents us with the possibility of reading the girls' questioning of Katie or indeed the entire sexualised battlefield of schooling as 'calm' and 'proper' responses to quite difficult situations. She tries to actively disinvest or disassociate from the idea of bullying. She also sheds light on how this reading is negated by the dominant discourses of schooling which read back individualised feminine pathology onto the events and indeed largely refuses to engage with the complexity and difficulty of sexualised competition between girls.

Gwyneth also challenged the ideal feminine and sought to challenge the designation of girls as inherently mean:

Gwyneth: I think girls can be mean but not like more than anyone else … like adults get mean and like, babies get mean because they like fight when they are toddlers and stuff, it's like everyone gets angry. Like dogs get angry, animals get angry, like boys get angry and I think everyone gets angry sometimes. I think they are just talking about girls, I don't know why … Like they are trying to spread it around, like all girls are horrible just because they've had something happen to them. Like I don't reckon it's true.

Gwyneth goes to the heart of the contradiction of femininity that girls in particular are not allowed to express anger and aggression in direct and open ways (Brown, 1998). As she puts it everyone gets angry, and what she points to is the imperative that girls must not, and the way this contradiction gets read as all girls are horrible. Faiza critiques the discourse of mean from a somewhat different angle:

Faiza: Mm. It's wrong yeah. We shouldn't be put out to the world like that.
Jessica: Mm.
Faiza: They don't say boys are mean.
Jessica: Not in the same way, no.
Faiza: Doing that just makes boys, I don't know feel great. Oh girls are mean …

Jessica:	Mm.
Faiza:	… Women have got to be careful on the streets just in case something happens to them. Men can walk freely until twelve o'clock at night and nothing will happen to them. Women have got to be careful about who they talk to and what they do and … men can do whatever they want any time.
Jessica:	Mm.
Faiza:	A man would know that he has a better life than a woman, because women can hardly do anything these days. It's better than what it used to be like but it's still not enough …
Faiza:	Ever since I have started playing football, because my dad has always said that it's boys' sport and my brother has always called me 'Oh you boy, you play football'… Say I wanted to be a footballer when I'm grown up, I would have to go all the way to America to get a scholarship and play football there because they wouldn't let me play football professionally over here … Boys can go to Manchester, Cardiff City and get a scholarship there and play football for the rest of their lives. I've got to go all the way to America and get a scholarship and play football professionally. I've got football every Friday with [local club], but it's not going to lead to anything big.

Here Faiza criticises the discourse of girls' 'mean-ness' pointing to heterosexualised violence against women as the real issue. We can see a poignant critique of the postfeminist mythologies of gender equality and sexual liberation for girls and women that I've been exploring in this book. I was struck by Faiza's worries about what will happen 'when I'm grown up' and her conviction that 'women can hardly do anything these days' which related to her resignation about not being able to play girls' football and pressure from her father and brother not to be 'boy-like', as well as the structural constraints of the male-dominated world of sport.

Challenging postfeminist discourses of sexual performance: troubling thongs and fancy-you-fighting

Throughout, Faiza strongly dis-identified with both feminine sexual passivity but also prioritising desirability to boys above the bonds of the peer group. I've considered how this operates simultaneously as a regulation of feminine sexuality (shouldn't show it off), but also as a mode of resistance to the competitive sexual relations that regulate how the girls are learning to perform feminine, heterosexual technologies of 'sexiness' (Gill, 2008; Evans *et al.*, 2010), further evident below:

Jessica:	We also talked a lot about girls who were sluts … remember?
Faiza:	A girl who shows too much of herself, a girl that tries too hard.
Jessica:	Tries too hard to what?
Faiza:	Impress people, especially boys. A girl that flirts with someone else's boyfriend. A girl that shows too much of herself.

Jessica: Like what, give me an example.

Faiza: Cleavage, there is a girl in my class, every time she bends over she pulls up her thong.

Jessica: Really?

Faiza: When she is walking past a boy, she'll suddenly start talking about how her thong is bugging her.

Jessica: Really? What do you think of that?

Faiza: It's disgusting, I wouldn't walk past a boy and say ah, my thong is giving me a wedgey.

Jessica: So why do you think she acts like that?

Faiza: Because the boys are like oh, she's wearing a thong.

Jessica: But like why do you think she would want, like what do you think she is after?

Faiza: A boyfriend.

Jessica: And do you think that kind of thing is working for her or …?

Faiza: Working for, as the boy wouldn't like her, they'd like her body, they wouldn't exactly like her, just from hearing oh my thong is giving me a wedgey, doesn't give much of her personality that does it? And a boy wouldn't go up to her and ask her out then just to know her personality, he'd want to know, what it's covering … I wouldn't like the idea of someone hitting me, smacking me on the arse, she probably would.

On the one hand Faiza is resisting the heterosexualised politics thrust upon her, which is the feeling that she should emulate the seeking of attention through the display of the thong – noted as the ultimate signifier of postfeminist sexualised culture (Duits and van Zoonen, 2006; Evans *et al.*, 2010). But the primary target of her criticism is the girl in question. What Faiza is questioning is how the girl's personality gets split off from her body through the male gaze upon her body parts (e.g. 'arse', cleavage). Again, what I am interested in here is how Faiza is both regulatory and pathologising of the individual girl, something which infects postfeminist popular culture en masse. It is also apparent that any expression of feminine bodily desire must be controlled, since Faiza says she wouldn't like someone smacking her 'arse', which emerged in previous discussion above as well. Again, Faiza and her sister Safa's problematisation of female sexual performance may relate to their Iraqi cultural background, as they are the only ones in the group explicitly not allowed to date boys. The interpellation of Faiza and Safa both as objects of desire and as possessing their own feminine sexual desires seemed more risky and dangerous than for the others. This is mediated by their raced, religioned (Shain, 2003; Youdell, 2006) background, which made their negotiation into teen heterosexual culture different and possibly more difficult than for the other girls.

And yet, Faiza actually deeply desires engagement with boys, and manages it another (perhaps more reciprocal) way through a discourse of being sporty, since she is highly active in the local girls' football club, which helps her be able to physically engage (Paechter, 2009) with and actively thrust smacking and hitting back upon boys:

Faiza: The girl got smacked on the arse, she turned around and said ha, ha and laughed. If a boy done that to me I would turn around and slap him one, kick him and slap him again.

Jessica: I get you ... What I want to know is like what you think makes the difference, like why would that girl just be like oh ha, ha, ha?

Faiza: Because she'll probably be like um ... oh he fancies me, I'm not going to do anything to that. Oh, let him tell his friends, something like that. There's a boy in my sister's year, he was walking past me and saying things like, saying my name and coughing and saying things like that, it just gets on my nerves. So one day I slapped him, so then he went, ran and went behind his friend and said it again. So I went up to his friend and goes move out of the way and he goes 'No'. So then his friend started saying my name. And ever since like that day which was about November, that boy comes up to me, says my name, hits me and expects me to run after him. He just, hits me, because the first couple of times, I started running after him, smacking him one and then running back and now he expects me to run after him again. I just can't be bothered any more.

Jessica: So it's like a form of flirtation then, this hitting?

Faiza: If they call it that, yeah.

Jessica: Do you think?

Faiza: I don't know. I wouldn't think he fancies me.

Jessica: You don't?

Faiza: Because me and the boy done football together and I wouldn't think he fancied me.

Via the intersubjective space of the interview it seemed to me that Faiza's investment in being this object of hitting was intensely pleasurable, despite her denial. The need to be above it and disinvested ('can't be bovvered') jostles with her pleasure in the telling of the story which she mentioned again during a follow-up focus group interview. In this case a psychosocial reading helps by pointing to how repetition and a fixation on displaying for me her own dis-investment in the boy's attention, contradicted her repeated accounts of the fighting, slapping and pushing with boys (Hollway and Jefferson, 2000: 37). Rather than simply taking the account as 'transparent' or at 'face value' (ibid.: 3) the narrative highlights her own desire to be constituted somewhat differently, as actively desiring agent (in control), as well as recipient of male desire. She resists and desires the sexual objectification and reduction of the girl's body.

However, the problem is that the primary means of doing this resistance is through 'slut shaming' or sexual regulation of other girls. My interest is in how we might address this dynamic in schooling, which I return to in my conclusion to the book. As noted, Faiza and Safa were caught in a cultural clash between religious, familial sexual norms (innocent, de-sexualised good girl) and those of the peer group (heterosexual performance and compliance to peer rules around female sexuality). I think Faiza in particular brought an insistence on a more active reciprocal form of desire to aspire towards. It is not surprising, however, that managing these contradictory spaces, being at once a 'good girl' and good friend against being constituted as an object of desire ('hit on' in competition with other girls) and trying to maintain some active (sexual) desire as a girl, constituted the single most important site of conflict among the girls.

Subverting pre- and postfeminist fantasies: who needs a prince?

The final data extracts I'd like to explore say something important about girls' friendships as places of survival within the complex affective terrain of heterosexual competition. They also tell us something age-specific about the importance of friendship as sites of passion and strength in this time of transition into teen sexual cultures. Despite the difficult terrain of love and hate informing girls' conflicts, their friendships formed an important site for challenging the increasingly heterosexualised tyranny of everyday tween/teen girl life and the reduction (or making small) of their subjectivity into object of sexually commodified gaze.

Over 25 years ago now, Valerie Walkerdine (1984) wrote about how girls' comics held out the dream of finding a prince to rescue working class girls from adversity. Bronwyn Davies (1997) showed in similar ways how children rejected the possibilities of feminist fairy tales where the princess was heroic, that is children re-read patriarchal ideals of male heroism and female pathology onto a feminist version of a princess who did not marry or get saved by the prince. The princess has re-emerged as a powerful postfeminist motif in popular culture. Diane Negra (2009) analyses films like *The Princess Diaries* and *Enchanted*, where for instance the teen girl is saved from wage labour through the fantasy of inheriting or marrying into wealth and title. This dream was recently writ large with Kate Middleton's marriage to Prince William, popularising narratives of princesses and ladies in waiting for a suitable mate to take care of them for an entire new generation of girls globally.

Faiza, however, appeared to embrace a different feminist utopia that was man-free, signalling perhaps her inability to imagine gender-equal relationships within the fabric of her cultural and familial ties. For Faiza, the prince seemed to fall by the wayside in the fantasies and imagined spaces for the future:

Faiza: I don't want to get married to a man. I don't want to get married. But I want children, but I don't want to get married.

Jessica: Why is that?

Faiza: I don't know, I always see marriages with problems, you break up, money problems, something problem. I want it to stay to myself.

Jessica: Okay, so that's why you want to have your career and …

Faiza: Because if I get married you'll be like, I'd be like not worried about my career but worried about what he wants to worry about and things he'd want to do. He wouldn't worry about my career exactly would he?

Jessica: So how do you think you would do that then? Have children but not be married?

Faiza: Adopt.

Jessica: Really?

Faiza: I wouldn't mind adopting a child.
Jessica: So tell me your whole scenario then. That you have worked out. Like ideally, it doesn't have to really happen but …
Faiza: When I grow up, first of all I want to live in a house with Lucy. We want to live in a house together. We both want to be doctors. I don't know and then I don't want to get married, I might adopt.

Not only did Faiza fantasise about being a doctor with Lucy, but Gwyneth described how Elizabeth and her would have a 'law firm' and be 'partners', while Faiza and Lucy had their joint 'doctor's practice'.

In previous writing with Emma Renold (Renold and Ringrose, 2008) we suggested that these classed fantasies of sharing high-flying careers, not marrying, not giving birth but adopting are forms of 'lines of flight' that congeal into a significant and sustained 'alternative figuration' (Braidotti, 1994) or way of doing girl. The ordinary, normative development into fertile, maternal woman is ruptured; the idea of compulsory hyper-heterosexual identities which will lead to conjugal marriage is usurped. Faiza's primary attachment to her female friend is projected into the future. A future phallogocentric, oedipal drama (Deleuze and Guattari, 1987) is in some ways usurped. We also explored additional research data on girls' fantasies of careers and living arrangements without men, in ways that rework oedipal-daddy-husband narratives (Ringrose and Renold, 2011). We thought about the possibility of such fantasies as sites of resistance and possibility for girls with as yet unknown effects (ibid.; Lawler, 2000). Jessica Willis (2009) has suggested that when girls' narratives of resistance remain at the level of fantasy this stands little chance of connecting with genuine collective struggle at the level of feminist political organising. I outlined an alternative theory of social-subjective change in Chapter 6, which takes account of the complex micro-politics of the affective terrain of relationships (like those of this friendship group) as spaces where hetero-normativity can be ruptured, with unknown future effects. These tween/teen fantasies operate as a space against normative trajectories, offering lines of flight away from the everyday exhaustion of coping with the heterosexual playing field. Of course, a fantasy does not necessarily imply follow through. Rather it illustrates an important level of critical awareness and consciousness that has political significance that we need to account for in how girls talk about and manage their everyday conflicts and realities. The way Faiza's fantasy resonates with older feminist utopias eschewing primary attachments to men (Wittig, 1969) illustrates some of the same battles are being staged by girls within the context of postfeminist discourses of girlhood.

Renold and I also suggested, however, that it would be a mistake to interpret these types of micro-acts as a 'molar' or grand, revolutionary second wave feminist narrative (Renold and Ringrose, 2008). Faiza is not simply eschewing all identifications with hetero-normative recognition. She was invested in boys finding her attractive, repeating at several points in the interviews the story of the boy that chased her around school and punched and how she 'hit back' on him at school. Maxwell and Aggleton (2010) questioned the value of such temporary moments of 'rupture', seeking 'sustained agency' in their narrative accounts. But the empirical mapping project that follows on from Deleuze and Guattari is doing something different than searching for sustained, rational accounts from unitary and coherent actors. It is looking at how we can make sense of how bodies interact in new and different ways, and underscoring critical moments of subjective flux in research accounts. This approach offers new ways to re-figure fantasy, for instance, as not just harnessed to individual lack but to the possibility of thinking and even acting something different (Ringrose and Renold, 2011). As these are teen girls we cannot know what their adult molar identities (Jackson, 2010) will hold, but mapping the nuance of their affective relations and their affective capacities to trouble (or not) the boundaries of the norm as girls in moments like these is important.

Conclusions

This chapter has mapped the narratives of an early teen girl friendship group discussing their tween transition to secondary school. I have illustrated the complex relational struggles and micro-politics around sex and power the girls negotiate in raced, religioned and class-specific ways. I argue that sexualised conflicts are dominant, normative and everyday, but generally not interpretable or addressable through the language of bullying used in schools, which means we have few institutional resources to work with girls on these issues. We need to grasp how sexual conflict is central to adolescence but *also* to adult gender relations, which possibly explains the defensiveness educators and policy makers have for delving into this messy and uncomfortable domain and the difficulty the mothers and teachers in this research had in managing these conflicts (Hadley, 2004; Ringrose, 2008b). Although girls' conflicts tend to be glossed over or naturalised, I have shown their dramatic effects since sexualised struggles led to the withdrawal of Katie (and also, it was implied, Hannah) from Herbert Secondary, influencing the market of parental choice and perceptions of school performance in important ways.

My concluding chapter will argue for the need to continue to work on an explicitly feminist approach to addressing heterosexual competition in schooling, but through a psychosocial lens that takes the intersectional, classed and raced dilemmas of struggles within and 'between femininities' into account (Gonick, 2004). I will argue that we need resources that can actually help girls navigate and challenge entry into the teen heterosexualised playing field, refusing the dual pressures to shame one another as sluts or frigid. First, however, in the following chapter I will explore how girls continue to navigate entry into adult sexualised, postfeminist media culture and 'sexy' femininity, as they proceed through the middle teen years.

8 Girls negotiating postfeminist, sexualised media contexts

Chapter 7 explored how tween to teen girls in Years 8 and 9 (age 12–14) were negotiating the heterosexualised playing field and peer group at school. In this chapter I explore how older teens in Years 10 (14–15) and 11 (15–16) are managing new challenges of navigating the sexualised and 'pornified' media cultures explored in Chapter 4. Here I continue to elaborate my psychosocial and affective approach by mapping how girls negotiate and 'perform' sexual identities in the context of new digital technologies. I aim to engage with and challenge the binaries of savvy agentic actor vs passive dupe or victim of sexual objectification outlined in Chapter 5. I will argue again that girls have not made any miraculous escape from their sexed body as 'successful' females, the discourse I examined in Chapter 2. Rather, they continue to be defined by their bodies and sexuality in highly classed and raced ways, with pressing implications for life at school. I aim to shift debate from moralistic statements about girls' sexuality and conflicts as wrong or bad, as documented in Chapters 3 and 4, to analysis of their embodied engagements and affective flows. I also challenge a simplistic online–offline divide, documenting how digital identity thoroughly mediates and shapes 'real' life experiences and relationships at school (Kearney, 2006; boyd, 2008).

I draw on research undertaken in 2008 with a team from the London Knowledge Lab exploring young people's negotiations of social networking sites.[1] We looked at the peer networks and representations of gender and sexuality in the teen-dominated social networking site Bebo. I will map some of the sexual content and idealised representations of femininity and masculinity (Nayak and Kehily, 2008) on the young people's Bebo assemblages. But I move well beyond analysis at the level of cultural representation to explore the gendered power dynamics among young people. I explore how girls relate to, produce and subvert sexualised text and images online and how this shapes their friendships, intimacies and relationships at school and beyond. The findings illustrate that social networking sites can operate as spaces of sexual (and other forms of) play, fantasy and experimentation, but also carry many of the same risks of sexual regulation over girls' bodies described at length in Chapter 7. I also focus on sexualised cyber-aggression (Grigg, 2010), examining how girls manage comments about their appearance and sexualised name calling, exploring where and when spaces of disruption become possible.

Online social networking sites, identity construction and gender

In the UK at the time of our research, 49 per cent of those aged between 8 and 17 had an internet profile on social networking sites (SNSs) such as Bebo, Facebook and MySpace (Smithers, 2008). As boyd and Ellison (2007) suggest, SNSs 'constitute an important research context for scholars investigating processes of impression management, self-presentation, and friendship performance'. SNSs are technological platforms where young people are performing their identity publically, hooked into local and global (glocal) virtual networks or what I call 'affective assemblages' (Ringrose, 2010a). Notably, school-age children's networks are mostly school-based (Livingstone and Brake, 2010), meaning kids have increased contact with known individuals from the school network (boyd, 2008). SNSs extend and intensify school-based relationships, and can take such relationships into a 24/7 form of never-ending contact with peers (Livingstone, 2008; Koefed, 2009b). This makes social networking sites a crucial educational issue (Selwyn, 2008). Schools now operate software security systems, they have developed new mobile technology policies, and are increasingly concerned with issues of online 'risk' and 'e-safety' including cyberbullying policies, as I discussed in Chapter 3.

Here, I am particularly interested in the gendered context of uses of these new often mobile technologies (Manago *et al.*, 2008). We are seeing increasing reports that it is girls and women who are the highest users of the online technologies and also in greater danger of abuses of these technologies (Livingstone *et al.*, 2009). For instance, girls have been positioned as more involved in cyberbullying than boys (Rivers and Noret, 2010) in ways that can re-essentialise notions of girls as relationally aggressive and pathological in problematic ways. Girls are also viewed as most 'at risk' of exposure to sexual 'grooming' from adult sexual predators, and 'self-sexualisation', and as victims of the exchange of sexually explicit imagery (for instance, alkeld and Hartley-Parkinson, 2011; Livingstone and Haddon, 2009; Hinduja and Patchin, 2009).

In some senses then new digital technologies like online social networking are understood to be 'feminised' and concerns about them have centred on the problems of girls' usage. We see a familiar tension outlined in this book between girls having powerful new opportunities, in this case through the democratisation of online space (Turkle, 1995; Kearney, 2006), and girls as victims and in crisis as a result of these very opportunities (Aapola *et al.*, 2005). Susannah Stern highlights this tension and the problem with demonising teen girls asking:

> Why is it reasonable to treat adolescents and girls in particular, as commodities to be sold to marketers and advertisers, but to disparage girls' own experimentations with self-commodification? ... The Internet provides a space – some would say a comparatively safe one – for this, even if it's uncomfortable for the rest of us to witness how American culture turns girls into women.
> (http://spotlight.macfound.org/blog/entry/susannah-stern-girls-gone-wild)

In my analysis I aim to balance a tension between girls as creators and producers of new media (Kearney, 2006), however, girls draw upon a limited range of normalised discourses (discursive conditions of possibility) which limit affective capacities with which they can forge their identity. My concern is also to break down Stern's notion that the internet provides a 'safe' space that is distinct from school life, and rather to understand how school relations and online identities intermingle in complex ways. I want to explore the embodied processes of 'self-commodification' from the girls' perspectives.

Beverly Skeggs' (2005) work on moral visual representation is useful for understanding self-commodification, as it looks at what types of representations have exchange value in what are always classed and racialised moral and visual economies of looking. Skeggs argues that visual representations are judged 'according to the symbolic values generated by [exchange] processes' (2005: 965). I analyse some content and imagery on Bebo including quizzes and applications, which appear on the personal profiles of our participants. I ask: What types of representations have specific value or currency on the social networking site Bebo? Which are the dominant gender and sexual discourses and which formations of femininity and masculinity are idealised? How do these plug into, replicate or disrupt dominant trends in the wider postfeminist, sexualised media sphere (Gill, 2008)? How do young people navigate these 'glocal' gender discourses? When is girls' self-sexualisation oppressive and when does it allow for new spaces of creativity, fantasy and desire (Tolman, 2002; Lerum and Dworkin, 2009)?

The research design and schools

The data drawn on in this chapter include group and individual interviews with young people in two year groups collected in two schools in England, one in rural Suffolk, the other in a deprived estate in Southern London. We studied one Year 10 Media Studies class in Thornbury Secondary,[2] a high-achieving specialist college in rural Suffolk, where the level of socio-economic disadvantage was well below average. The most recent Ofsted[3] report described Thornbury as a Church of England voluntary controlled secondary, smaller than average comprehensive school serving a rural area. Thornbury was regularly over-subscribed; although it has students from a mix of economic backgrounds the vast majority of students are from White British backgrounds. The level of socio-economic disadvantage and students eligible for free school meals is well below average and attainment on entry to school is above average. However, this school was interesting because the village was being 'gentrified'. It has students from some of the long-standing families in the village who were traditionally working class, based on parent occupation, but this was mixed with newer families who had bought cottages and commuted to London to work (for instance one participant's father was a wealthy business man). The high achievement of the school was a steady attractor for the new families. The school occupied a low-rise building on an attractive country road with open fields in front of it.

Our second research school, New Mills Secondary, was in contrast an estate school in an Outer Southern London borough, in an area of 'high deprivation'. This school was a newly appointed 'Visual and Media Arts College' and we worked with Year 11 students from a Media Studies class. The most recent Ofsted report describes New

Mills as a mixed comprehensive secondary school serving an urban area with high deprivation. The school was located on a typical estate with cookie cutter identical red brick low-rise houses spreading out as far as the eye can see. Half the pupils were eligible for free school meals, with a similar number with learning difficulties and disabilities. Very few local families had experience of higher education. Although one quarter of pupils were from ethnic minority groups, with the percentage of pupils whose first language is not English higher than average, we worked primarily with White working class girls.[4]

The economic and social differences in the schools are important for the arguments about how sexual identity is negotiated in relation to background and aspirations of girls. I look briefly at the narratives of a more middle class friend group at Thornbury, as well as a working class group, and then two working class groups at New Mills.

We began the field work through some observations of the media classroom where social networking was already being discussed by the Media Studies teachers. Next, focus group interviews were conducted in each school to discuss students' use of SNSs (11 boys and 12 girls, all aged 14–16). The focus group interviews involved general discussion about how young people were using and engaging with social networking sites, given it was becoming an area of policy concern and regulation in UK schools (Selwyn, 2008).

During the focus group we discovered that most participants were using the SNS Bebo, and we asked for consent to view participants' Bebo pages. We then conducted online observations (boyd, 2008), studying the Bebo sites and friend networks[5] for a period of a few weeks. We then returned for in-depth individual interviews with key participants (six girls and one boy). Finally, we observed the SNSs of the case study participants over a period of a few months while we analysed the interview data. I will focus on case study data collected with girls, although I will touch on some of the issues around gender, sexuality and romance that emerged from the data with boys.

Bebo 'skins' and applications: what are the dominant gender/ sexual discourses?

As noted, at the time of the research in 2008 we found that Bebo was the most popular teen social networking site, used predominantly by the 13- to 24-year-old age group (Livingstone, 2008; Smithers, 2008; Willett, 2009).[6] Bebo, like other social networking sites, is a commercial product with a specific teen target audience for constructing a semi-public 'friend' network, depending on privacy settings selected. Bebo has a 'virtual architecture' (Papacharissi, 2009) that codes engagement through identity categories (age, relationship status, hometown, etc.) to be filled in. It is also a platform for video clips, music 'play lists', applications, blogging and posting, tagging and commenting on photos. Bebo pages are a form of 'bricolage' construction of self-identity via complex uses of branding and consumer culture (Chandler and Roberts-Young, 1998). I am interested in how commercialised content circulating on Bebo is gendered and sexualised through 'skins' and quiz applications, which will channel affect in particular ways.

Bebo, like Myspace, is much visually richer than Facebook as the user can choose a colourful and personalised 'skin' or background that covers the generic site.[7] Skins are a visual template that can only be modified with specialised technical skills, so they exist as commodities themselves that young people find, 'choose' and trade through Bebo networks. A search at the time of the research (using the application 'Top 50 Bebo skins') showed Louis Vuitton background to be the number one skin, with others showcasing celebrities, such as the singers Kelis and Alicia Keys, boxer Ricky Hatton, and footballer Michael Owen.

Discussion of some of our participants' skins can offer insight into the dominant discourse of normative/idealised masculinity, femininity and sexuality circulating on Bebo. For instance, a top 50 skin used by a male student (16) at New Mills features a picture of a man in Adidas shoes pressed against by a woman in stiletto heels with her knickers around her ankles. The Playboy Bunny motif was used by one of our case study research participants Marie (16, New Mills) as discussed further below. Another focus group participant Jen's (16, New Mills) skin read 'Boom chicka Wah Wah' which is a reference to a 2007 advertising campaign for Lynx male deodorant spray, which featured men (including Ben Affleck) attracting hundreds of semi-naked women in various scenarios after applying the spray, but also, according to the urban dictionary, refers to 'Music played in old porno films right after the first penetration or little bit before a blow job by the bass guitar and also used to describe someone that is very hot'. In interview, Jen described finding the skin online and liking it, pointing to the 'bricolage' construction, where consumer branding is appropriated.

Two of our participants (Daniela, 14; Sally, 14) used a Marilyn Monroe skin. Daniela's Bebo profile, which is a case study discussed at length below, featured a picture of a naked Marilyn in bed, with the quotations 'It's all just make believe isn't it?' and 'A wise girl kisses but doesn't love, listens but doesn't believe, and leaves before she is left'. Sam (15, Thornbury), the boy Daniela was 'seeing' during the research, had a skin with a mini-skirted woman posing in platform heels beside a Ford GT, an exotic sports car (price approx. £100,000). Girls' displays of experienced sexual 'knowingness' (Bragg and Buckingham, 2009: 132) about intimate relationships, like Daniela's use of Marilyn Monroe's 'wise girl' quotes, were common. Another skin featured a picture of a little girl attempting to read a book that reads 'Th, the ca … cat in the … Oh fuck this I'll be a stripper' (Kristy, 14, Thornbury), which subverts notions of girlhood innocence, with an ironic take up of stripping for money. Many skins made references to sexually aware game playing such as 'she falls for players, but she plays the same games' with giant lipstick kisses as the visual background (Marni, 14, Thornbury). Sexual conquests were also contrasted with innocence such as the 'I'm a heartbreaker' skin with a pastel cupcake motif (Tanya, 14 Thornbury). Pamela's (16, New Mills) skin said 'hold me in your arms and tell me that I'm your baby girl'. Some girls' skins featured explicit 'girl' products like 'Tinkerbell', 'Hello Kitty' and 'Little Miss Naughty'. There were also several boys whose skins incorporated their love for their girlfriends, such as 'I love Sarah more than words can say' (Nate, 14, Thornbury).

The way gender and sexuality are represented in the participants' skins illustrates a digital, gendered and sexualised assemblage. Users plug into and have to negotiate 'idealised' forms of teen masculinity and femininity on the network in complex ways. In some of the cases, masculinity is epitomised as sexually predatory, and achievable through buying consumer goods (i.e. cars and shoes) with which to gain access to the sexually commodified female body (leaning against the sports car). Ideal femininity was constructed in some of the skins through images of the sexually commodified female body via symbols like the Playboy Bunny, performing as knowing, irresistible sexual subject (Marilyn Monroe, 'Boom Chicka Wah Wah' girl or 'heartbreaker'), but also some position themselves as sexually vulnerable and innocent 'baby girl'. These discourses of idealised masculinity and femininity are also played with and disrupted, in some skins, like the reference to becoming a stripper if you can't read, or with boys who proclaim their romantic 'luv' for their girlfriends via their skins. Another male friend of one of our participants (16, New Mills) called himself 'piano whore' subverting normative notions of whore as a term of female sexual regulation.

There are further technical applications on the virtual assemblage of Bebo such as game and quiz applications which circulate and are played. Popular Bebo applications on participants' pages included 'make a baby', which allows you to 'Make babies with your friends!' by choosing appearance, clothes and accessories, and 'Celebrity look a likes', which uses face recognition technology to help users 'Discover your celeb twin among thousands of top celebrities'. There were also 'sexy' femininity, sex/romance-related quiz and interactive applications, which included 'What type of kisser are you?' and 'Kiss me', which 'lets people kiss you in various ways and places'. The most popular sex quiz on our participants' pages was 'Are you sexy, flirty, or a slut?' (which appears on MySpace and Facebook also), which quizzes girls on how many guys they've slept with, how short they wear their skirt, whether (penis) 'size' is important, and whether they like strip and lap dances, among other questions. As the quiz title suggests, it offers three subject positions: sexy, flirty, slut. Results are posted onto your Bebo page accompanied by randomised pictures mostly of girls in bras or bikinis. Heather (16, New Mills) got the quiz result 'sexy' on her site, which featured a sweaty woman in towel and exercise bra. Marie's (16, New Mills) result was 'flirty', which posted a different woman also in exercise gear suspended on a pole onto her Bebo site.

Similar quizzes include 'What kind of lingerie are you?' which offers a range of barely differentiated results such as 'v-string panties', with a close up of a woman's crotch wearing a yellow G-string with a diamante studded 'sexy' on it. 'What kind of girl are you?' generates the response 'eye candy'. 'What sexual fantasy are you?' creates the image 'sexy schoolgirl' with a grown woman posing – much like Britney Spears first number 1 video 'Hit me baby one more time' – in pigtails, a kilt mini skirt and a white shirt tied underneath her large circular fake breasts, with a chalkboard with A, B, C behind her. This quiz explicitly invokes a sexy/innocent binary inhering in the motif of sexualised schoolgirl. The quiz 'What sexual position r u?' gets a range of results such as: 'classic doggy', 'perfect for maximising penetration'; ironically, however, the image shows two women in this position, perhaps referencing the 'hot lesbian' fantasy (Gill, 2009).

These quiz applications are thus 'sexualised' in specific ways that shape the 'performative', 'identificatory' possibilities (Butler, 1993) and affective flows (Deleuze and Guattari, 1987) of the users. Some quizzes references to stripping, lap and pole dancing and sexual positions are part of the normalisation of 'porno-chic' in this online network. The popular 'Are you sexy, flirty, or a slut' quiz in particular points to the production of a dominant discourse of 'compulsory sexual agency' (Gill, 2008) depicting the embodied moves girls/women can perform to be 'sexy' and as 'up for it', including pole dancing as part of their sexual repertoire. Girls do not passively absorb these, however, but rather actively negotiate these in ways that are crucial to map and explore.

Photos and producing a 'sexy' visual display

Sites are further personalised through the use of images, usernames, taglines and blogs on one's page. The all-important display photo is the first thing one sees when searching or looking at the Bebo page:

Daniela: (14, Thornbury)	Girls, I think, take more care over how it looks and like their pictures.
Marie: (16, New Mills)	You don't really want to put, put a picture on there that makes you look like you just woken up in the morning!
Nicola: (14, Thornbury)	You only put a nice picture up. Not one of you looking awful.
Louisa: (16, New Mills)	You can airbrush yourself... you can make yourself look better then, well – what can I say? – I've been doing it all the time!

Indeed, there was considerable anxiety about having a bad picture posted:

Heather: (16, New Mills)	That Trudy girl her Bebo got hacked didn't it? Have you seen it? ... And they've changed all of her pictures and that and put the most horribillist one of her as her display picture!

Comments about how good or bad someone looks in a photograph were common, such as 'you're well fit', 'nice pic' or 'Hello Sexy'. Jen (16, New Mills) told us 'saying you're sexy just means you look good'. There was also, however, the danger of 'rude comments' being posted such as 'fat' or 'ugly', or even of Bebo profiles and display photos being 'hacked' and manipulated as mentioned above.

In focus groups we asked 'what can you tell about a person by looking at his or her Bebo page?' to get at how young people were evaluating each other's profiles. What emerged immediately were tensions for girls around sexual representation:

Daniela: (14, focus group 1, Thornbury)	I think like if you've got like say a slutty girl, she'll take a picture of her body or whatever and have it as her image ... If I came across a Bebo that's someone's got a picture of their cleavage and their body, and nothing else. And I'll think, 'Well, they obviously think too much of themselves'.

Sally (14), Alice (14) and Clare (14) (focus group 3 Thornbury) had similar responses:

Sally: There are loads of really slutty pictures. And the boys on Bebo always take pictures of their stomach. It's like, 'Oh, great!'

Alice: Yeah.

Clare: Because they could be really ugly, couldn't they?

Sally: And they don't just take pictures – I get really annoyed when people have like alcohol and stuff and they're taking pictures purposely.

Alice: Yeah, they're like, 'Oh, look at me!'

Sally: Yeah, and they're like, you know, when they go for parties or something and they're sleeping over, they take really slutty pictures. And then they've got the alcohol in their hands and they're just taking pictures and they're just like [makes an impression] with the alcohol, and it's really stupid.

Clare: I think it's funny because they're like, 'Oh, I'm so gorgeous because of this.' And half the time it's like empty or the cap's on and stuff. It's really funny.

Jessica: You don't do that, then? You don't take pictures at parties or …

Sally: No.

Clare: I did! But like not … I pose for pictures but …

Alice: Really funny. Not slutty.

Sally: Yeah, not like nearly naked and with alcohol and stuff.

Here embodied display and alcohol drinking are viewed as 'slutty' and subject to ridicule. Louisa (16, New Mills) had a very similar response:

> If you put pictures on like that people are just going to think oh look you're like a bit of a slut or you're gagging to have sex, I had to make that choice because I thought I don't want people to see me like that.

And again Marie (16, New Mills) responded with a nearly identical narrative:

> It's like you, if you go on some people's pictures … you see pictures of girls in their bras, bikinis and all that … It's like putting yourself down, it's making everyone think, oh, she's a slag … they're trying to impress everyone. Like get all the boys thinking … they're up for anything … I could but … I don't really like going round in short skirts, bikini tops and that 'cause one it's too cold, and two … I think it makes the boys think you'll do anything if you're walking around like that … making yourself look desperate.

The comments indicate the complex gendered and sexualised negotiations that have to be undertaken as part of self-representation of sexualised femininity on the Bebo assemblage. As I illustrated in Chapter 7, sexual regulation around not being too 'slutty' is well documented in research on girls' friendships (Hey, 1997; Lamb, 2002), but this takes on new contradictory dynamics with online social networking profile displays (boyd, 2008). Online identity performances are made within a context of new pressures to display the self in line with celebrity norms of idealised femininity. Marie discussed pressures for girls to post 'pictures of girls in their bras, bikinis and all that' (see also Patchin and Hinduja, 2010). Heather (16, New Mills) had posted a series of bikini shots on Bebo, which her focus group described as 'normal' because she was in a holiday context. Girls commented at length about not wanting to be seen as 'slutty', a classed dynamic of sexual regulation. Heather also said girls had to be careful not to come across as a 'fucking diva' from the photos you post. Thus importantly, the online incitement to present as 'sexy' sits in contradiction to the sexually regulative peer group at school.

Online pressures were also racialised in important ways. Where displays of breast and cleavage were the biggest issue among the white girls, buttocks emerged as a locus of 'sexiness' of Black femininity. For instance, a user photo of a black teen girl who was friends with one of our participants at New Mills featured a side profile only of her buttocks from the waist down.[8] This sexualised emphasis on her buttocks signals a key marker of racial difference in idealised femininity in relation to globalised 'Black' hip hop, R&B and rap celebrity culture, which celebrates big 'booty' (Battle and Barnes, 2009). In addition, both Sally (14, Thornbury) and Marie (16, New Mills) described the prevalence of some boys wanting to post photos of their 'six packs'. The difference being, however, that boys seem to be mostly rewarded and not sexually regulated in the same ways as girls by revealing their torso and chest and stomach muscles (Ringrose *et al.*, 2011).

Various girls negotiated the pressures of online display differently. Alice's (14, Thornbury) parents and older siblings regulated her use of Bebo and Facebook, commenting on her photos, which restricted her forms of display. Louise (16, New Mills) told us her mother said 'you should not exploit yourself' online' and regulated her online and mobile phone usage. Daniela discussed her parents wanting her to limit her online usage, but she spent considerable time constructing a 'sexy' online Bebo identity, which her parents were not aware of.

Performing digital 'slut'

In this section I focus on the case study online observations and interview data from two Year 9 girls, Daniela (14, Thornbury) and one of her best friends Nicola (14, Thornbury), to explore how teen girls enact self-sexualisation performances online and how these can hold both sexist and transformative meanings. Daniela was from one of the traditional working class families in the village of Thornbury. She described a complicated family structure in which her father is working full-time to support two families. She lives with her dad, step-mum and step siblings. She was in middle to low academic set at school, and describes herself as a 'ditsy blonde' in 'hard' lessons like 'English and maths'. She was planning to do a qualification in beauty therapy, something she describes as a better career choice than a hairdresser, since she saw her older sister 'do hair' which 'seems like a bit of a boring life to start with … you have to sweep hair like for ages'. Daniela is popular, with a close group of friends called the 'Mini Plastics' after the group 'Plastics' in the movie *Mean Girls*. She is also part of a girls group in the village who play football, are called the 'Thornbury Girls' and have their own Bebo site, featuring photos of the girls at sporting and social events. Daniela spends a great deal of time on SNSs telling us that she goes on them as much as possible although her parents are concerned 'because literally when I got in from school until I go to bed I'm on MSN ... so they said ... you are going to break the computer so you won't be able to use it at all ... limit yourself'.

Recall Daniela's extremely pointed comments about 'slutty girls' who post 'cleavage' and 'body' shots and 'think too much of themselves' during the first group interview at Thornbury. Yet when we looked at Daniela's Bebo page her profile picture was her in heavy gothic style make-up and a low cut vest top, accompanied by many other photos in her albums focusing on her breasts including images with shadowing to enhance the cleavage. One image had been put through a Bebo application to place flashing stars around her breasts. In interview she described how her profile photo was taken when she and her friends got together and did their make-up like the 'dollies' in the popular children's musical, Chitty-Chitty Bang Bang. Most girls described these joint photo construction sessions – as Daniela said: 'it's just a thing that girls do when they have a sleepover, and it's like, ah, let's take a picture of us ... in the mirror.'

Resignifying 'slut' and 'whore'?

Daniela worked hard to channel her affect around producing a recognisable form of idealised feminine corporeality. Her bodily properties such as long blond hair and visible breasts act as a form of currency in the Bebo network. But she also used the space to experiment with and speak back to the forms of sexual regulation I have been exploring in Chapter 7. For instance, Daniela's username, which sat beside her profile photo was 'Slut'. The username/tagline looked like this: 'Slut <Da- Da- Daniellaaaa> 'Aчччҷeeeeee ..♥ 'Hi Im Daniela And ii Like It Up The Bum .. Just Like Your Mum! And I Suck Dick for £5'.

Although this was sexually explicit in relation to our sample, it is important to foreground discussion of Daniela's pictures, username and tagline in relation to the larger Bebo network. At the time of the research over 25,000 Bebo users used 'slut' or had reference to 'slut' in their usernames or taglines. So it is not an unusual finding. Indeed, a cursory look at Bebo reveals many variations on the slut username such as 'Kinky Slut', 'Lisa McSlut', 'Sluts on Speed', accompanied by pictures of girls in their underwear, two girls kissing, cleavage shots etc. Rather than being unusual, these types of images and textual representations are normal on the Bebo assemblage, so our focus was to explore how the girls in our research engaged with and used such forms of performance and what this meant to them. In our individual interview Daniela brought up the username fairly quickly herself:

Daniela: I didn't know what you would think, because like my username is slut ...
               but I don't mean it as like I'm a slut. Because if you look down on my
               friends list ... One ... username is Whore ... We have this little thing,
               like she's my slut, I'm her whore. Because loads of people used to call us
               it, so we just thought whatever, we'll just be them then. And like one day

	we just found a [Bebo] background like it, and we were like, oh, that's quite nice. And people are like, 'why have you got slut?'… and it's like, I don't mean it like that. But 'cos I didn't know, like if you read it if you'd be thinking, 'oh my god!'
Jessica:	So you mean that people used to say that you were a slut and so you … what … what … what do you mean by that?
Daniela:	Well, 'cos our group, like some people, like older girls that saw us, like with someone would be like, 'oh you slag or you slut' … Just because they didn't know us … because they wanted to insult us … so we just got a bit like, 'oh I don't care'. 'Cos we used to really care about it, and then we just got a bit like 'oh I don't care any more' … we just got used to it, and then … I don't really know what happened but it was just a random thing of where we were just like, I'd be like 'your, she's my whore and I'm her slut. Whatever. Get over it!' and then she'd say the same.
Jessica:	Okay. And how do you think other girls perceive that in your group? What do they think?
Daniela:	I don't know. I haven't had anybody say anything, like girls being bitchy about it to me.
Jessica:	How … how do you think, like, 'cos … I remember you said, you know, other, older guys contact you and stuff, like how do you think that might affect how people see you, like wider than your school community?
Daniela:	I suppose that probably entices them a bit. But … but like if they do say anything to me I just literally tell them to 'Fuck off!'
Jessica:	Yeah?
Daniela:	Because … Like I say, I'll look at their Bebo and if they're like over 17 I'm just like, 'well you look like a bit of a perv to me, can you leave me alone?' or something.

In this dialogue we see a complex negotiation and several competing accounts of 'slut'. First, Daniela says I don't mean it as slut, suggesting slut and whore have another meaning besides what she assumes I am thinking. She then she tells me that older girls called her and Nicola slut so they took on these labels. She talks about looking around at Bebo skins and finding good backgrounds, which enabled them to embrace the notions further. She then describes the way she and Nicola 'got used to' calling themselves slut and whore – it became a 'random' thing, 'whatever'.

The way Daniela describes taking up these terms is complex, since the girls are actually producing their friendship through these notions – they are not sluts or whores in general, but each other's slut and whore. This relates to Deleuze and Guattari's important caution against reading representation as cultural reproduction and mimicry, and the need for detailed mappings of mimesis, where difference disrupts repetition (Renold and Ringrose, 2008). Feona Attwood (2007) has argued the term 'slut' has shifted meanings culturally, having been appropriated and re-worked in wider popular culture and by particular groups of women/girls, and can be taken on as a term of defiance and pride rather than shame (see also Ringrose and Renold, 2012). Daniela and Nicola's reframing of slut and whore shows the form of discursive re-signification I discussed in Chapter 6. They appropriate and reverse the injurious meanings of 'slut' towards a positive extolling of solidarity and identity (Butler, 1993; Hey, 2006). Positioning themselves as each other's slut and whore changes the terminology from one of masculine control and operates as a 'fun' and pleasurable way for Daniela and Nicole to perform intimacy and closeness with each other. They respond to girls who sought to slut-shame them. In a sense it 'queers' these tags (Butler, 1993) and operates as a 'line of flight' from other girls' sexual regulation (Deleuze and Guattari, 1987).

Daniela also indicated that the tagline 'Hi Im Daniela And ii Like It Up <u>The Bum</u> … Just Like Your Mum! And I <u>Suck Dick</u> for £5' had come out of her relationship with Nicola. One weekend they traded Bebo passwords and started writing on one another's sites. First off Daniela made a rhyme on Nicola's site about how she cheated on her boyfriend with a boy who:

> gave her an org … because his name rhymed with org … and then it was just running, like where we basically swapped Bebos and she'd write loads of comments.

When Nicola wrote the 'I like it up the bum' tagline, Daniela retaliated with 'I suck nipples for free but you have to ask nicely'. Daniela said:

> I didn't mind because I know she was only joking. 'Cos I was on the phone to her at the same time so she was going, like, ha ha, look what I've thrown on your Bebo … So I was like, no, look at your Bebo. It was just like that, so it just started building up and got worse and worse.

This incident marked a specific interchange between these close friends, happening in real time on the phone as well as on each other's Bebo sites – a complex virtual and embodied assemblage through which friendship and identity is being staged. The tagline was, however, left as a semi-permanent reminder (artefact) and 'joke' for others to witness.

So there are multiple ways of reading the scenario. On the one hand one can see how her Bebo site might be a 'fantasy space' where Daniela is trying out sexual identity (Thomas, 2004). Researchers have suggested such online platforms provide a relatively 'safe' space to experiment (Stern, 2006) and to perform as 'wise', 'knowing', and 'cool' about sex and relationships. Talking porn with her best friend positions these two as knowing, experienced and 'sexy', rather than innocent, passive and weak. Daniela also dismisses the idea of outside 'pervs', whom can just be told to 'fuck off', illustrating a certain confidence and knowingness about 'stranger danger' which is rejected as unproblematic (Livingstone, 2008). On the other hand, the tagline is informed by 'porno-scripts' (Paasonen *et al.*, 2008), and her body is assembled in particular ways with holes (sucking mouth and bum) that can be plugged into and which can service other parts of other machines (the phallus). Deleuze and Guattari's focus on the body help us to see how the tagline has an affective force and channels sexual affect and possibility in particularly striated and indeed 'pornified' ways.

In one sense their Bebo pages help them to reject the sexual regulation of the slut tag in the teen assemblage. But if we think about Gill's (2008: 53) theories of new technologies of 'sexy' and how a 'performance of confident sexual agency' has shifted to become a key regulative dimension of idealised femininity in postfeminist media contexts, we can think about new pressures to perform this way and how girls and women are 'required to be skilled in a variety of sexual behaviours'. We have to ask, why *these particular* discourses of sexuality are used to talk back to slut, given they link back to prostitution and sexual commodification and selling sexual services for money (see also Ringrose and Erikson-Barajas, 2011). It is not the status of these speech acts as truth claims (Davies, 1997) in this temporal moment (e.g. do they 'really' like anal sex, sell oral sex or suck nipples) that is as important, but rather how these discourses shape ideas of female sexuality in particular ways.

Unpacking the reference to 'sucking dick' for money, this relates to dominant cultural themes of fellatio as a prime vector of girls as 'skilled' sexual performances. This is widely evident, for instance, in Paris Hilton's sex video, dominated by a prolonged session licking and sucking a penis; or the popular 2003 Kelis song 'My milkshake brings all the boys to the yard', featured in the *Mean Girls* teen movie in 2005. This song is another well-known example of references to mastery at performing blow jobs with milkshake referring to ejaculate (see also Coy, 2009). Importantly the Kelis Bebo skin was in the top 10 at the time of writing. As I reviewed in Chapter 4, Canadian commentator Sharon Azam (2009) wrote an entire popular book implying the normalisation of blowjobs: *Oral Sex is the New Goodnight Kiss* (although she conveniently forgot to qualify that it is girls giving fellatio not the other way round, which equalises what is a highly sexist typically one-directional flow of affect shaping the girl as sexual performer for the male other).

Similarly, the normalisation of anal sex as a heterosexual practice should not be surprising, given its wide representation and discussion in popular culture from UK women's magazines such as *Marie Claire* (in advice columns), to the teen-oriented Hollywood *American Pie* movies (which introduces anal sex into several story lines). The normalisation of 'hetero anal sex' is part of a dynamic of 'pornification' or the leakage of pornographic text and imagery into everyday vocabulary and usage (Paasonen *et al.*, 2008). The content of the chain of signifiers (Lacan) or codes (Deleuze and Guattari) 'I like it up the bum …' contains the discursive incitement (Foucault) to perform and enjoy anal sex, but as I've indicated we need to unpack the mimesis in this. It is not a case of straightforward reproduction. The girls evoke the codes in ways that partly make a joke or irony of the utterances. While many adults have been shocked about the 'up the bum' statement, invoking their own sexual innocence at Daniela's age (e.g. 'I had no idea that existed'), moral righteousness and invoking of idealised sexual innocence (typical of the sexualisation moral panic) is not academically useful. Rather we need to understand what these trends mean and potential effects/implications for teen girls' bodily and affective states.

As a feminist commentator, there are two pressing issues. First, we have to ask questions about girls' genital pleasure. What was striking was while Daniela and Nicola's Bebo sites featured talk about the anus, the mouth, the dick, breasts and nipples there was no reference to female genitals or the clitoris. There was reference to the mystical notion of having an 'org' but the bodily mechanics of this act for girls or how they themselves or their partners would achieve this was absent (in contrast to explicit references to servicing the phallus through sucking 'dick' or having it 'up the bum'). Michelle Fine and Sarah McClelland (Fine, 1988, Fine and McClelland, 2006) discuss the 'missing' discourses of adolescent female desire, and in the data set there was a discursive absence around the vagina or clitoris, in contrast to prominence of the 'dick', illustrating the primacy of male bodily functions and an affective dynamic of male sexual parts penetrating or being sexually serviced by the girls' body parts, creating a normative heterosex assemblage. We need to ask about the possible bodily and affective effects for young people of this channelling of phallogecentric energies into a normal sexual assemblage on Bebo.

Second, those working in sexual health education have raised health concerns about the mechanics of facilitating the possible heightened demands for anal heterosex as it becomes a more normalised heterosexual practice, raising questions about gendered power relations in sexual relations among young people (Grimes, 2008). It is crucial to underscore that my discussion about the discourse of anal hetero-sex is not a rejection of different consensual sexual practices from a moral perspective that seeks to re-innocent the girl child as in sexualisation panics. Rather, I am asking questions from a poststructural feminist perspective that is interested to understand how girls' and boys' body parts are being constituted and related to in ways that could be potentially painful and life and energy destroying (as Deleuze and Guattari think about these processes) if it impedes the development of sexual health and pleasure (particularly for girls). Feminist promotion of sexual health means enabling girls to become competent and familiar with finding bodily sexual pleasure (Lerum and Dworkin, 2009) – rather than knowledgeable only about servicing the male erection and bodily functioning. These concerns, as outlined in Chapter 4, are crucial in relation to sex education curriculum and practice in the UK and internationally (Allen, 2004; Alldred and David, 2008), where emphasis continues to be on condom usage to facilitate male penetration (of either vagina, mouth or anus), rather than knowing how to create enjoyable sexual interaction (with self and others) for girls (female masturbation is also a discursive silence across many sexual education materials) (Alldred and David, 2007: 79). Daniela's tagline, therefore, written as a 'joke' between two 14-year-old girls, raises some important questions that need further inquiry around the construction of female sexual pleasure, desire and agency both within the networked publics of social networking sites and in everyday life, which I will return to in my concluding chapter.

The final issue I would like to explore in relation to Daniela is how her Bebo identity shaped her bodily affect and relationships offline at school. Recall that Daniela's condemnation of 'slutty' girls in the group interview at school contrasted with her online self representations as slut on Bebo. Although there were aspects of resignification of 'slut' as a 'line of flight' away from sexual regulation, as I explored, it did not seem possible to entirely shift the slippery hold of 'injurious' norms like slut and whore that work to sexually regulate girls (Butler, 2004a; Ringrose, 2008a).

Re-signification is not, therefore, a one-way completed process as Butler would agree, and through a Deleuzian lens, lines of flight can be easily re-territorialised. For instance, despite her knowing and confident displays of 'sexy' online, Daniela's relationship with Sam at school and offline seemed to be characterised not by sexual confidence but by hetero-normative dating rituals of female passivity (Nayak and Kehily, 2002). Although online Daniela fills in 'relationship status' as 'married', and the Bebo category of 'hometown' as 'Sam's bed' implying strong intimacy, Daniela commented she was worried that she could not call Sam her 'boyfriend', since he had not yet formally 'asked her out' after weeks of dating. She was also concerned Sam found it 'weird' getting Bebo messages from 'slut, slut, slut' (her username). A few weeks after the interviews, Sam started getting increasingly intimate Bebo messages from another girl, Daisy, and then appeared to break it off with Daniela and state his 'luv' for Daisy much more strongly than he had for Daniela.[9] After the tenuous relationship with Sam ended, it is significant that Daniela changed her Bebo profile. She dropped the 'slut' username and 'suck dick, up the bum' tagline, as well as references to Sam. She also changed her profile photo to a picture of her and her friends lying on their stomachs in their uniform skirts on a grassy hill, with their feet up behind them, invoking discourses of childhood/girlhood innocence.

In addition, it did not seem that the production of online sexually confident display disrupted intense bodily pressures and anxieties in real life at school that Daniela and other girls were constantly negotiating. Daniela told me in her individual interview about her body worries, saying she 'hated' her legs and felt 'huge' and 'fat' compared with her friends. She discussed the pressures informing the production of the ideal visual feminine to be performed online and worried about whether or not she could sustain the 'perfect' self offline:

> popular boys in this school, you don't see them going out with girls that they would probably see as ugly … puts a lot of pressure on girls to make themselves look pretty, to make themselves just look perfect to that one boy that they really want; because, otherwise, if they don't try or make an effort they're not going to want to go out with them.

Rather than constructing some transformative sexual confidence for girls, online displays of visually sexy femininity and textual displays of being 'up for it' seemed to offer little in shifting the impact of deeply regulative beauty norms and pressures to be 'perfect' at school as well as online. Daniela describes the complex effects of disciplinary effects of body politics at school:

> to show off, to show that they have the power … I think if all girls were the same and didn't do that sort of thing, then it would just be a bit of a boring world … we'd all be so dull and quiet and boring … it just wouldn't be worth living in! But, I think, if girls had more confidence and were happy with how they looked, then I think it would better, because there wouldn't be so much complaining and so much, like, anorexic people … like you'll sit there at lunch and you'll see somebody who is not eating, and it'll be like, it's 'cos they think they're fat.

Here Daniela describes both the excitement of girls competing and using their sexual 'power', as well as the affective experience of lacking body confidence and not wanting to eat, describing a contradictory, conflicted terrain. So while SNSs can offer new spaces for sexual expression, there is also the possibility that the visual performance of the self online can heighten the pressures of 'perfectionism' to be performed at school and increase a sense of 'abject' bodily lack, around being 'too fat' for instance (Ringrose and Walkerdine, 2008).

The data also illuminate, however, how some working class white girls are carrying out trajectories of low educational aspiration and devoting considerable energy to their sexual identity online, which both contradicts and raises important question about the reductive discourse of all girls as 'successful' in school. Daniela's work trajectory in the beauty industry, and poor performance in academic subjects (she called herself a 'ditsy blonde' in maths and science), is notable. We need to conduct further research into how relative class mobility may shape investments in performing 'sexy' (Coy and Garner, 2010; Evans *et al.*, 2010) and also how specific forms of cultural/visual erotic capital on social networking sites are classed (Hakim, 2010; Skeggs, 2005).

Performing Playboy Bunny

Where Daniela and Nicola played with their sexual identity and at least temporarily took up the labels of 'slut' and 'whore' together to partially transform their meanings, challenging sexual regulation from older girls at school, not every girl could legitimately take up the identity of sexually confident 'slut'. At New Mills we studied a slightly older age group of 15–16 year olds in Year 11. A media studies college, none of the girls in our sample were going on to university. All of them were going for jobs in the beauty or caring industry, although one girl, Rachel (16), wanted to take on a male trade in brick-laying. We worked with two different groups, a higher status more popular group (which included Heather who posted herself in bikini on Bebo) and a lower status group that struggled with competition and conflict, particularly in the case of two girls: Marie and Louise. Here I focus on this 'friend' pair first, exploring how Marie coped with physical pressures to perform as 'sexy' online. Next I will look at the dynamics of heterosexual competition explored in Chapter 6 that emerged between Marie and Louise who got into a physical fight after Marie was said to call Louise a 'fat slag' to another friend online on MSN (instant messaging).

Unlike Daniela, Marie appeared to be located much further down the affective, social hierarchy of the school peer group assemblage. In interviews she recounted a difficult set of circumstances where she had moved the previous year from a school in one town where she lived with her mother to her new school where she was living with her father's new family, including several step-siblings. She described moving being due in part to what she called 'bullying', on-going incidences of violence and ~ression with her girl peer group in the previous school. She was already by the interview involved with violent peer conflict at New Mills as I'll

a's Bebo profile photo, which boldly displayed her face, hair and
d a photo in a baseball cap with a pony tail, cut at the shoulders,

which partially hid her face. As discussed above, Marie expressed concern about girls who put up photos of themselves in 'bras, knickers and bikinis' saying 'it's out of order … makes you look like a slag … [and] look desperate'. She responded to further questions about displaying one's body on the site by saying:

> I don't like walking round in bikini tops 'cause I don't like my stomach. And people say, oh, that's stupid, you've got the most skinniest stomach ever. And I was like, yeah … Like when I was 11 I used to be fat … not proper fat, but I used to be proper chubby. Chubby cheeks, chubby belly, everything … And I used to try and walk round with my stomach breathed in, everything. I've never liked my stomach … Even now that I'm skinny.

She was also very concerned about being 'small', a 'midget' and 'having nothing' which I read as a bodily anxiety over lack of sexual development of breasts in particular. In relation to these bodily anxieties it was interesting that the most noticeable feature of Marie's Bebo page was the Playboy Bunny skin. The Playboy Bunny symbol features frequently in the Bebo assemblage with many using this skin backdrop. Not only did Marie have the Playboy Bunny skin, however, but she had a photo of her in fluffy bunny ears featured prominently on her Bebo page. Marie had turned the picture into a cartoon-like image through a Bebo application to 'cartoonise' photos.

The Playboy Bunny has become a contested symbol of feminist critique against commodification of women's/girls' bodies, given its mass production and the massive success of marketing the bunny for women and younger and younger girls (Tankard Reist, 2009). Our aim was to explore what using the Playboy Bunny symbol meant to Marie. She explained having a virtual folder with 'loads of pictures of Playboy Bunny', including the skin that she picked. She told us her mum had given her and her 12-year-old sister the bunny ears, to which I asked:

Jessica: Yeah, and what does it mean to you, the symbol?
Marie: To most people it means like the Playboy mansion and all the girls and that but with girls it's just the bunny and like girls like rabbits and.
Jessica: So do you, are you thinking that about, you know, the Playboy Bunny mansion or anything like that?
Marie: No, it's just a good cartoon.
Jessica: You, so you think of it more like a cartoon?
Marie: Yeah.
Jessica: And do you have like the shirts and.
Marie: Yeah … I've got two tops with the Playboy Bunny on it.
Jessica: Ok, so you know other people might think of it as like the Playboy mansion?
Marie: Yeah.
Jessica: And how do you, what do you think about that, the fact that you see it one way and other people might see it another way?
Marie: It's other people's opinion, it's completely up to them. I just like it because of the picture.

The Playboy Bunny symbol is taken up and used in multiple ways by Marie. The tangible Playboy Bunny T-shirts and bunny ears products are added to by a virtual folder with a collection of Playboy Bunny pictures, the Playboy Bunny skin and the cartooning application, which Marie uses specifically to cartoonise herself into a bunny. Bebo appears to intensify her relationship to the Playboy Bunny symbolism and commercial products. The symbol also operates as marker of sexiness, an escape to glamour and material wealth (to most people it means the Playboy mansion) *and* a symbol of childhood innocence (to girls it's just a 'rabbit' and a 'good cartoon'). It is a symbol with 'condensed', layered meanings (Erassari in Hey, 2005). The Playboy Bunny signifies both sexiness and innocence and has commercialised symbolic value 'generated by [exchange] processes' (Skeggs, 2005: 965), through a long history of use and normalisation in the public domain. Marie, however, seizes onto the discourse of childhood innocence to discount any implied discourse of inappropriate sexualisation; Marie is also wearing a sweatshirt in her cartoonised bunny ears photo, so her body is not on display. Again, this is not merely reproduction of a unitary Playboy Bunny identity but a complex mimesis. In one reading Marie uses the Playboy Bunny symbolism to associate herself with 'sexy', since she does not feel she has the requisite bodily properties (e.g. big breasts) to perform in bras and knickers or bikini on Bebo. The Bunny symbol also does work to shield her body from scrutiny. Marie is managing her bodily insecurities in creative ways on Bebo.

Sexual cyber-aggression

Marie was in some ways, however, highly invested in her bodily 'smallness'. She used 'lil' repeatedly, for instance her user name and tagline was 'Marie L <xlilxmissxMariex> 'lil miss Marie ere aka ratface lol', which she later changed to 'lil miss bitch'. Ratface and bitch gesture towards the violent peer conflicts she was embroiled in. Critical of her own either too 'fat' or 'skinny' body she also projected these bodily regulations onto others. As mentioned, during the first focus group interview it emerged that Marie had apparently called Louise a 'fat slag' through instant messaging with other girls. This then escalated into face-to-face violence the following day at school when Louise confronted and attacked Marie:

> On the day of the fight I was talking to my mate in Drama and she was telling me all this stuff she said to Louise over MSN that I said that she was a fat slag, and that I'd been spreading rumours about her and all this. So, my dad drove to me to school, I've gone in through reception and I've gone, through the gates with my tuba and loads of people come running up to me going, your dad's gone, come out the front gates cos everyone wants to speak to you, so I've gone down there thinking nothing was wrong and I've got pinned up against the wall by Louise, saying why have you called me a fat slag, ra, ra, ra, ra, and I've gone to walk off and she's pulled me back by the hair and she started screaming at me again so I've pushed her away, walked off, she's come running after me, punched me in the back, then a teacher came out and split it up ... it bruised most of my back and it was hurting to walk and that but, it's not the first time I've been hit and that so.

What is significant is how the online rumour escalates into school yard violence so that cyber-aggression has manifold impacts upon peer culture and educational experience. Like the younger girls in Chapter 7, Marie also reported this level of conflict as completely banal and normalised, also telling me that girls from her previous school has contacted her through Bebo and were now 'bullying' her online, indicating the difficulty in separating out victim and bully subject positions in the affective complexities of cyber-experiences.

Resisting 'fat slag'

Louise's Bebo profile and interview illustrated, more than for any other girl in our data, the effects of the types of exclusions and affective injuries happening in the online/offline peer networks. Louise's case study illustrates how digital technology can intensify issues of social rejection, exclusion, and peer hierarchies hardening into embodied physical affect, such as violence at school.

Like Marie, Louise described her disdain over girls who look like their 'gagging to have sex' on SNSs. Her site contained no body-revealing pictures. Her refusal to expose her body is also, however, part of constraints of 'choices' around self-representation discussed by writers like Gill (2008). Girls have to manage the visual criterion for being 'sexy' – a 'well fit', 'skinny' body (Focus group, New Mills). New technological forms of sexual regulation of bodies via tropes of popular culture organised the types of visual display idealised and normalised on Bebo, as I've been illustrating.

After the encounter with Marie, Louise was left struggling with the label of 'fat slag' for the remainder of the school year. Fat slag seemed a particularly difficult subject position to negotiate, given smallness is revered (Walkerdine, 1997) and fatness is abject. Louise also used 'lil' in her username, which was 'XxlilLouisexx Mwah'. Louise had also chosen the beauty industry for work and was going into hairdressing the following year. She talked about cultivating a 'pretty' photograph online and was one participant who explicitly reported 'airbrushing' her photos. However, they were mostly of her face taken from angles that minimised attention to her body and Louise told me she did not expect comments on her Bebo that she was 'well fit'.

Like Marie, Louise's Bebo skin was pink, but had swirls and hearts and read 'When Santa asks me what I want for Christmas I know exactly what I'll say … I don't want presents I want a boy who will take my breath away'. Set against this explicit desire, Louise discussed a 'complicated' relationship with a boy Jay:

Louise: I do like someone but at the moment things are just a bit complicated with school and I'd rather leave it until out of school.

Jessica: Does he, do you talk to him on-line?

Louise: Yeah, he's one of my closest mates.

Jessica: And how does that help or how does that affect it?

Louise: He, it doesn't really affect it because he knows how I feel and he feels the same but he understands that I want to wait until I leave so I can get all my studies out of the way. So, it's like that.

Jessica: OK. So how often do you talk to him?

Louise: Every day. [online]

Jessica: And does he go to the school?

Louise: No, he's left school ... but he's only 17.

Jessica: And when you see him in real life, are you guys like kissing or.

Louise: No, we don't do that. We leave that for our private self, like if it's just me and him one night going out somewhere.

Jessica: OK.

Louise: But if we're going out with a group of friends, we may give each other the odd hug but then we'd do it to everyone else as well so no one else would get suspicious if we don't want people to know.

Jessica: You don't want people to know.

Louise: At the moment no, not until we are or not. So it's like that.

Jessica: And do you feel OK with that?

Louise: Yeah. I do feel OK with that but it's whether the fact that I don't know whether he doesn't want people to know? Maybe he might be embarrassed and doesn't want to tell me? But I don't think he would be. I think he just wants to keep it private for now in case like, he doesn't want me going round saying to everyone oh, we might be going out but then we might not be. So that's why we want to leave it.

The online space allows for the relationship to continue since Jay has left school. But despite Louise's protestations that they have mutually decided to keep their relationship 'private' because they 'don't want people to know', 'because of her studies', Louise goes on to describe feeling concerned that Jay might be embarrassed of her. This relates in important ways to how the visual culture of Bebo commodifies affect and relationships through new categories like 'relationship statuses' and 'other half' (and other categories which fix ties with others). For instance, there was a dominant culture at both schools of 'sharing the luv' on Bebo, sending virtual luvs, hugs and kisses (Ringrose and Willett, 2008).[10] Students at both schools discussed how it was becoming 'a competition to see who can get more' (Heather, 16, New Mills), 'who can get the most "luvs"' (Daniela, 14, Thornbury). In Louise's case the hard and fixed categories demanded on Bebo ('in a relationship' status) are not fulfilled. She cannot meet the quantifiable measures of desirability, popularity and 'luv', also worrying that her girlfriends were not equally reciprocating friendship:

Louise: You've got to be careful who you pick because if you pick certain people, other people will get upset that you haven't picked them ... you have to pick people over other people ... It can cause a lot of arguments actually.

Jessica: You have to choose your top friends?

Louise: Yeah, well ... it's weird because they want them to be your first. But then why aren't you their first? You want me to be my first? Why, why am I your third or second? It's what I don't understand.

Jessica: So how do you negotiate that?

Louise: You don't, you just don't do it back. I just let them go round doing it to everyone else and it's like, well, I'm not going to do it back. Why should

I do it back? You want me to be my first? Why, why am I your third or second?

Jessica: So you don't, so you don't have one where you're the first and she's the first?

Louise: No ... It's choosing really because, when you're sitting there choosing you have to think about, of, if I don't choose this person what argument can it cause? Will it cause an argument? Will it? Will it? Will it? It's just like ... I have to explain myself and then what they would do is the other person would say, 'well you said this' and I'd be like, 'no, I didn't, you said that', trying to blame it on me.

Jessica: Mm.

Louise: It's very difficult when it's with MSN and then you have to approach them the next day. Very, very difficult.

Jessica: Do you think it causes stress at all?

Louise: Mm. Does. A lot of stress ... 'Cause, well, you do really because it's like when you're lying there sleeping, you're thinking I can't believe I just had that conversation. Such a stupid argument and now I've got to face it tomorrow at school.

Jessica: Mm.

Louise: And you sit there and you think about it and then you wake up the next day and you're still thinking about it. It's like ... I don't want to go anywhere.

This section details hierarchies in orders of friends, being neglected, overlooked, being chosen behind others, and not being chosen by anyone as a 'top friend', which can lead to arguments. The channelling of affect and desire in relation to intimacy and friendship can intensify peer hierarchies leading to risks of rejection, and life-destroying anxieties (stress, interfering with sleeping). Significantly, however, students still have to wake up and go to school, another visceral reminder of how the online affective connections and constant contact are mediating and transforming face-to-face relationships offline. A Deleuzo–Guattarian analysis shows how these online sites striate affective possibilities, hardening the flows of energies into quantifiable orderings (like top friends and relationship status) with painful emotional effects and losses that follow negotiating this new affective economy. There are immediate and real effects as we saw with the physical confrontation with Marie:

Jessica: Your fight with Marie ... could you kind of tell me what happened again?

Louise: I was talking to one of my other mates on MSN.

Jessica: Mm.

Louise: As well as Marie. And my other mate said to me, 'oh, Marie has called you a fat slag and she doesn't want nothing to do with you no more and she said you go round with everyone, you try and get with everyone's exes and everything like that' or something. So I said to her on MSN, 'have you been saying stuff about me?' She says 'no ... I've got to go now because it's my time to come off but if you're still on later on I'll talk to you then'. I looked back on, she wasn't on. So I waited for her outside the school the next day and I, I'd been so angry 'cause more people had been coming to me, telling me what she's been saying. And the more people that come and tell me against one person kind of gets me thinking that well, she's obviously been saying it.

Jessica: Mm.

Louise: So I asked her and she said, 'no, no, no, no, I haven't said nothing. I promise you I haven't said anything'. I said 'well you must have because I've had about five or six people coming to me saying you've been calling me a fat slag and everything'. She goes 'why would I say that?' 'I don't know. Why would you?' And she said, 'at the end of the day, you know, you're one of my best friends. Why would I want to do that?' And I ended up hitting her, 'cause I got so stressed because everyone was telling me while I was trying to talk to her. 'She's been saying this. She's been saying that. Ra, ra, ra, ra.' All in one ear.

Jessica: All around you, at the time?

Louise: Yeah, yes. I got so stressed I hit her and I regret, regret it to this day that I hit one of my best friends ... So horrible.

It is important to contextualise this fight in relation to the chain of cyber-events that have informed it, and the general affective state of insecurity Louise has described. As we've seen, Louise has had to negotiate being no-one's top friend and a refusal to solidify attachment from her romantic interest. Within the specific chain of relations in the school assemblage she is vulnerable to attack. As we've seen, fat marks her out as abject and combined with slag this works to sexually regulate Louise in classed ways. Less ambiguous than slut, slag is a classed category implying she is dirty, loose and desperate (Cowie and Lees, 1981). Indeed, Marie is noted as having said Louise is 'going round with everyone and trying to get with other girls' exes (leftovers, making her second choice). Fat slag works to disavow Louise from having qualities that legitimise her as desirable in the peer-networked assemblage. Because Louise is positioned as undesirable, she should not desire (chase around boys). She is constituted through this lack. As Deleuze and Guattari say 'desire does not express a molar lack within the subject; rather, the molar organisation deprives desire of its objective being' (1984: 29). Because Louise does not fit the molar technology of 'skinny', 'well fit' femininity, she is constituted as lacking, depriving her of 'objective being' as qualified either to seek out attention from or to desire the male subjects in question.

What does the fight mean and what does the school do?

In this final section I look further at Louise's response to being called a fat slag and how the school responds. Comparable to the examples I explored in the previous chapter, Louise's bursting out of violence onto Marie is diagnosed through the behavioural interventions at school as highly problematic because it violates conditions of normative, middle class passively aggressive femininity. Marie's calling of Louise 'fat slag' behind her back is a more of the normative display of covert and manipulative aggression in the psychological typologies I've reviewed in Chapter 3. Thus Louise's violence is pathologised, while Marie's cruelty is 'normative' (Ringrose and Renold, 2010) and so largely over-looked. This is evident in Louise's description of how the school addressed the fight:

Jessica: Can you tell me a little bit more about that? Like what, what if, like how you dealt with that experience.

Louise: Well, I didn't really deal with it. Sally went to Miss Taylor, one of our teachers, and told her about it. Miss Taylor pulled me out of a lesson and we had to deal with it like that. Me and Marie were sitting there crying in front of each other. Marie was explaining to me that, 'look, I'd never do that, I promise you I'd never ever, ever say anything about you, I'd never want to hurt you'. And I said to her 'well, I've got about seven or eight people coming to me saying that you said this and they're all saying it to me while I'm trying to talk to you, kind of gets me thinking'. And Miss Taylor said, 'well you didn't need to lash out and hit her'.

Jessica: Mm.

Louise: And I said, 'Miss, but I got so stressed, it was so hard not to'.

Jessica: Mm.

Louise: We had to deal with it like that.

Jessica: OK. And I want to ask you how you feel, 'cause, let's face it like, if you hit someone when you're a girl, it's like worse, you know? … Has there been any reaction about that?

Louise: Nothing's changed really. People know that I haven't … an anger problem when I get angry I can hit people like that but doesn't really change … because if people know what I'm like they should be able to accept me for it.

Jessica: Mm, mm. Just, so you, do, do you feel that you have an anger problem?

Louise: When I have a really bad argument, yeah. When it's just like some, he said, she said, it's like that one time, I lashed out but I've never ever done it again.

Jessica: Mm. Yeah. It's hard.

Louise: Very.

In this excerpt we can see that Miss Taylor's intervention works to pathologise Louise, while whatever part Marie may have played in the fight is glossed over. The symbolic violence of the norms around appearance and behaviour are not in question. Being called 'fat slag' is dismissed and internal reasons in Louise's psyche and background are drawn upon to explain her violence. Louise describes how she is known to have an 'anger-management' problem. She is constructed as a subject in psychological deficit in need of treatment. The way Marie is constructed as the victim and Louise as the aggressor/bully was also evident in Marie's interview account:

Miss Taylor sat us both down and made Louise apologise to me and explain why she hit me and that. And Louise said sorry and that she was never going to do it again and that. She, she promised me that she would never, that she would listen to me from now on and would never go like that.

Deleuze and Guattari's schizoanalysis suggests we deconstruct the schizoid social conditions that led to this assessment, the affective striations of the online and at-school assemblage, being called injurious names, and feminine imperatives to not act out, as a 'girl', at school. The school intervention does nothing to get at these underlying sexualised competitive dynamics, nor the content of the cyber-gossip which led to the physical altercation. Louise and Marie are encouraged to smooth everything over and acquiesce to the anti-bullying codings of the school. They vow to 'get along' and that 'things are fine' in the interviews. Indeed, they play an elaborate game of love and hate in the group interview:

Louise: We've literally been in a fight before because things have been ... said that's like, one of my mates told me on MSN that she called me a fat slag and everything like that so then I ... waited for her outside before school one day and I said 'Why are you saying this for?'
Marie: She punched me in my back.
Louise: I punched her in the back, she razzed in my face, she tried walking away, I grabbed her, punched her again, everything right, because all these things that people say to ... wind people up ... she sits there and cries their eyes out, right and I beg to differ that – I will never, ever do it again and I promise.
Marie: Because you love me!
Louise: I love you! But the things that people say they don't realise what, how much trouble it can actually cause.

After the fight, Louise's Bebo page also declares Marie as her 'other half'. Marie's site, however, had a photo of Marie with another girl Chantelle as her profile photo and Chantelle as her 'other half', signalling the same lack of reciprocity in her relationship with Louise.

Louise continued to manage the events through recourse to pathological blaming of her own personality. Indeed, she also writes on Bebo 'some bad things have happened to me leaving me with brain damage mentally' as way of explaining 'to all my friends ... what happens' – the rationale for her behaviour. Louise's social networking site, Bebo, offers a space for her to construct an explanatory narrative, but biomedical discourses of mental illness are drawn on to legitimise and explain her classification into 'damaged', violent, pathological girl.

Lines of flight: from rage to rupture?

In contrast, however, Louise also posted the following blog on her Bebo site:

Them things that i effin hate would have to be them spitefull bitches and bastards when they say stuff and then they shit stir and then there two faced about it and then they backstab you ... i cannot believe why some people would be such pains in the effin asses u get me let me know in message if you have ever had this as i have been through this alot so i have alot of advice to give towards all you ppl.

In this instance the online assemblage enables her to express her rage and appeal to others, to take up the position of knowing – 'I have a lot of advice to give'. In interview Louise suggested this comment related specifically to Marie:

> it relates back to the Marie thing. I hate people that are spiteful and stab you in the back and that are, are two-faced. You don't know whether this person has said it but you can get out of it by saying I don't want to know … And just being, and walking away. Walk. Being myself.

Louise's Bebo site therefore offered some space to continue the energy of refusal mobilised when she psychically responded to the violent capture of her signification as 'fat slag' – a space to point to the hypocrisy of betrayal and verbal attack. I want to think about how her rage is a 'line of flight' (Deleuze and Guattari, 1987: 4–5) which is both destructive (violent in the interaction with Marie) but also life affirming in that it enables her to speak back and construct alternative narratives. Given the 'impossible' contradictions of living femininity in a site like school (Griffin, 2005), where you are not meant to act out against symbolic violence, schizoanalysis suggests rage might be a useful and positive response (see also Austin, 2005) if harnessed in life-affirming ways. By mapping Louise's Bebo activities after the end of the school year we could see the potential of SNSs as assemblages and visual, discursive spaces with immanent possibilities.

After leaving New Mills, Louise constructed a new Bebo site. First, Marie was absent from her site and friend list. Louise has not repaired the relationship, she has 'walked away', freed from the constrictive sediments of school affective space. Second, on the new page Louise had fulfilled the terms of recognition of performing as loved and desirable. Her profile photo is of herself and Jay, lying down and embracing for the camera. Relationship status is 'in relationship' with Jay, who is now her 'other half'. This is all solidified with a purple swirling background and her tagline: 'I love my baby boy … I love you so much'.

How do we interpret these affective declarations and visual signifiers? Are they a recuperation into the molar norms of recognition of heterosexualised desirability demanded through the online assemblage? Or is it a resistance to and talking back to the hateful condemnations and lines of subjection of her body (as fat), her sexuality (as a slag) and her brain (as mentally damaged) mobilised through the affective community at her high school? To be a desiring machine, to defy, survive, to love and to be, despite the injuries of hierarchies orienting school life – does this constitute a line of flight from oppressive formations of feminine sexual identity (Renold and Ringrose, 2008)?

Conclusions

In this chapter I have explored how young people's SNS Bebo sites are replete with increasingly normalised and intensified examples of sexually explicit representations of girls' bodies, which supports the claims about postfeminist norms of female sexual embodiment discussed throughout this book (Gill, 2007; McRobbie, 2008).

I explored normative discourses of heterosexual femininity and masculinity in Bebo which are plugged into a wider globalised hetero-pornified media sphere (Paasonen *et al.*, 2008). I also looked at how the 'glocal' digital identities and groupings in school peer groups are class, racial and culturally specific. By mapping the conditions of possibility that are normative and dominant in the 'networked public' (boyd, 2008: 119) in question, I was able to also find places of disruption where girls navigated highly sexist content and relational sexual regulation from peers in creative ways. This ranged from Daniela and Nicola appropriating and partially re-signifying the categories of 'slut' and 'whore', to Marie taking up the Playboy Bunny symbol in ways that signalled 'sexy' without revealing her body, therefore shielding her from some of the technologies of looking and gazing that predominate in the postfeminist mediascape (Evans *et al.*, 2010). With Marie and Louise we saw how sexualised regulation and competition between girls led to cyber-gossip that Louise was a 'fat slag', which held particular injury around bodily abjection and classed sexual illegitimacy as desirable to and/or desirer of boys. Louise expressed anger, rage and violence, becoming pathologised at school, but also spoke back to events on her Bebo sites. I also raised questions about the meanings of her romantic resolution on Bebo. This brings us back to Walkerdine and questions raised in Chapter 7 about girls' primary desire to find a prince. When the princess defies the normative conditions of 'sexiness', is the sought-after visual affirmation of love a feminist-style victory?

What is crucial in all of this for educators is to get to grips with how thoroughly girls remain defined by their sexualised bodies, and how bodily performance mediates the minutia and molecularity of their everyday lives on and offline. New technologies like SNSs have enormous gendered and sexual implications for schooling, because they can intensify the visual hierarchy of looking upon and bodily scrutiny through new cyber-processes and spaces of identity performance that must be managed in school space. In the concluding chapter, I will explore the implications of this for educators, considering further what could happen in PSHE, sex education and media studies curricula, and through bullying and cyberbullying policies, to address these new forms of sexual politics that form the backdrop to contemporary schooling.

9 Conclusion
Ways forward for feminism and education

In this book I have looked at the relationship between the media, dominant gender and sexual discourses, educational research and policies and teen girls' lived experiences. I've argued that postfeminist 'presumptions' of gender equality obscure on-going issues of sexual difference and sexism that girls experience in the classroom, playground and beyond. These are the 'sexual politics' of schooling I have sought to underline and return our analysis to. As part of the dynamic of the media-charged landscape, we are often faced with the problem that issues facing girls and women are either invisible/neglected *or* they become sensationalised. I have explored a range of what I positioned as postfeminist panics over girlhood, each of which reproduce ideas of feminine 'excess' (Walkerdine, 1991) including concerns over girls as too academically successful, too indirectly mean or overtly aggressive and too sexual.

In this chapter, I will further outline the implications of my arguments about postfeminist panics over girlhood for education, considering what could happen differently in PSHE, sex education, media studies, and through behavioural policies to try to address the everyday sexual politics that form the backdrop to schooling. Educational policies are changing rapidly and in contradictory ways in a climate that Stephen Ball (2008) says is plagued by 'policy overload'. My analysis, then, is not at the micro level given rapid policy shifts. Rather I look broadly at what might be done around particular areas of schooling in relation to feminism and gender equality, raising a series of questions for moving our thinking forward. First, however, I want to outline a final example of media sensationalism that encapsulates the type of postfeminist discourses that demonise feminism and calls for gender equality in schools in the UK political landscape.

Revisiting the affective charge of postfeminist politics

On Saturday morning, 9 August 2008 I awoke to find that the research project I explored in Chapter 8 had been highlighted in the *Daily Mail* in an article entitled 'Girls should be taught feminism at school "to counter negative influence of celebrity role models"'; the electronic tagging system to this headline online read more provocatively 'Girls who call themselves sluts need feminism lessons.' My research on teen girls and social networking had been profiled in the *Times Educational Supplement*[1] which came out on Friday afternoon, was picked up by the *London*

Evening Standard by Friday night and then used for Saturday editions of the *Daily Mail* and *The Daily Telegraph*.[2] Whilst my work had appeared in the press in other instances this was the most extensive and invasive, given that the *Daily Mail* had included a photograph of me in the coverage that they lifted from my work web profile. Displayed prominently on page 9 of the Saturday edition, I sat in a rather strange ménage between Christina Aguilera in a pair of leather chaps with 'nasty' on the butt of her undies, on my right, and Virginia Woolf and Emmeline Pankhurst flanking me to the left. The *Daily Mail* article read:

Teenage girls should be taught feminism at school to stop the growing trend of giving themselves abusive 'male' nicknames such as 'slut' and 'whore', an expert said yesterday. Dr Jessica Ringrose, who has studied the social habits of schoolgirls, found they increasingly linked their personal worth to their ability to be sexually attractive. Sexualised insults were common in chatrooms and social networking websites and young girls even boasted of being good at sex acts. Dr Ringrose, of London's Institute of Education, found examples of girls choosing usernames such as 'slut', 'whore' and 'freesex' on social networking sites. She called for teachers to discuss feminism and suggest positive role models, who could include figures such as Virginia Woolf, suffragettes' leader Emmeline Pankhurst and even the cartoon character Lisa Simpson. She said they are needed to overcome the negative influences of celebrities such as Paris Hilton, Britney Spears and Christina Aguilera. Dr Ringrose said: 'If you look at the images and representations girls have to identify with, they are primarily defined through their bodies – being thin, having fake boobs.' The trend was true of almost all women in the magazines and music videos that were central to young girls' social lives. Debates in class could raise pupils' use of language and what it says about girls' self-esteem. 'It's important for girls to have a forum for discussing these issues so "feminism" isn't such a dirty word,' said Dr Ringrose. Lessons in feminism could also help overcome the myth that men and women are now equal. Dr Ringrose said most schools see gender equality in terms of exam results, where girls now outshine boys in most subjects. But in the adult world, women are still paid far less and face dilemmas trying to balance work and family life. Feminism needs to be 'reinvigorated', said Dr Ringrose. 'Pupils shouldn't assume that we've met every target in gender equality. How do you explain the ways popular culture portrays women?' But the study also found that while girls rely on their sex appeal to create their identities, they tend to see themselves – and others – as 'slutty' if their behaviour goes too far. Dr Ringrose's research, published in the *Times Educational Supplement*, comes at a time of growing concern over the sexualisation of childhood through teen magazines, advertising, films and music videos. Ministers have launched an inquiry into the commercialisation of childhood and teachers' leaders have warned that highly sexualised clothes and toys are being marketed at primary school children.

(*Daily Mail*, 9 August 2008)

I want to highlight this reporting of my research 'findings', in what is widely understood to be a right-wing, populist broadsheet for several reasons. First, it helps in thinking about the central dynamics I've been exploring throughout this book – that is the relationship between the media, dominant gender discourses, and educational research, policies and politics. Second, it is immediately evident from the article that the nuance of the psychosocial approach I have outlined for thinking past slotting girls into the victim or liberated binaries is absent from the news story. It actually seems impossible for the news media to engage with these complexities because their goal is to generate sensationalised claims and stimulate either/or debates around issues like feminism.

Unpacking the logic of the article, it suggests first that my research argued girls continue to link personal worth to their ability to be sexually attractive (the visual nature of this hegemony is highlighted later in the quote about girls being defined through bodily aspects of 'thin' and 'fake boobs' in magazines and music videos). Relatedly, it also raises the issue of how girls use 'sexualised insults' and used abusive 'male nicknames' such as 'slut' and 'whore'. While the first claim was accurate, the second claim then reduces girls' approaches to this to girls abusing one another, reducing girls to victims. The reporter has missed the nuance of my argument that what girls were doing with names like 'slut' was in some cases to reclaim these labels. Instead it seizes on the victim side of the binary where 'slutty' is only a site of risk and danger for girls.

The report then suggests girls have to 'overcome negative influences of celebrities such as Paris Hilton, Britney Spears and Christina Aguilera' so they can have better 'self-esteem'. Whilst I had argued that the visual hegemony of idealised femininity is oppressive in new ways, this presents a simplistic psychological self-esteem 'at risk' of media effects type of argument (Coleman, 2008) that I have tried to move beyond in this book, particularly in Chapter 8, where I thought about how teen girls have complex affective relationships to images of celebrities and themselves, where they rework and restage sexualised imagery (as in the case of Marie's use of the Playboy Bunny symbol for instance).

What was most significant about the story however, was the suggestion that exam scores could not be used as a performance indicator for gender equality and my call for feminism to be taught in schools. Indeed a similar headline appeared in the *Telegraph*: 'Schools should teach feminism in the classroom' (although note again what gets taken up in the subtitle is 'Girls should be taught feminism at school to stop them being disrespectful to each other, according to a leading academic'). This call in UK broadsheets for feminism in schools and the response from readers and other media commentators marks the article out as significant in the context of what I am arguing is a postfeminist socio-political scene in the UK. I received rabid comments to both the *Daily Mail* (18 comments) and the *Telegraph* (33 comments) stories, some of which I would like to reproduce and explore here to illustrate the discursive nature and affective potency of postfeminist discourses:

> I fell out of my chair laughing while I read this article and the comments that followed. I thought Feminism died in the educated community after women were given equal rights. Boy was I wrong … You see, not all women are 'suppressed' by

society, there are some with the self-esteem and intellect to rise above it. Likewise, some young men are 'suppressed', and forced to become the society's idea of masculine. So, it is not women who are weak, and inferior, and easily corrupted by culture, it is those with little pride or intelligence. The difference is not between the sexes, it is between those people who individually DECIDE to rise above society, and those people who individually DECIDE to let it control them.

(*Daily Telegraph*, Objectivist)

I suspect the good lady may be part of the problem rather than the solution. Why have I suddenly got this image of dungarees, sandals, an amateur haircut and the Guardian and just how much does the taxpayer fork out each year for a lecturer in the sociology of gender at London's Institute of Education?

(*Daily Telegraph*, O Zangado)

A lecturer in the sociology of gender at London's Institute of Education. If this Ringrose woman had any self-esteem, she would get a proper job. Why is the Daily Telegraph devoting column inches to this nonsense? The Telegraph's Comment pages are full of execrable left-wing garbage … And to add insult to injury, the Telegraph's hacks seem to think that it is acceptable to give press coverage to some bra-burning feminist who has views 100 years out of date. This is not news-worthy and it is not worthy of the Telegraph's readers. It is time for the Telegraph to get a grip or lose what is left of its readership.

(*Daily Telegraph*, Paul, Southampton).

These comments illustrate a range of discursive threads that characterise a postfeminist view. First, there is the view that 'bra-burning' feminism is '100' years out of date, as another reader commented 'Glory be!! Backwards to the future!' (*Daily Telegraph*, DMAR). Feminism is viewed a 'bunch' of 'left-wing garbage' and therefore laughable and a waste of time. The comments reflect assumptions about gender equality in society and anxiety that women have taken 'too much power'. Indeed, we see the vehement disavowals of feminism, yet commentators go beyond attacking outmoded feminism to demonising me as an academic and personally. That I am paid a salary is called into question and I am imagined to be un-feminine, and out of fashion with an 'amateur haircut', the exact opposite of the postfeminist masquerade of hyper-femininity (McRobbie, 2008).[3]

We also see a neo-liberal, individualising trend where we can no longer talk about groups of girls and women or boys and men only 'individuals' who are 'weak' and 'inferior', yet somehow purposefully 'decide' to let culture control them. The issues are reformulated as psychological problems of self-esteem on the part of individual girls and women who do not 'respect' themselves:

No, schoolgirls need to stop behaving like sluts and whores. Walking around any town centre on these summer days, especially when even slightly warm, reveals gangs of tartily dressed early teens, with loads of slap on.

(*Daily Mail*, Alan, Australia)

Forget about feminism, teach women about manners, respect and decency.

(*Daily Telegraph*, wherehaveallthemannersgone)

These comments return us back to Officer Sanguinetti's comments at York University in Toronto explored in the introduction to the book. Sanguinetti positioned the real problem of sexual violence against girls and women as an issue of how they act and what they wear – girls and women should stop behaving like sluts and whores wearing 'tarty' clothes. Although girls' dress and indecent behaviour is identified as a problem in the above comments, however, the idea that gender norms and cultures may therefore be usefully discussed at school is considered a ridiculous waste of time. This is in line with much problematic educational policy, readers separate out 'academic' performance from the emotional and behavioural aspects of school:

Girls are at school to be educated, not fed political feminist propaganda.

(*Daily Mail*, Dave, UK)

I do wish these kind of people would just put a sock in it. How about bloody well teaching them to read, write, and add up?

(*Daily Telegraph*, Richard, Holloway)

Would it not be better for schools to teach numeracy and literacy instead … Schools aren't suppose [sic] to educate, silly, their role is to enforce left wing / liberal propaganda. Labour does not want a population to think for themselves, Labour wants a population to go on voting Labour.

(*Daily Mail*, Pinkie)

One doesn't know whether to laugh or weep. Does this crazy woman really think that our girls can be induced to swoon over Emily Pankhurst? And to think that we, as taxpayers, pay Dr Ringrose's salary. Being that the Institute of Education is our premier Education school, it's no small wonder that our schools are in such a parlous state. And, I should add, if Dr Ringnose [sic] really wants to find out why girls have such trashy values, she should look no further than to her colleagues, who for years have been preaching that schooling must be made 'relevant' to children's interests, and that EastEnders is just as 'valid' as Shakespeare.

(*Daily Mail*, Sparafucile)

Overall, this micro 'media event' (my findings, the news reports and the audience responses) illustrates the extraordinarily contested space of schooling, raising the core dilemmas of this book, of articulating an alternative vision of what schooling is for and what we imagine can be taught and engaged with inside school walls. The media event highlights the contested political ideologies and discourses around gender and sexuality and just how threatening feminism continues to be for some.[4] Indeed, we witness strong affects in the form of vehement disgust over feminism. That the broadsheets felt the topic would be provocative to its readers indicates a journalistic knowledge of the affective resonances around feminism, but also 'slut' and 'whore', which were viewed as juicy enough signifiers to rile up the readers.[5] The comments also indicate the limitations of such media as a space for productive debate about educational research, given the modus operandi of such broad sheets is to generate controversy through extreme opinion (Gill, 2008). It throws up again the need to investigate the relationship between academic research and the popular press and media for what is possible and impossible in these mediums. The media event is also an excellent jumping-off point for discussing what is possible in schools from a feminist perspective as we look to the future of education.

Re-thinking achievement, conflict and sexual competition in schooling

Throughout this book I have explored and critiqued a range of gendered educational discourses. First I looked at the educational crisis of 'failing boys', when girls apparently closed the 'gender gap' in the UK (Arnot *et al.*, 1999). I explored the corollary discourse of 'successful girls' (Ringrose, 2007b), which still forms a dominant gendered educational discourse in the popular political consciousness and UK governmental policy to the present day. I raised the issue of affect: that the failing boys discourse is organised around a gender war mentality (Jackson, 1998) and paranoia that girls might overshadow boys at school. Statistical analysis comparing gendered bodies, which Foucault argued was the basis of bio-political control and what Gillborn (2008) calls 'gap talk' in education works as a way to divide and conquer, so that particular groups are isolated out as the most marginalised as a means for competing for educational resources. It also silences attention to the particular issues facing racial minority (Osler *et al.*, 2002) and working class girls (Jackson, 2006). Most significantly, this statistical gap talk has operated to reduce our imaginations about what a relevant gender issue can be in schools (Connell, 2010).

In neo-liberal, competitive, performative audit cultures (Ball, 2008) student/ school performance in league tables takes precedence over all aspects of socio-political life. The 'successful/failing' educational discourses operates to push anything outside the core remit of academic-based educational attainment as peripheral, as locatable in the realm of pastoral care and/or behavioural policy, rather than the 'core business of schooling'. We see a split between academic and the emotional and behavioural dimensions of learning in educational policies. Renold and Epstein (2010) have used a Deleuzian frame to think about how policies are actually operating in contradictory competition with each other in 'schizoid' fashion, so that performative targets may undermine policy discourses like 'Every child matters' focused on children's well-being.

The effects for PSHE, an area where a range of issues related to gender can be explored, have been quite dramatic. In a school I have been working at recently PSHE has been transformed from timetabled weekly lessons, reduced to four themed inset days a year. This is in part because many tutors have felt uncomfortable teaching some of the 'sensitive' topic material, including domestic violence. However, when PSHE has a low value in the subject status and priorities of schooling as with the neo-liberal, test performance driven school, then it is unsurprising that there will be a lack of motivation to work with and deliver 'sensitive' materials around emotional well-being (Maxwell *et al.,* 2010; Parkes, Ringrose and Showunmi, 2011).

This relates to the problems with both conceptualising and then managing 'behavioural' issues in school where girls' conflicts tend to be constructed as either 'not a problem' or as a crisis (Osler and Vincent, 2003; Aapola *et al.*, 2005). In Chapter 3, I explored how educational psychology discourses about girls as 'relationally' aggressive set up the normative conditions of idealised femininity, against which violent girls are re-constituted as pathological problems. I argued panics over girl's aggression operate to erase contexts of heterosexualised power and sexism as well as race and class differences among girls.

In my data chapters I explored problems with anti-bullying interventions, viewed as largely ineffective, by girls themselves. In some ways interventions may operate through a dynamic of under- and over-exposure. Much cruel gender play is viewed as normal and expected and largely unchallenged by children and adults (Ringrose and Renold, 2010). When something does come under the radar of the school it can escalate, potentially placing the child at more 'risk' by turning the light on the event, making it a 'luminosity' (Deleuze in McRobbie, 2008) that then has to be dealt with and managed. The categories of victim and bully do nothing to alleviate this. I illustrated how Faiza and Louise both in different ways were constructed as female bullies, which had both racialised and classed implications. Both girls were positioned as objects of fear, and both were left coping with pathologising psycho-educational discourses: 'bullying' in Faiza's case and 'anger management' in Louise's.

What we need to think through further is: What scope is there in schools to address gendered conflict differently? What would help in better managing the sexualised name calling and regulation of girls through notions of 'slut', 'whore', and 'slag'? Can we move past the simplistic, reparative logic of 'just be friends' mobilised at Herbert Secondary? Are there resources to help young people sit with and 'walk away' from conflict? How can we better address the types of sexualised cyber- and school-based conflicts happening at Thornbury High and New Mills secondary?

I will consider these questions in relation to the other strand I have been addressing in this book which is the on-going dilemma of how to deal with sexuality and sexual competition in the regulative spaces of schooling, typically infused by desires to sanitise, purify and erase sexuality (Epstein and Johnson, 1992; Atkinson and DePalma, 2009). I explored how femininity and girlhood sexuality has re-emerged as a site of crisis in the past few years as part of the sexualisation of children moral panic – a highly gendered crisis discourse, where specific concern over premature sexualisation of girls has overtaken the public imagination in the UK but also internationally (Egan and Hawkes, 2010). Chapter 4 put this sexualisation panic in the context of morally conservative and regressive sex education policies in UK schools, which focus on parts and plumbing and managing the phallus in ways that totally neglect girls' sexual rights, including those of sexual pleasure.

My data chapters explored how heterosexual competition and sexual regulation of girls' bodies are central to teen peer culture across ages and contexts. In Chapter 8, I looked at real-life examples of what Angela McRobbie calls the performance of 'porno-chic' as part of the 'postfeminist masquerade'. I looked at how new technologies like social networking sites have important gendered and sexual implications because they can intensify the visual hierarchy of looking upon and scrutinising the body through new cyber-spaces of identity performance. I also challenged the online/ offline divide showing how digital sexual identity practices thoroughly saturate and mediate experience at school.

My analysis illustrates an urgent need for tools for getting to grips with new visual cultures, norms of femininity and masculinity and new modes of intimacy online which mediate school life. This has to go beyond the banality of much e-safety, safe-guarding guidance, for instance posters reminding children to 'report inappropriate messages',[6] to explore the content of celebrity, media cultures, and indeed pornography itself, so young people can cope with issues more effectively, given these cultural engagements are such enormous sites of pleasure and interest.

Feminists are now pointing to the need to re-frame debates on sexualisation, for example, towards spaces that open up a 'sex-positive' (and I would add pleasure-positive) but 'anti-sexism' forms of feminism (Gill, 2008). We need to think about how sex-positive, anti-sexism feminism can be brought into schools through the curriculum of media studies as well as in PSHE and in policies addressing conflict and violence. We need resources that can actually help young people navigate sexual competition in ways that do not individualise and pathologise femininity and offer tools for deconstructing the postfeminist discursive terrain under exploration in this book.

Rather than trying to re-innocent young people the aim should be to develop a critique of complex formations of sexism across wider society among adults as well, and the continuing sexual regulation of girls *and* adult women's bodies. We need to create space in PSHE and sex and relationship education to think about discussing issues like pornographic fantasy and thinking about the issue of respect and consent in relationships negotiated in real life, and exploring ideals of femininity (like the digital slut and Playboy Bunny subjectivities I looked at in Chapter 8). There may also be space in the media studies curriculum. We cannot try to push girls into some fictive box of sexual innocence (which certainly is the desire in schools in general and in SRE in particular, which represents a renewal and intensification of familiar forms of sexual regulation over girls). We need to give all girls and boys tools to deal with the specific discourses of sexualisation circulating at present, in ways that relate to the 'glocal' that is globalised media cultures including pornography, as well as the cultural, race and class specific differences in local peer cultures.

Indeed, in my analysis I consistently raised the issue of class and femininity. We need discussion about the sex industry and its offshoots including, glamour modelling, and lap dancing, and to be asking questions about realities of economic viability for working class young women in a class-segregated society with unequal access to educational capitals, a situation worsening with the now escalating higher education fees in the UK (Coy and Garner, 2010). Race and religioned differences between girls also need further attention. Where hypersexualised displays are positioned as increasingly normative and even liberatory for many Western girls and women the headscarf and hijab are viewed (in many Western contexts) as backwards, sexually repressive and sexist (Duits and Van Zoonen, 2006; Gill, 2007). We need further research exploring these racialised, cultural dynamics of how the female body continues to be sexually regulated in different ways, without slipping back into binaries about good and bad girls.

There are exciting innovations in 'pornography education' (Crabbe and Corlett, 2011) in Australia for instance, exploring the actual political economy of pornography from the perspectives of the producers, performers and teen consumers of pornography, that could form a crucial point of discussion for young people and adults around 'pornification', of course paying careful attention to age specificity and cultural tensions. We also need to find ways to prioritise and understand girls' sexual pleasure as part of an ethical project of gender equity in schools and society capable of challenging the continuing bias of sexual desire as constructed through a masculine and phallic bound 'imaginary' (e.g. wet dreams and condoms), to bring in the important critiques of French feminists like Kristeva (1982) to bear on the dilemmas I'm exploring. We need feminisms capable of attending to complexities and of finding new spaces for feminist political imaginaries, which garner hope and mobilise change.

Towards a feminist political imaginary: finding spaces of hope

I draw hope from the feminist, poststructural, psychosocial theoretical and methodological approach that grounds this book. For instance, drawing on Butler (2004a), as well as Deleuze and Guattari (1984, 1987) has helped me to reconceptualise and reimagine what resistance might mean and look like in research encounters with young people in school and beyond. Rather than always searching for easily discernable resistant acts (or revolts) through our research narratives, we need to track the regulative rhythm of the normative to find some spaces where gender 'undoings' emerge, and other understandings and convictions jostle for authenticity (Butler, 1997; Renold and Ringrose, 2008). We also need to explore how girls' experiences and narratives are plugged into wider popular culture and where counter-narratives (like the global SlutWalks or gender equality curriculum at school) make new spaces for thinking and doing 'girl'.

The girls in my research challenged the simple truth claims that girls are overly successful, mean or sexual, rupturing these types of continual pathologisations of the feminine. They pointed to the on-going dilemmas and brutal conflicts involved in navigating the sexual politics of schooling. Their contradictory narratives indicate the problems with the postfeminist, celebratory mythologies of alpha and super girls as well as crisis narratives of girls at risk (Aapola *et al.*, 2005). But they also narrated complex relational struggles and micro-politics around sex and power and conflict, sometimes refusing their interpellation into compliant and passive feminine sexuality at the same time they enacted highly regulative discourses around feminine sexuality. The girls' narratives therefore offer feminist inflected 'hope' (Coleman and Ferreday, 2011) indicating important spaces of possibility for more active and reciprocal forms of feminine desire, in schooling and beyond, moving us beyond the postfeminist panics of girlhood critiqued in this book.

However this type of analysis needs to be in tune with mass political protest (Willis, 2009) and the changing nature of the socio-cultural assemblages in particular contexts. As discussed in my introduction, the UK SlutWalks (London, Cardiff, Edinburgh, and Birmingham)[7] represented a new political space/time where new possibilities for girls and women opened up. The SlutWalks powerfully illustrated that feminism is not fixed in a cultural 'freeze frame' (Massumi, 1994), but in constant movement. We are witnessing many new forms of feminist politics that challenge the complex dynamics of sexual regulation: from men marching with 'consent is sexy' on their chests in the global North SlutWalks;[8] to the Green movement activists in Iran fighting the legal requirement of women to wear the hijab through savvy strategies like men donning the headscarf;[9] to French women wearing beards to protest a political culture of chauvinism like IMF head Dominique Struass-Khan's response to charges of sex crime as 'a bit of hanky panky'.[10] Women and men are working together to challenge heteronormative gender and sexual oppressions and bodily regulations in exciting new ways.

We have also witnessed a rise in popular cultural texts disrupting gender equality myths such as the *Equality Illusion* (Banyard, 2010), and questioning the vilification of feminism, such as Redfern and Aune's (2010) *Reclaiming the F Word: The New Feminist Movement*. It is important to ask, therefore, are we seeing a new face of feminism? What difference do these new discourses of feminist political action make? How do we theorise feminist resistance in such contradictory and confusing postfeminist neo-liberal times, where newness is typically co-opted and re-marketed (Braidotti, 2006)? What are the implications for education and schooling and feminist pedagogies (Luke and Gore, 1992)? How can we harness this political energy to revitalise discussion of feminism within schools?

I want to conclude by briefly discussing some consultancy work for a UK women's charity I did during the past several years, exploring their educational interventions around gender equality and gender-based violence in several schools. In particular I have followed the trajectory of one school and initiated a follow-on research project exploring a 'girl power' group established at the school.[11] The remit of the girl power group, which started with girls in Year 8 (age 13), was to 'empower' girls who were noticeably disengaging from formal schooling. This group mainly learned about local and global 'women's rights' and engaged in a series of activities around sexual bullying, sexual relationship education, lesbian, gay, bisexual, transgender, queer (LGBTQ) issues and domestic violence – all of which led to their involvement in national conferences and the delivery of some PSHE lessons (i.e. on healthy relationships) to younger students in their school. We were conducting research with the girls just prior to the SlutWalk in their city, and it transpired through discussion and negotiation with the group that some of the girls and their mothers as well as teachers from the school were able to attend the SlutWalk. We are still tracking the implications of this initiative, exploring the complex tangle of experiences when a 'girl power' group of teen girls goes on a largely adult-defined 'SlutWalk', particularly in the midst of a panic over girls' premature 'sexualisation' (Ringrose and Renold, 2012).[12] What is significant for concluding this book, however, is the progressive, feminist inspired imaginary enacted by this school, which has taken on board a gender equality agenda and treats it seriously. This enabled significant 'lines of flight' for the students, teachers and parents, including participating in the local SlutWalk, opening hope and space for rupturing and resignifying the sexual regulation of girls' bodies at school and beyond.

When gender equality is taken as a whole-school approach (Maxwell *et al.*, 2010; Parkes *et al.*, 2011; Ringrose and Renold, 2012) something very different is possible than schools oriented towards academic achievement in ways that split off emotional and behavioural issues as disciplinary problems to be dealt with on the side. We need to keep pressing for these types of initiatives around gender leadership in schools, and not become hopeless in the context of governmental cuts and dismantling of the welfare state.

As educators, practitioners, teachers, and researchers we are operating in a discursive space where to think differently and otherwise about issues like gender equality can be difficult as gender can be viewed as a 'luxury' issue and less significant than attaining academic-based performance. The neo-liberal logic of practicality in the context of accountability, audit cultures and performance targets of schooling shuts down thinking. So where can we find the space to move forward and challenge this? Drawing on Deleuze and Guattari's model of transcendental empiricism I would suggest we need to search through every space that we are operating in to find where thinking, hoping and becoming otherwise might be possible: from the teacher struggling to deliver PSHE lessons on relationships that tackle the nuances of gendered and sexualised relationships and health, to the academic writing data and then communicating this to the academic community, working this knowledge into teacher and professional educational training, and hopefully communicating with policy makers.

The neo-liberal logic of individualised competition makes academics compete with each other for funding sometimes from sources that compromise the intellectual integrity of the 'findings' (Ball, 2008). It also transforms schools into entrepreneurial actors competing for performance-based results to garner resources. We need to resist what Beck calls the 'acid bath of competition' that individualism and neo-liberalism enacts and ask whether it is possible to harness the performative logic at work in our institutions (Ball, 2008) and use it towards the ends of social justice. Could we reward and incentivise equalities measures in schools (like innovative approaches to sex education and bullying that cover an intersectional framing of race, class, gender and sexual equalities)? In the UK we need to think further about how spaces in school inspection criteria may offer space for measuring how schools deal with well-being in gender sensitive ways in line with the Gender Equality Duty. Can we draw on leadership discourses to create 'equalities leaders' in schools? Schools *can* lead on gender issues, as the school above demonstrates, but how do we reward, incentivise and mobilise others? How do we stop equalities boxes simply shutting down spaces for thinking and doing?

These are issues I am pursuing at my own university, fighting to create a space of understanding around how Ofsted school inspectors could be interested in the gender and sexual nuances of my research on bullying and cyberbullying. This I would argue could be done in ways that can help them address the mandates of the

UK 2010 White Paper in relation to discipline in schools, but not simply in order to penalise schools who actually admit that they are dealing with complex problems and dilemmas around coping with bullying and cyberbullying (Davies and Bansel, 2007), but rewarding those schools taking positive steps and making more room for coping with the daily difficulties of negotiating gender inequalities and sexism in the networked online and offline peer cultures in schools.

The many questions I've raised in this concluding chapter are certainly not easily answered with a one-answer-fits-all logic. Rather we have to repeatedly grapple with them as we attempt to work within and enact progressive change as educators and practitioners in the multiple educational sites we are engaging with at the present political moment. This is a task I urge readers to take forward with them as part of engaging with the theoretical and methodological tools outlined in this book as they work to address, reimagine and transform the sexual politics at play in their own educational spaces.

Notes

1 Introduction: postfeminism, education and girls

1 Fin Cullen http://www.genderandeducation.com/issues/feminism-trumps-egalitarianism-the-twisted-logic-of-david-willets/

2 Foucault (1982) suggested a shift from a repressive to a disciplinary society where norms come to be established through statistical measures (bio-power), and these norms are internalised and enacted through self-policing and policing of others. Foucauldian governmentality theorists (e.g. Rose, 1999a) suggest neo-liberalism is a primary discourse through which subjectivity is governed (though understood as 'free') at present.

3 There has been a significant amount of educational writing on neo-liberal trends in Western educational systems, suggesting neo-liberalism is an ideology which supersedes classical liberal free market ideologies because contrary to popular belief the state has shifted from a nation state to a 'market state' (Hoffman in Sears, 2011: 19), and plays a significant regulatory role in ensuring beneficial terms for corporate interests for fear of capital fleeing around the globe. For interesting accounts of neo-liberal trends in education internationally see Hursh, 2005 (USA/UK), Hill, 2002, (UK), for analysis of schools and policies; and see Lynch, 2006 (UK) for analysis of implications of neo-liberalism for higher education.

4 Recent exceptions to this trend include work from Allan, 2010 and Pomerantz and Raby, 2011.

5 The site of this exchange is particularly important to me as I completed my MA and PhD at York University in Sociology and Women's Studies.

6 There have been SlutWalks in Toronto, Vancouver, New York, Boston, Dallas, Montreal, Sydney, Buenos Aires, New Delhi, London, Cardiff, Newcastle, Manchester, Glasgow, Edinburgh, and Gallaway. Further SlutWalks have happened or are planned in the US states of Arizona, California, Colorado, Florida, Georgia, Illinois, Indiana, Louisiana, Maine, Maryland, Massachusetts, Michigan, Nevada, New Jersey, New Mexico, New York, North Carolina, Oregon, Pennsylvania, Texas, Utah, Washington and Wisconsin; and in the countries of Argentina, the Netherlands, New Zealand, Sweden, Singapore and Malaysia.

7 For a fuller analysis of the clothing and placards at some of the UK marches, please see Ringrose and Renold, 2012.

2 Successful girls? Exploring educational media and policy 'scapes' and the postfeminist panic over feminine 'success'

1 UK headlines ranged from 'Girls doing well while boys feel neglected' to 'Is the future female?', with reports claiming that boys' 'under-achievement … has become one of the biggest challenges facing society today' (*Guardian*, 1995; Panorama, BBC1, 1995; *Times Educational Supplement*, 1997, cited in Cohen, 1998).

2 The evidence of gender disparity in grades in Canada was not as clear as in the UK case because of regional differences in the test data, but it still sparked governmental concern.

3 Canadian concern has been sustained via the media with broadsheet headlines like 'School system failing boys' (CBC, 2006); 'Girls outperforming boys, tests show' (Metro, 2006); and TV 'Gender gap' specials focused on boys' failures (CBC News, 2003).

4 http://www.aare.edu.au/98pap/lin98245.htm

5 Further Australian 'failing boys' media coverage includes (in Lingard, 1998): 'The trouble with boys' (*Sydney Morning Herald*, 19 August 1995), 'Suspensions from school: boys top the class' (*Sydney Morning Herald*, 27 July 1996), 'How to keep the beast out of the boy' (*The Australian*, 23 May 1997), 'Closed book boys: chapter and verse' (*Courier-Mail*, 4 October 1996), 'Nobody loves us, everybody hates us...Why today's teenage boys have become pariahs' (*Sydney Morning Herald*, 22 November 1997).

6 Davison *et al.* (2004) have reported similar findings in Canada.

7 As Valerie Walkerdine (1989) has found, the reason that girls were rarely identified as 'brilliant' in the past had nothing to do with the quality of their performance in comparison with boys; rather, teachers and parents alike assumed only boys possessed such innate intellectual properties (Walkerdine, 1988; 1989;).

8 Although I do not have space to explore it here, another worrying trend has been the allocation of UK HE grant allocation around girls, gender and education almost exclusively to research on 'high achieving' girls in recent years (Allan, 2010; Maxwell and Aggleton, 2010; Francis *et al.*, forthcoming)

9 http://www.girleffect.org/learn/faq

3 Mean or violent girls? Exploring the postfeminist panic over feminine aggression

1 Having had my own research findings taken up in the popular press as I explore in my conclusion, I am not asserting that Besag's research or quotes are 'accurately' represented in the press. It is the relationship between academic research and news articles and indeed the discursive tropes of gender in media that shape and frame the discursive 'conditions of possibility' (Foucault, 1982) of constructing a newsworthy story about girls that can be sensationalised and sold to an audience that interests me throughout this book.

2 http://www.athealth.com/consumer/disorders/aggressivegirls.html

3 http://en.wikipedia.org/wiki/Relational_aggression

4 http://www.clubophelia.com/clubophelia/ra.php

5 Quoted from http://www.opheliaproject.org/resources/resources_print.shtml (accessed 23 July 2004 [really?!]).

6 Quoted from http://www.cbc.ca/ideas/features/girls_world/index.html (accessed September 2004).

7 http://www.ucdsb.on.ca/Schools/School+Directory/Secondary/ADS/School+Council/About+School+Council/Parent+Resources.htm

8 http://www.girlshealth.gov/bullying/whatis/cyberbully.cfm

9 Cyberbullying is increasingly being understood as a particularly feminine problem, where girls use the indirect tools of digital networked communication to 'wound from afar', the ultimate vehicle for indirect 'relational' aggression (Noret and Rivers, 2006). The internet is also a site of perceived sexual risk for girls as I explore in the next chapter. I critique and respond to these assumptions about risky and at-risk girls and 'cyber' experiences in Chapters 7 and 8.

10 Research Briefing: School Bullying. (NSPCC) http://www.nspcc.org.uk/inform/research/briefings/school_bullying_pdf_wdf73502.pdf

11 Unfortunately more recent data are not differentiated by race and gender to update these findings.

12 http://www.daventrytoday.co.uk/news/School-praised-for-zerotolerance-policy.5692668.jp
13 Croyden is a suburb of London with a 'working class reputation', noted as one of Britain's top ten 'chav towns' http://www.chavtowns.co.uk/2004/07/croydon-2
14 http://www.abc.net.au/am/content/2011/s3289676.htm
15 To flesh this out in theoretical terms: the developmental discourse of girls' indirect aggression reproduces a split, binary construction of the feminine and masculine that is (re)constitutive of the feminine as pathological – as universally different from and 'other' to male subject (Grosz, 2004). However, femininity itself is also split between those girls and women that turn on themselves internally and through manipulation and social coercion (indirect and repressive) and those girls and women who externalise aggression (direct physical violence), which is constituted as not feminine, masculine, deviant (Austin, 2005). The discourse of indirect aggression is therefore organised along a nice/mean continuum, so that repressive niceness can/will lead to indirect manipulative mean-ness. But this is more 'normal' than violence emerging from girl bodies which is constituted as deviant in that women do not fulfill a normative developmental path (Motz, 2001).

4 Sexy girls? The middle class postfeminist panic over girls' 'sexualisation' and the protectionist discourses of sex education

1 http://www.swc-cfc.gc.ca/med/news-nouvelles/2009/0716-4-eng.html
2 I sat on the advisory committee of the UK sexualisation report, and was also an academic adviser to the Scottish report, and therefore have some inside knowledge of the process. Government representatives suggested that high profile media figures are now specifically targeted to lead such reports because of their media presence which is thought to generate greater awareness. The choice of Linda Papadopoulos, seen regularly on reality TV programmes such as UK Big Brother and Celebrity Fit Club, to lead the sexualisation review was similar to Tania Byron leading the 'Safer children in a digital world' review in 2008. Instead of critiquing the figurehead chosen to author the report, perhaps academic analysis should attend to how the government's increasing dependence on media savvy experts/'academics' tells us something about the postfeminist media context itself, where, particularly when women are chosen to lead on such projects, glamour and celebrity kudos appear to count as much as the content and arguments of reports. The way this sits in contrast to men chosen to lead on relevant reports, e.g. David Buckingham on the UK 'Commercialization of Childhood' report (2009) and Scottish sexualised goods aimed at children report (2009) and Reg Bailey on the Bailey Review (2011), needs further analysis.
3 http://www.timeshighereducation.co.uk/story.asp?storyCode=410913&sectioncode=26
4 http://www.google.co.uk/search?hl=en&defl=en&q=define:skank&ei=qYMnS5j5DNG24QaH-pSxDQ&sa=X&oi=glossary_definition&ct=title&ved=0CAcQkAE
5 Egan and Hawkes have particularly attacked Azam's text 'Oral sex is the new kiss goodnight' in a recent paper (2011), as mobilising a panic-based, universalising logic that all young people are engaging in oral sex on their first encounters. My argument in this chapter and elsewhere in the book, in line with the views of other academics, is that we require much more empirical research to engage with the complexity of such debates over children and 'impacts' of sexualisation (see also Buckingham, 2009; Albury and Lumby, 2010). My own (Ringrose and Erickson-Barahas, 2011) and other research findings suggest there is a lack of understanding around oral sex in youth culture, but there do appear to be worrying trends in a rise of demands for girls to be performing fellatio at younger ages (Weekes, 2002) whilst cunnilingus is constructed as horrific and disgusting in some teen cultures (Ringrose *et al.*, 2012). This is actually a feminist problem relating to issues of male domination, consensual sex and reciprocity in sexual encounters. Azam's book

should have signified the blow-job as the sexual act that is increasingly normalised and expected in teen peer cultures, not the gender neutralised 'oral sex'. The issue with many of these sensationalist texts is there is some truth behind their impetus, which leads to their uptake and celebration in the popular media. Azam was featured on Good Morning America, to profile 'A provocative and frightening look into the lives of teenagers' as well as being endorsed by celebrity US psychologist Dr. Phil.

6   http://theorwellprize.co.uk/longlists/natasha-walter/

7   http://www.amazon.co.uk/Living-Dolls-Return-Natasha-Walter/dp/1844087093/ref=pd_sim_b_1

8   http://accordcoalition.org.uk/2011/07/14/peers-debate-the-importance-of-statutory-pshe-in-lords-debate/

9   This is taken from SRE Core Curriculum for London, a set of schemes of work with detailed lesson plans and suggested resources for the foundation stage, primary and secondary curriculum. It has been put together by Young London Matters, an initiative sponsored by the Government Office for London in response to the new statutory curriculum for PSHE (Young London Matters, 2009).

10 There is also the heteronormative assumption that girls will be heterosexual, there is little consideration of sex with other women, or of anyone stepping outside the sex they were assigned at birth (e.g. trans-identities) (DePalma and Atkinson, 2008).

11 http://www.drpetra.co.uk/blog/unpacking-the-bailey-review-on-commercialisation-and-sexualisation-of-childhood/

12 http://archive.scottish.parliament.uk/s3/committees/equal/reports-10/eor10-02.htm#2

13 http://www.drpetra.co.uk/blog/unpacking-the-bailey-review-on-commercialisation-and-sexualisation-of-childhood/

14 http://www.politics.co.uk/news/2011/05/04/abstinence-based-sex-education-bill-passes-co

5 Rethinking debates on girls' agency: critiquing postfeminist discourses of 'choice'

1   Intersectional thinking has become increasingly popular in educational research with a greater number of researchers looking at multiple variables of class, race and gender in issues like educational attainment, inclusion and exclusion in schooling and higher education (Archer *et al.*, 2007, Gillborn and Mirza, 2000; Lucey and Reay 2003; Phoenix and Pattynama, 2006; Reay, 2004, Ringrose, 2007a; Youdell, 2006; Ali *et al.*, 2010).

2   It is also important to underscore that Maxwell and Aggleton's data are with upper and middle class teens attending a 'private school', meaning the teen girls' subjective relationship to voice and narratives will be shaped and read in particular ways, also depending on the class positionings of the researcher.

3   McRobbie outlines different formations of femininity including a 'phallic girl' who performs drunken excess, swearing, sexual promiscuity and general laddishness, a new classed formation of femininity. But like the office girl who adopts masculine traits of professional success, these phallic shows or the up-take of masculinity must be balanced with an outward masquerade of femininity lest the girl fall into undesireable object of fear, like, for instance the violent, hoodie wearing laddette gang girl I discussed in chapter three. I will explore these classed formations further in my data chapters.

4   The reference to disciplinary technologies of the self here indicates a Foucaudian concept of regulative, subjectivating power. Foucault's work has been key in illuminating disciplinary discourses that regulate subjectivity. Biopolitics refer to the processes through which new norms emerge and are taken on by the subject (Rose in Sears, 2011). Foucault theorized processes of internalization and normalization of disciplinary forms of subjection through panopticon processes of surveillance of the self and others. He described processes such as separating normal from abnormal as biopolitical 'dividing

practices',; and discussed the rise of new technologies of subjectification that developed in the eighteenth century to observe, watch, regulate and correct (1980: 215).

5 We need to generate theoretical and methodological reflexivity and awareness of the possibilities and limitations of the theoretical approaches that we are adopting and the political implications of the analysis and theorizations we do (Skeggs, 2005). We are never free from the 'albatross' of theory.

6 Indeed, the debate between Duit and van Zoonen (2006, 2007) and Gill (2007) revealed the cultural differences being drawn between young women wearing thongs as a marker of sexual liberation vs. young racialized and Muslim women who are wearing headscarves or hijabs to cover the body in line with religious ideals of modest femininity. These sorts of complexities of feminine subjective positionings and negotiations need to be unpacked.

6 Towards a new discursive, psychosocial and affective theoretical–methodological approach

1 While elaborating the various psychoanalytic traditions from Freud to Klein and Lacan is beyond the scope of this chapter, it is important to note that some of these frameworks try to use poststructural discourse analysis with humanist forms of psychoanalysis such as object relations (Klein), with problematic outcomes where essentialised notions of self-hood lie at the base of theorisations of defensiveness, for instance (e.g. Hollway and Jefferson, 2000). Those more influenced by the structural psychoanalysis of Lacan have offered accounts of 'poststructural psychoanalysis' outlining psychical processes informing being and doing girl or boy in ways that elaborate theories of how discourses are psychically navigated both by research participants and the researcher (Walkerdine *et al.*, 2001).

2 While detailed discussion of Freud's psychosexual theories is beyond the scope of this chapter, the Oedipus complex is a theory of masculine infantile desire organised around overcoming a desire to kill the father to sexually possess the mother. The Electra complex is the female variant of psychosexual development for girls, which sees the girl compete with the mother for the affections of the father. Both complexes involves the child's unconscious desire to possess the opposite-sexed parent and to eliminate the same-sexed one, and their resolution was to be found in the eventual identification with the same-gendered parent, posited as the normal, healthy, heterosexual route (Freud, 1956).

7 Sexual regulation and embodied resistance

1 All names in my data chapters are pseudonyms.

2 My background as a Canadian appeared very useful for gaining access and facilitating discussion during interviewing, since my classed background is not easily read off my accent or embodiment, and the girls appeared to relate to me as a novelty, asking me to speak to their mates on the phone so they could hear the 'American', for instance, or commenting at points that they 'loved' my accent, and I sounded like someone from 'Friends' (the US sitcom).

3 ESTYN is the acronym for 'Her Majesty's Inspectorate for Education and Training in Wales', which inspects schools.

4 Staff I interviewed at the community centre did not have this impression of the school and had a heightened sensitivity to the needs of the culturally diverse families and young people in the area.

8 Girls negotiating postfeminist, sexualised media contexts

1 The research was conducted with Rebekah Willett. Andrew Burns assisted by carrying out one of the focus groups with boys.

2 All names in this chapter are pseudonyms.

3 Ofsted is the 'Office for Standards in Education, Children's Services and Skills', the English equivalent to ESTYN discussed in the previous chapter.

4 This was due to the selection process by the media studies teacher at the school, who shaped the sample in relation to high usage of digital technology, which shaped the findings.

5 In addition to the sites of our research participants, we considered some sites of the significant friends and romantic interests of participants specifically discussed in interviews. Studying the friend network poses ethical issues as friends had not agreed to participate, so we were limited to publically available friends. We also looked at the wider Bebo assemblages, exploring representational gendered trends on sites to pinpoint some dominant discourses of masculinity and femininity.

6 Use of Bebo has now greatly diminished, indicating the speed and changeability of the technology and applications of digital mobile technology. Now Facebook dominates with teen as well as adult groups and in some regions Blackberry messaging networks are more popular than public internet-based profiles for teens (Ringrose *et al.*, 2011).

7 Originally there were a range of images to accompany the analysis in this chapter. But, unfortunately, the complexity of the origins and uses of images on social networking profiles, ownership rights and branding have led to a range of copyright concerns that have prohibited publishing the visual images of BEBO skins, applications and quizzes. Moreover, due to ethical protocols the personal profiles, particularly the photos of the young people cannot be published.

8 This pictorial reference to the buttocks (booty or 'back-off') as a higher priority sexual signifier over breasts is highly visible in research on networks of urban Black teens in some London communities (Ringrose *et al.*, 2012).

9 Indeed, Sam's Bebo page existed as a complex what I call 'love log' that documented various exchanges with girls including Daniela, then Daisy, illustrating an archive into his dating relationships.Our research team did not have an opportunity to interview Sam, making it difficult for me to elaborate in a meaningful way further upon how he performed masculinity and sexuality via his site, but the way Bebo sites operate as an artefact of dating history if the posts are not erased is significant methodologically and for theories of contemporary digitised gendered/sexualised identities.

10 'Share the luv' is a unique application to Bebo. In 2007, near Valentine's Day, the application was introduced which allowed each user to 'share the luv' with one user per day. The 'luv' appears on profiles as a small red heart, and there is a counter which shows how many people have 'shared the luv' with that user.

9 Conclusion: ways forward for feminism and education

1 The first story was written by Adi Bloom for the TES, which reported on an upcoming BERA presentation and draft paper on my research findings.

2 It later appeared on numerous websites (Yahoo, UPI, *The Gulf Times*) and then was taken up again the following week by *The Times* and again by the *Daily Telegraph* (and online by the Londonist and others). I was also asked to go on the Richard and Judy afternoon chat TV show, which I declined due to lack of media training but I did go on BBC Radio 4 Woman's Hour for a segment called 'Feminism on the Curriculum' http://www.bbc.co.uk/radio4/womanshour/04/2008_33_tue.shtml

3 Deborah Finding (2010) has written about having research misreported in the press and receiving abusive comments about appearance, being out of touch, unfeminine, man-hating etc., suggesting this type of 'symbolic violence' is an experience shared by many feminist scholars.

4 It would be unwise, however, to relegate this discussion as the purview of ignorant, uneducated blokes or harmless right wing ideologues, given the comments that began this book from Universities Minister David Willetts.

5 The provocative tagging to the online version of the *Daily Mail* article ('girls who call themselves sluts need feminism lessons') demonstrates further the tactics of antagonism employed by the tabloid press in a climate of diminishing returns, increasing reliance on advertisers who require specific levels of associated 'hits', which is important to flag up given how my research became (ab)used in this particular attention economy. Thanks to Tracey Jensen for this point.

6 http://ceop.police.uk/

7 http://www.palebluenews.co.uk/2011/05/10/slut-walks-come-to-the-uk/; http://www.guardian.co.uk/world/2011/may/09/SlutWalking-phenomenon-comes-to-uk

8 http://www.genderandeducation.com/issues/london-SlutWalker/

9 http://www.rferl.org/content/Men_In_Hijabs_Iranian_Green_Movements_New_Tactic/1900501.html

10 http://gothamist.com/2011/05/23/french_feminists_protest_chauvinism.php#photo-1

11 This research was conducted with Emma Renold.

12 The findings of this research project are written up in much greater detail in a *Gender and Education* article, Slut-shaming, Girl power and 'Sexualisation': Thinking through the Politics of the International SlutWalks with Teen Girls (Ringrose and Renold, 2012).

References

Aapola, S., Gonick, M., and Harris, M. (2005) *Young Femininity: Girlhood, Power and Social Change*. Basingstoke, UK: Palgrave.

Adkins, L. (2002) *Revisions: Gender and Sexuality in Late Modernity*. Buckingham and Philadelphia: Open University Press.

Ahmed, S. (1999) Phantasies of becoming the other, *European Journal of Cultural Studies*, 2(1): 47–63.

Aikman, S. and Unterhalter, E. (eds) (2005). *Beyond Access: Transforming Policy and Practice for Gender Equality in Education*. Oxford: Oxfam GB.

Alaimo, S. and Hekman, S.(2006) *Material Feminisms*. Bloomington, IN: Indiana University Press.

Albury, K. and Lumby, C. (2010) Too Much? Too Young?: The Sexualisation of Children Debate in Australia, *Media International Australia,* 135: 141–152.

Albury, K., Carmody, M., and Lumby, C. (2011) Playing by the Rules: Researching, teaching and learning sexual ethics with young men in the Australian National Rugby, *Sex Education* 11(3): 339–351.

Ali, S., Benjamin, S., and Muthner, M. (2004) *The Politics of Gender and Education: Critical Perspectives*. Basingstoke, UK: Palgrave.

Ali, S., Mirza, H. S., Phoenix, A., and Ringrose, J. (2010) Intersectionality, Black British Feminism and Resistance in Education: A Roundtable Discussion, *Gender and Education*, Special Issue: Rethinking Gendered Regulations and Resistances in Education, 22(6): 647–660.

Allan, A. J. (2010) Picturing success: young femininities and the (im)possibilities of academic achievement in selective, single-sex education, *International Studies in Sociology of Education*, 20(1): 39–54.

Alldred, P. and David, M. (2007) *Get Real About Sex: The politics and practice of sex education*. London: McGraw Hill/Open University Press.

Allen, L. (2004) Beyond the birds and the bees: constituting a discourse of erotics in sexuality education, *Gender and Education*, 16(2): 151–167.

Allen-Mills, T. (2006) Free at last: alpha teenage girls on top. October 15 http://www.timesonline.co.uk/tol/news/world/article600902.ece (accessed 15 July 2008)

American Psychological Association (2007) *Report of the APA Task Force on the Sexualization of Girls:* APA.

Andrews, M., Sclater, S. D. and Squire, C. (2001) *Lines of Narrative: Psychosocial Perspectives*. London: Routledge.

Appadurai, A. (1996) *Modernity at Large: Cultural Dimensions of Globalization*. Minneapolis: University of Minnesota Press.

Apple, M. (2006) Understanding and Interrupting Neoliberalism and Neoconservativism in Education. *Pedagogies*, 1(1): 21–26.

Archer, L., Halsalb, A., and Hollingworth, S. (2007) Inner-city femininities and education: 'race', class, gender and schooling in young women's lives. *Gender and Education*, 19 (5): 549–568.

Arnot, M. (1984) How shall we educate our sons? In R. Deem (ed.) *Co-Education Reconsidered.* Milton Keynes and Philadelphia, PA: Open University Press.

Arnot, M., and Phipps, A. (2003) Gender and Education in the UK. Background paper for the UNESCO Global Monitoring *Report Education for All: The Leap to Equality*, available at http://www.efareport.unesco.org/.

Arnot, M., David, M., and Weiner, G. (1999) *Closing the Gender Gap: Post-war Education and Social Change.* Cambridge: Polity Press.

Asthana, A. (2008) Crackdown on schoolgirl bullying epidemic, *The Guardian*, 20 January. http://www.guardian.co.uk/uk/2008/jan/20/pupilbehaviour.gender (accessed November 2008).

Atkinson, E. and DePalma, R. (2009) Un-believing the matrix: Queering consensual heteronormativity, *Gender and Education,* 21(1): 17–29.

Attias, B. A. (1998) To each its own sexes? Toward a Rhetorical Understanding of *Molecular Revolution*. In E. Kaufam and K. J. Heller (eds) *Deleuze & Guattari: New Mappings in Politics, Philosophy, and Culture.* Mineapolis: University of Minnesota Press.

Attwood, F. (2007). Sluts and riot grrrls: Female identity and sexual agency. *Journal of Gender Studies*, 16(3) 231–245.

Atwood, F. (2006) Sexed up: Theorizing the sexualization of culture, *Sexualities*, 9(1): 77–94

Atwood, F. (2009) *Mainstreaming Sex: The Sexualisation of Western Culture.* I. B. Taurus: London/New York.

Austin, S. (2005) *Women's Aggressive Fantasies: A post-Jungian exploration of self-hatred, love and agency,* New York: Routledge.

Azam, S. (2009) *Oral Sex Is the New Goodnight Kiss: The Sexual Bullying of Girls.* Bollywood Filmed Entertainment.

Bailey, R. (2011) *Letting Children Be Children.* London: Department for Education. https://www.education.gov.uk/publications/standard/publicationDetail/Page1/CM%208078 (accessed September 2011).

Baker, J. (2008) The ideology of choice. Overstating progress and hiding injustice in the lives of young women: Findings from a study in North Queensland, Australia, *Women's Studies International Forum*, 31(1): 53–64.

Baker, J. (2010) Great expectations and post-feminist accountability: young women living up to the 'successful girls' discourse. *Gender and Education*, 22(1): 1–15.

Ball, S. J. (2008) *The education debate: policy and politics in the 21st Century.* Bristol: Policy Press.

Ball, S. and Vincent, C. (1988) I heard it on the grapevine: 'Hot' knowledge and school choice, *British Journal of Sociology of Education*, 19(3): 377–400.

Banet-Weiser, S. (2007) What's your flava? Race and Postfeminism in media culture. In Y. Tasker and D. Negra (eds) *Interrogating Postfeminism.* Durham, NC and London: Duke University Press

Banyard, K. (2010) *The Equality Illusion: The Truth About Women and Men Today.* London: Faber and Faber.

Barker, M. and Duchinsky, R. (2012) Sexualisation's four faces: Sexual and gender stereotyping in the Bailey Review. Special issue: 'Making sense of the sexualisation debates: Schooling and beyond', *Gender and Education*, 24(3).

Barter, C., McCarry, M., Berridge, D. and Evans, K. (2009). *Partner exploitation and violence in teenage intimate relationships.* London: NSPCC.

Batchelor, S. (2007) "Prove me the Bam!" Victimization and agency in the lives of young women who commit violent offences. Unpublished doctoral thesis, University of Glasgow.

Batchelor, S. (2009) Girls, gangs and violence: assessing the evidence, *Probation Journal*, 56(4): 399–414.

Battle, J. and Barnes, S. (2009) *Black Sexualities: Probing Powers, Passions, Practices.* New Brunswick, NJ: Rutgers University Press.

Bauman, Z. (2001) Pariahs and parvenus. In P. Beilharz (ed.) *The Bauman Reader.* Oxford: Blackwell.

BBC News (2007a) Sexualisation 'harms' young girls. 20 February. http://news.bbc.co.uk/1/hi/health/6376421.stm (accessed June 2011).

BBC News (2007b) The future is female. http://news.bbc.co.uk/1/hi/business/6518241.stm

BBC News (2008) Violent girls making the headlines. 14 July. http://news.bbc.co.uk/1/hi/uk/6552177.stm (accessed June 2011).

BBC News (2011) Nottingham riots: Girl aged 11 admits damaging shops. 11 August. http://www.bbc.co.uk/news/uk-england-nottinghamshire-14490603 (accessed September 2011)

Beck, U. (1992) *Risk Society: Towards a New Modernity,* New Delhi: Sage.

Beck, U. and Beck-Gernsheim, E. (2002) *Individualization.* London: Sage.

Beddoes, D. J. (n.d.) Breeding Demons: A critical enquiry into the relationship between Kant and Deleuze with specific reference to women, http://www.cinestatic.com/trans-mat/Beddoes/BD6s4.htm, accessed 12 November 2008.

Benjamin, J. (1998). *Shadow of the other: Intersubjectivity and gender in psychoanalysis.* New York: Routledge.

Benjamin, S. (2003) What Counts as 'Success'? Hierarchical Discourses in a Girls' Comprehensive School, *Discourse*, 24(1): 105–118.

Bergen, V. (2010) Politics as the orientation of every assemblage. *New formations: A journal of Culture/Theory/Politics: Deleuzian Politics,* 68, 34–41.

Besag, V. (2006) *Understanding Girls' Friendships, Fights and Feuds: A Practical Approach To Girls' Bullying.* New York: Open University Press.

Bibby, T. (2010) *Education – an 'impossible profession'? Psychoanalytic explorations of learning and classrooms.* London: Routledge.

Bjorkqvist, K. (1994) Sex differences in physical, verbal, and indirect aggression: A review of recent research, *Sex roles*, 30(3/4): 177–188.

Bjorkqvist, K. and Niemela, P. (1992) New trends in the study of female aggression, pp. 3–15. In K. Bjorkqvist and P. Niemela (eds) *Of Mice and Women: Aspects of female Aggression.* London: Academic Press.

Bjorkqvist, K., Lagerspetz, K., and Kaukiainen, A. (1992) Do girls manipulate and boys fight? Developmental trends in regard to direct and indirect aggression, *Aggressive Behaviour*, 18: 117–127.

Blackman, L. and Walkerdine, V. (2000) *Mass Hysteria.* London: Routledge.

Blackmore, J. and Thompson, P. (2004) Just 'good and bad news'? Disciplinary Imaginaries of head teachers in Australian and English print media, *Journal of Educational Policy*, 19(3): 301–320.

Bonta, M. and Protevi, J. (2004) *Deleuze and Geophilosophy: A Guide and Glossary.* Edinburgh, Edinburgh University Press.

Bouchard, P., Boily, I. and Proulx, M. (2003) School Success by Gender: A Catalyst for the Masculinist Discourse. At http://www.swccfc.gc.ca/pubs/pubspr/0662882857/index_e.html.

Bourdieu, P. and Wacquant, L. J. D. (1992) *An Invitation to Reflexive Sociology*. Chicago: Chicago University Press.

boyd, d.m. (2008) Why Youth Social Network Sites: The Role of Networked Publics in Teenage Social Life. In D. Buckingham (ed.) *Youth, Identity, and Digital Media*. Cambridge, MA: MIT Press, pp. 119–142.

boyd, d.m. and Ellison, N. B. (2007) Social network sites: Definition, history, and scholarship. *Journal of Computer-Mediated Communication*, 13(1), article 11.http://jcmc.indiana.edu/vol13/issue1/boyd.ellison.html.

Bracchi, P. (2008) The feral sex: The terrifying rise of violent girl gangs. *The Daily Mail*, http://www.dailymail.co.uk/news/article-566919/The-Feral-Sex-The-terrifying-rise-violent-girl-gangs.html#ixzz1oA41gXzq (accessed June 2011).

Bragg, S. and Buckingham, D. (2009) Too much too young?: Young people, sexual media and learning. In F. Atwood. *Mainstreaming Sex*. London: I. B. Taurus.

Bragg, S., Buckingham, D., Russell, R. and Willett, R. (2011). Too much, too soon? Children, 'sexualisation' and consumer culture, *Sex Education*, 11(3): 279–292.

Braidotti, R, (1994) *Nomadic Subjects: Embodiment and Sexual Difference in Contemporary Feminist Theory*. Cambridge: Columbia University Press.

Braidotti, R. (2003) Becoming Woman: Sexual Difference Revisited, *Theory, Culture and Society* 20 (3): 43–64.

Braidotti, R. (2006) Affirming the affirmative: On Nomadic Affectivity, *Rhizomes* 11/12.

Braidotti, R., (2008) Of poststructuralist ethics and nomadic subjects. *The Contingent Nature of Life, Part I*. International Library of Ethics, Law, and the New Medicine, 1, Volume 39. New York: Springer.

Bray, A. (2008) The Question of Intolerance: 'Corporate Paedophilia' and Child Sexual Abuse Moral Panics, *Australian Feminist Studies*, 23(57): 323–342.

Britzman, D. P. (1998) *Lost Subjects, Contested Objects: Toward a psychoanalytic inquiry of learning*. Albany, NY: SUNY Press.

Brock, D. (1998) *Making Work, Making Trouble: Prostitution as a Social Problem*. Toronto: University of Toronto Press.

Brown, L. M. (1998). Performing femininities: Listening to white working class girls in Maine, *Journal of Social Issues*, 53: 683–701.

Brown, L. M. (2003) *Girlfighting: Betrayal and rejection among girls*. New York: New York University Press.

Brown, L. M. and Gilligan, C. (1992) *Meeting at the Crossroads: Women's Psychology and Girls' Development*. Cambridge, MA: Harvard University Press.

Bryson, Valerie (1992) *Feminist political theory: An introduction*. New York: Paragon House.

Bryson, V. (2002) Gender. In G. Blakeley and V. Bryson (eds) *Contemporary Political Concepts. A Critical Introduction*. London: Pluto.

Buckingham, D. (2000) *After the Death of Childhood: Growing Up in the Age of Electronic Media*. Cambridge: Polity Press.

Buckingham, D. (2009) *The Impact of the Commercial World on Children's Wellbeing: Report of an Independent Assessment*. London: DCSF/DCMS.

Buckingham, D., Willett, R., Bragg, S. and Russell, R. (2009) Sexualised goods aimed at children, Scottish Parliament Review. At http://www.scottish.parliament.uk/s3/committees/equal/reports-10/eor10-02.htm.

Burke, P. J. and Jackson, S. (2007) *Reconceptualizing Lifelong Learning: Feminist Interventions*. Abingdon: Routledge.

Burman, M. J., Batchelor, S. A., and Brown, J. A. (2001) Researching girls and violence: Facing dilemmas of fieldwork, *British Journal of Criminology*, 41: 443–459.

Butler, J. (1990) *Gender trouble: Feminism and the subversion of identity*. New York: Routledge.

Butler, J. (1993) *Bodies That Matter: On the Discursive Limits of 'Sex'*. New York: Routledge.

Butler, J. (1997) *The Psychic Life of Power: Theories of Subjection*. Stanford, CA: Stanford University Press.

Butler, J. (2004a) *Undoing Gender*. New York: Routledge.

Butler, J. (2004b) *Precarious Life: The power of mourning and violence*. London: Verso Books.

Byron, T. (2008) *Safer children in a digital world: The report of the Byron Review*, Department for Children, Schools and Families, and the Department for Culture, Media and Sport, United Kingdom.

Carby, H. (1982) White Women Listen! Black Feminism and Boundaries of Sisterhood, pp. 212–235. In P. Gilroy, (ed.) *The Empire Strikes Back*. London: Hutchinson.

Carter, H. (2009) Teenage girl is first to be jailed for bullying on Facebook, *The Guardian*, 21 August. http://www.guardian.co.uk/uk/2009/aug/21/facebook-bullying-sentence-teenage-girl (accessed, June, 2011).

CBC News (2003) Gender Gap. At http://www.cbc.ca/news/background/gendergap/.

CBC News (2006) School System Failing Boys. At <http://www.cbc.ca/canada/saskatchewan/story/2006/06/07/sk-boys-schools060607.html, accessed 4 May 2007.

Chandler, D., and Roberts-Young, D. (1998) The construction of identity in the personal homepages of adolescents. Available at http://www.aber.ac.uk/media/Documents/short/strasbourg.html.

Chesney-Lind, M. and Brown, M. (1999) Girls and violence: An overview, pp. 171–199. In D. J. Flannery and C. R. Huff (eds), *Youth violence: prevention, intervention, and social policy*. Washington, DC: American Psychiatric Press.

Chesney-Lind, M. and Irwin, K. (2004) From badness to mean-ness: Popular Constructions of Contemporary Girlhood, pp. 45–56. In A. Harris (ed.) *All About the Girl: Culture, Power and Identity*. New York: Routledge.

Chesney-Lind, M. and Irwin, K. (2008) *Beyond Bad Girls: Gender, Violence and Hype*. New York: Routledge.

Clarke, L. (2006) Boys are being failed by our schools. *The Times*. 13 June. http://www.dailymail.co.uk/news/article-390319/Boys-failed-schools.html.

Clough, P. T. and Halley, J. (2007) *The affective turn: theorizing the social*. Durham: Duke University Press.

Clout, L. (2008) Violent women: Binge drinking culture fuels rise in attacks by women, *The Telegraph*, 31 July.

Cohen, M. (1998) A Habit of Healthy Idleness: Boys' Underachievement in Historical Perspective. In D. Epstein, J. Elwood, V. Hey, and J. Maw, (eds) *Failing Boys? Issues in Gender and Achievement*. Buckingham, UK: Open University Press.

Cohen, J. (2010) Teachers in the news: a critical discourse analysis of one US newspaper's discourse on education, 2006-2007. *Discourse,* 31(1): 105–119.

Cole, D. (2011) The Actions of Affect in Deleuze: Others using language and the language that we make, *Educational Philosophy and Theory*, 43 (6): 549–561.

Coleman, B. (2008) The becoming of bodies, *Feminist Media Studies*, 8(2): 163–179.

Coleman, B. and Ferreday, D. (eds) (2011) *Hope and Feminist Theory*. London: Routledge.

Coleman, B. and Ringrose, J. (eds) (2012) *Deleuze and Research Methodologies*. Edinburgh: Edinburgh University Press.

Collins, Patricia Hill (1998) *Fighting Words: Black Women and the Search for Justice*. Minneapolis: University of Minnesota Press.

Connell, R. W. (1987) *Gender and Power*. Cambridge: Polity.

Connell, H. (2005) We're leaving the boys behind. *The London Free Press*. http://www.lfpress.com/ (accessed April 23 2007).

Connell, R. W. (2010) Kartini's children: On the need for thinking gender and education together on a world scale. Special issue 'Rethinking gendered regulations and resistances in education', *Gender and Education*, 22(6): 603–616.

Conolly, A. (2008) Challenges of generating qualitative data with socially excluded young people, *International Journal of Social Research Methodology*, 11(3): 201–214.

Cook, T. D. (2005) The dichotomous child in and of commercial culture, *Childhood*, 12(2): 155–159.

Cowie, C. and Lees, S. (1981) Slags or Drags, *Feminist Review*, 9: 17–31.

Cowley, P., and Easton, S. T. (1999) Boys, Girls, and Grades: Academic Gender Balance in British Columbia Secondary Schools. The Fraser Institute. At http://www.fraserinstitute.org/Commerce.web/publication_details.aspx?pubID=2528.

Coy, M. (2009) Milkshakes, lady lumps and growing up to wait boobies: how Sexualisation of popular culture limits girls' horizons, *Child Abuse Review*, 18 (6):372–383.

Coy, M. and Garner, M. (2010). Glamour Modelling and the Marketing of Self-sexualisation: Critical Reflections. *International Journal of Cultural Studies*, 13(6): 657–675.

Coy, M. and Garner, M. (2012) Definitions, discourses and dilemmas: Policy and academic engagement with the sexualisation of popular culture, Special issue 'Making sense of the sexualisation debates: schooling and beyond', *Gender and Education*, 24(3).

Crabbe, M. and Corlett, D. (2011) 'So, this is what sex is like?': Porn, young people and sexuality. Pornified? Complicating debates on the sexualisation of culture conference, Institute of Education London, December 2.

Crick, N. R. (1996) The role of overt aggression, relational aggression, and prosocial behavior in the prediction of children's future social adjustment, *Child Development*, 67(5): 2317–2327.

Crick, N. R., and Grotpeter, J. K. (1995) Relational aggression, gender, and social-psychological adjustment, *Child Development*, 66(3): 710–722.

Crick, N. and Rose, A. (2000) Toward a gender-balanced approach to the study of social-emotional development – A look at relational aggression, pp. 153–168. In P. Miller and E. K. Scholnick (eds), *Toward a feminist developmental psychology*. New York: Routledge.

Cruddas, L., and L. Haddock (2005) Engaging Girls' Voices: Learning as Social Practice, in G. Lloyd. *Problem Girls: Understanding and Supporting Troubled and Troublesome Girls and Young Women*. London: Routledge-Falmer.

Cullen, F. (2010) 'Two's up and poncing fags': young women's smoking practices, reciprocity and friendship, *Gender and Education*, 22(5): 491–504.

Cullen, F. (2011) Feminism trumps egalitarianism: the twisted logic of David Willetts. Gender and Education Association http://www.genderandeducation.com/issues/feminism-trumps-egalitarianism-the-twisted-logic-of-david-willets/ (accessed June, 2011).

Currie, D. H., Kelly, D. M. and Pomerantz, S. (2007) 'The power to squash people': Understanding girls' relational aggression, *British Journal of Sociology of Education*, 28(1): 23–37.

Currie, D. H., Kelly, D. M. and Pomerantz, S. (2009) *Girl Power: Girls Reinventing Girlhood*. New York: Peter Lang.

David, M. (2004) A Feminist Critique of Public Policy Discourses about Educational Effectiveness. In S. Ali, S. Benjamin, and M. L. Muthner (eds), *The Politics of Gender and Education: Critical Perspectives*. Basingstoke, UK: Palgrave.

David, M., Ringrose, J. and Showunmi, V. (2010) *Browne Report + the White Paper = A Murky Outlook for Educational Equality*, A GEA Policy Report, October–December 2010, http://

www.genderandeducation.com/wp-content/uploads/2011/01/GEA_Policy_Report_October_December_20101.pdf (accessed June 2011).

Davies, B. (1997). The subject of post-structuralism: A reply to Alison Jones, *Gender and Education*, 9, 271–283.

Davies, B. (2006) Subjectification: the relevance of Butler's analysis for education, *British Journal of Sociology of Education*, 27(4): 425–438.

Davies, B. and Bansel, P. (2007) Neoliberalism and education, *International Journal of Qualitative Studies in Education*, 20(3): 247–259.

Davies, B. and Harre, R. (1990) Positioning: The Discursive Production of Selves, *Journal for the Theory of Social Behaviour*, 20(1): 43–63.

Davies, B., Dormer, S., Gannon, S., Laws, C., and Rocco, S. (2001) Becoming schoolgirls: The ambivalent project of subjectification, *Gender and Education*, 13, 167–182.

Davison, K. G., Lovell, T. A., Frank, B. W. and Vibert, A. B. (2004) Boys and underachievement in the canadian context: No proof for panic. In S. Ali, S. Benjamin, and M. L. Muthner (eds) *The Politics of Gender and Education: Critical perspectives.* Basingstoke: Palgrave.

DCFS (2007) Gender and Education: The evidence on pupils in England. Available at: http://www.dfes.gov.uk/research/data/uploadfiles/RTP01-07.pdf.

Deeley, L. (2008) I'm single, I'm sexy and I'm only 13. *The Times,* 28 July.

Deleuze, G. (1986) *Difference and Repetition.* London: Continuum.

Deleuze, G. and Guattari, F. (1984/2004) *Anti-Oedipus: Capitalism and Schizophrenia.* London: Continuum.

Deleuze, G. and Guattari, F. (1987/2004) *A Thousand Plateaus: Capitalism and Schizophrenia.* Trans. and Foreword by Brian Massumi. London: Continuum.

Deleuze, G. and Negri, A. (1990) Control and Becoming. In G. Deleuze, *Negotiations* [Pourparlers], M. Joughin trans. Available at: http://www.generation-online.org/p/fpdeleuze3.htm.

Deleuze, Gilles and Parnet, Claire (1977/2002) *Dialogues II*, translated by Hugh Tomlison, Barbara Habberjam and Eliot Ross Albert, London: Athlone Press.

Delphy, C. and Leonard, D. (1992) *Familiar Exploitation: A New Analysis of Marriage in Contemporary Western Societies.* London: Polity Press.

DePalma, R., and Atkinson, E. (eds) (2008*) Invisible Boundaries: Addressing Sexuality Equalities in Children's Worlds.* Stoke on Trent: Trentham.

Department for Children, Schools and Families (2003) Raising Boys' Achievement. At http://www-rba.educ.cam.ac.uk/index.html.

Department for Children, Schools and Families (2007) Confident, Capable and Creative: Supporting Boys' Achievements. London: DCSF.

Department for Education (2010a) *The Importance of Teaching*, White Paper, http://www.education.gov.uk/ (accessed June 2011).

Department for Education (2010b) What is the Department doing to address the gender gap? http://www.education.gov.uk/popularquestions/schools/curriculum/a005576/what-is-the-department-doing-to-address-the-gender-gap (accessed June, 2011).

DfES (2000) Sex and relationship education guidance, https://www.education.gov.uk/publications/standard/publicationDetail/Page1/DfES%200116%202000 (accessed, September, 2009).

Dillabough, J. (2009) To be or not to be (a gendered subject): was that the question? *Gender and Education*, 21(4): 455–466.

Dines, G. (2010) *Pornland: How Porn Has Hijacked Our Sexuality*, Boston, MA: Beacon Press.

Dobson, R. and Hodgson, M. (2006) The truth about tweens: Parents 'clueless' about what their children are up to, says new report. *The Independent.* http://www.independent.co.uk/

news/uk/this-britain/the-truth-about-tweens-parents-clueless-about-what-their-children-are-up-to-says-new-report-413551.html (accessed July 2011).

Driscoll, C. (2002) *Girls: Feminine Adolescence in Popular Culture and Cultural Theory.* New York: Columbia University Press.

Duits, L. and van Zoonen, M. (2006) Headscarves and Porno-Chic: Disciplining Girls' Bodies in the European Multicultural Society, *European Journal of Women's Studies,* 13: 103–117.

Duits, L. and van Zoonen, M. (2007) Who's afraid of female agency? A rejoinder to Gill, *European Journal of Women's Studies,* 14(2): 161–170.

Duncan, N. (1999) *Sexual Bullying: Gender Conflict and Pupil Culture in Secondary Schools.* New York: Routledge.

Duncan, N. (2006) Girls' violence and aggression against other girls: femininity and bullying in UK schools. In F. Leach and C. Mitchell (eds) *Combating gender violence in and around schools.* Stoke-on-Trent: Trentham Books.

Durham, G. (2008) *The Lolita Effect.* Duckworth.

Durham, M. G. (2009) Lost youth: turning young girls into sex symbols, *The Guardian,* 18 September. http://www.guardian.co.uk/lifeandstyle/2009/sep/18/lost-youth-young-girls (accessed June 2010).

Duschinsky, R. (2011) The 2010 UK Home Office 'sexualisation of young people' Review: A discursive policy analysis, *Journal of Social Policy.*

Egan, D. (2011) Touched by the 'Skank Fairy'? Deconstructing social class in the discourse on sexualisation. Pornified? Complicating debates on the sexualisation of culture conference, Institute of Education London, December 2.

Egan, D. and Hawkes, G. (2008) Endangered girls and incendiary objects: Unpacking the discourse on sexualization, *Sexuality and Culture,* 12: 291–311.

Egan, D. and Hawkes, G. (2010) *Theorizing the Sexual Child in Modernity.* New York: Palgrave-Macmillan.

Egan, D. and Hawkes, G. (2011) Sexualisation, Splitting and Innocence as Reparation, Girls, Sexuality and Sexualisation: Beyond Sensationalism and Spectacle Conference, Cardiff University, Wales. June, 11, 2011.

Eisenstein, H. (1996) *Inside Agitators: Australian Femocrats and the State (Women in the Political Economy).* Philadelphia: Temple University Press.

Epstein, D. and Johnson, R. (1998) *Schooling Sexualities.* Buckingham: Open University Press.

Epstein, D., Elwood, J., Hey, V. and Maw, J. (1998) *Failing Boys? Issues in Gender and Achievement.* Buckingham, UK: Open University Press.

Epstein, D., O'Flynn, S. and Telford, D. (2003) *Silenced Sexualities in Schools and Universities,* Stoke-on-Trent: Trentham Books.

Evans, R. (2009) Bullies 'jeered at leap girl as she lay dying', The Free Library, http://www.thefreelibrary.com/BULLIES+JEERED+AT+LEAP+GIRL+AS+SHE+LAY+DYING%3B+ Teen+jumped+50ft+to...-a0210623939 (accessed June 2011).

Evans, A., Riley, S. and Shankar, A. (2010) Technologies of Sexiness: Theorizing Women's Engagement in the Sexualization of Culture, *Feminism and Psychology,* 20(1): 114–131.

Eyre, L., and Gaskell, J. (2004) Gender equity and education policy in Canada, 1970–2000'. *Orbit: OISE/UT's Magazine for Schools* 34, 1.

Fairclough, N. (2000) *New Labour, New Language?* London: Routledge.

Fimyar, O. (2008) Using governmentality as a conceptual tool in education policy research. *Educate – The Journal of Doctoral Research in Education,* available online at www.educatejournal.org.

Finding, D. (2010) Living in the Real World? What Happens when the Media covers Feminist Research? In Róisín Ryan-Flood, and Rosalind Gill (eds) *Secrecy and Silence in the Research Process: Feminist Reflections.* London: Routledge.

Fine, M. (1988) Sexuality, schooling and adolescent females: The missing discourse of desire, *Harvard Educational Review,* 58(1): 29–53.

Fine, M. and McClelland, S. I. (2006) Sexuality education and desire: Still missing after all these years, *Harvard Educational Review,* 76(3): 297–338.

Foster, V. (2000) Is Female Educational 'Success' Destabilizing the Male Learner-Citizen?' In M. Arnot and J. A. Dillabough (eds) *Challenging Democracy, International Perspectives on Gender, Education and Citizenship.* London: RoutledgeFalmer.

Foucault, M. (1980a). Two lectures. In Colin Gordon (ed.) *Power/Knowledge: Selected Interviews.* New York: Pantheon.

Foucault, M. (1980b) *Power/Knowledge: Selected Interviews and Other Writings, 1972–77.* C. Gordon, L. Marshall, J. Mepham, and K. Soper (eds), trans. C. Gordon, New York: Pantheon Books.

Foucault, M. (1982) The Subject of Power. In H. Dreyfus and P. Rabinow (eds) *Michel Foucault: Beyond Structuralism and Hermeneutics.* Brighton: Harvester.

Francis, B. (2005) Not Know/ing Their Place: Girls' Classroom Behaviour, pp. 9–22. In G. Lloyd (ed.) *Problem Girls: Understanding and Supporting Troubled and Troublesome Girls and Young Women.* London: RoutledgeFalmer.

Francis, B. (2001a) Beyond postmodernism: feminist agency in educational research. In B. Francis and C. Skelton (eds) *Investigating Gender: Contemporary perspectives in education.* Buckingham: Open University Press.

Francis, B. (2001b) Commonality and difference? Attempts to escape from theoretical dualisms in emancipatory research in education, *International Studies in Sociology of Education,* 11(2): 157–172.

Francis, B. and Archer, L. (2004) The problematization of agency in postmodern social theory: as feminist educational researchers, where do we go from here? (The London Feminist Salon Collective), *Gender and Education,* 16(1): 25–33.

Francis, B. (2006) Heroes or Zeroes? The Construction of the Boys' Achievement Debate within Neo-liberal Policy Discourse, *Journal of Education Policy,* 21: 187–199.

Francis, B. and Skelton, C. (2005) *Reassessing Gender and Achievement: Questioning Contemporary Key Debates.* London: Routledge.

Francis, B., Skelton, C. and Read, B. (forthcoming) *The Identities and Practices of High Achieving Pupils.* London: Continuum.

Freud, S. (1956) *On Sexuality.* Penguin Books.

Froese-Germain, B. (2004) Are Schools Really Shortchanging Boys? Reality Check on the New Gender Gap. *Orbit: OISE/UT's Magazine for Schools* 34, 1.

Frosh, S. (2003) Psychosocial Studies and Psychology: Is a Critical Approach Emerging? *Human Relations,* 56: 1547–1567.

Frosh, S., Phoenix, A., and Pattman, R. (2001) 'But its racism I really hate': Young masculinities, racism and psychoanalysis, *Psychoanalytic Psychology* 17(2): 225–242.

Gagnon, L. (1999) La Misère scolaire des garçons. *La Presse,* 16 & 25 October.

Gamble, S. (2001) *The Routledge Companion to Feminism and Postfeminism.* New York: Routledge.

Gavey, N. (2005) *Just Sex? The Cultural Scaffolding of Rape.* London and New York: Routledge.

Genz, S. (2006) Third way/ve: The politics of postfeminism, *Feminist Theory,* 7(3): 333–353.

Geoghegan, T. (2008) 'Why are girls fighting like boys?', BBC Online, 5 May.

Gerwitz, S., Dickson, M., and Power, S. (2004) Unravelling a 'spun' policy: A case study of the constitutive role of 'spin' in the education policy process, *Journal of Education Policy*, 19(3): 321–342.

Giddens, A. (1984) *The Constitution of Society: Outline of the Theory of Structuration*. Berkeley, University of California Press.

Gilbert, J. (2004) Signifying nothing: 'culture', 'discourse' and the sociality of affect. *Culture Machine*. http://culturemachine.tees.ac.uk/

Gill, Z. (2005) Boys Getting it Right: The new disadvantaged or 'disadvantage' redefined, *The Australian Researcher*, 32(2): 105–124.

Gill, R. C. (2006) Critical Respect: The difficulties of agency and 'choice' for feminism, *European Journal of Women's Studies*, 14(1): 65–76.

Gill, R. (2007) Post-feminist media culture: Elements of a sensibility, *European Journal of Cultural Studies*, 10 (2): 147–166.

Gill, R. (2008) Empowerment/sexism: Figuring female sexual agency in contemporary advertising, *Feminism & Psychology*, 18(1): 35–60.

Gill, R. (2009) Beyond the 'Sexualization of Culture' Thesis: An intersectional Analysis of 'sixpacks', 'midriffs' and 'hot lesbians' in Advertising, *Sexualities*, 12(2): 137–160.

Gill, R. (2011) Sexism Reloaded, or, it's Time to get Angry Again! *Feminist Media Studies*, 11(1): 61–71.

Gill, R. and Koffman, O. (forthcoming) Girl power goes global. *Feminist Review*.

Gill, R. and Scharff, C. (2011) Introduction. In R. Gill and C. Scharff (eds) *New Femininities: Postfeminism, Neoliberalism And Subjectivity*. Basingstoke: Palgrave.

Gillborn, D. (2004) Anti-racism: from policy to praxis. In G. Ladson-Billings and D. Gillborn (eds) *The RoutledgeFalmer Reader in Multicultural Education*. New York: RoutledgeFalmer.

Gillborn, D. (2008) *Racism and Education: Coincidence or Conspiracy?* London: Routledge.

Gillborn, D. and Mirza, H. (2000) *Educational Inequality: Mapping Race, Class and Gender*. London: HMI.

Gilligan, C. (1982) *In a different voice: Psychological theory and women's development*. Cambridge, MA: Harvard University Press.

Gilligan, C. and Brown, L. (1992). *Meeting at the Crossroads: Women's Psychology and Girls' Development*. Cambridge, MA: Harvard University Press.

Gonick, M. (2003) *Between Femininities: Ambivalence, Identity and the Education of Girls*. Albany: SUNY Press.

Gonick, M. (2004) The 'Mean Girl' crisis: Problematizing representations of girls' friendships, *Feminism & Psychology*, 14 (3): 395–400.

Gonick, M. (2006) Between 'Girl Power' and 'Reviving Ophelia': Constituting the Neoliberal Girl Subject, *NWSA Journal*, 18 (2): 1–23.

Gonick, M., Renold, E., Ringrose, J. and Weems, L. (2009) Rethinking Agency and Resistance: What Comes After Girl Power?, *Girlhood Studies*, 2(2): 1–9.

Gorard, S. (1999) Examining the Paradox of Achievement Gaps, *Social Research Update*, 26.

Gordon, T. (2006) Girls in education: citizenship, agency and emotions. *Gender and Education*, 18(1): 1–15.

Griffin, C. (2005) Impossible Spaces? Femininity as an Empty/Depopulated Category. Paper presented at ESRC New Femininities Seminar Series, University of East London, December.

Griffin, C. (2011) Inhabiting youthful femininity as an impossible space: Hypersexual femininity and the culture of intoxication. Pornified? Complicating debates on the sexualisation of culture conference, Institute of Education, London, December 2.

Grigg, D. W. (2010) Cyber-aggression: Definition and concept of cyberbullying, *Journal of Guidance and Counselling*, 20(2): 143–156.

Grimes, J. C. (2008) Increase in Anal Intercourse Involving At-Risk Teens and Young Adults. *Medical News Today*. MediLexicon, Intl., 22 Nov. At http://www.medicalnewstoday. com/releases/130181.php (accessed 12 December 2011).

Grosz, E. (1994) *Volatile bodies: Toward a corporeal feminism*. Bloomington, IN: Indiana University Press.

Grotpeter, J. K. and Crick, N. R. (1996) Relational aggression, overt aggression, and friendship, *Child Development*, 67(5): 2328–2338.

The Guardian (2007) Girls more likely to suffer cyberbullying. 22 March. http://www. guardian.co.uk/technology/2007/mar/22/news.pupilbehaviour, (Accessed, June 2011).

Hadley, M. (2003) Relational, Indirect, Adaptive or Just mean – Recent work on aggression in adolescent girls – Part I, *Studies in Gender and Sexuality*, 4 (4): 367–394.

Hadley, M. (2004) Relational, indirect, adaptive or just mean : Recent studies on aggression in adolescent girls – Part II, *Studies in Gender and Sexuality*, 5(3): 331–50.

Hains, R. (2007): Inventing the teenage girl: The construction of female identity in Nickelodeon's 'My Life as a Teenage Robot', *Popular Communication: The International Journal of Media and Culture*, 5(3): 191–213.

Hakim, C. (2010) Erotic capital, *European Sociological Review*, 26(5): 499–518.

Hamilton, M. (2009) *What's Happening to Our Girls?: Too much, Too soon, How our kids are overstimulated, oversold and oversexed*. New York: Penguin.

Haraway, Donna, (1991) A cyborg manifesto: Science, technology and socialist-feminism in the late twentieth century. In *Simians, Cyborgs and Women: The Reinvention of Nature*, Routledge. First published in the Socialist Review, 1985.

Harker, R., (1984) On reproduction, habitus and education. In D. Robbins (ed.), *Pierre Bourdieu Volume II*. London: Sage Publications.

Harmon, A. (2004) Internet Gives Teenage Bullies Weapons to Wound From Afar, August 26, http://www.nytimes.com/2004/08/26/education/26bully.html?ex=1251172800&en=75fc c217518a0daf&ei=5090&partner=rssuserlan, accessed 28 August 2004.

Harris, A. (2004) *Future Girl: Young Women in the Twenty-first Century*. New York: Routledge.

Haydon, H. (2011) Olympics girl is London 'riot yob', *The Sun*, http://www.thesun.co.uk/sol/ homepage/news/3747365/Olympics-girl-is-London-riot-yob.html (accessed September 2011).

Hazlehurst, N. (2009) The right of children to be children. In M. Tankard Reist (ed.) *Getting Real: Challenging the Sexualisation of Girls*. North Melbourne: Spinefex.

Henriques, J., Hollway, W., Urwin, C., Venn, C., and Walkerdine, V. (1984/1998) *Changing the Subject: Psychology, social regulation, and subjectivity*. London: Methuen.

Hey, V. (1997) *The company she keeps: An ethnography of girls' friendships*. Buckingham: Open University Press.

Hey, V. (2005) The contrasting social logics of sociality and survival: cultures of classed belonging in late modernity. Special issue on 'Class, culture and identity', *Sociology*, 39(5): 855–872.

Hey, V. (2006) The Politics of Performative Resignification; translating Judith Butler's theoretical discourse and its potential for a sociology of education, *British Journal of Sociology of Education*, 27 (4): 439–457.

Hickey-Moody, A. and Malins, P. (2007) *Deleuzian Encounters: Studies in contemporary social issues*. London: Palgrave.

Hill, A. and Hellmore, E. (2002) Mean girls, *Observer: Guardian,* 3 March, http://observer. guardian.co.uk/focus/story/0,6903,660933,00.html (accessed 17 August 2004).

Hill, D. (2004) Books, banks and bullets: Controlling our minds – the global project of imperialistic and militaristic neo-liberalism and its effect on educational policy, *Policy Futures in Education,* 2 (3&4): 504–522.

Hinduja, S. and Patchin, J. (2009). *Bullying beyond the Schoolyard: Preventing and Responding to Cyberbullying.* Thousand Oaks, CA: Sage Publications.

Hoff-Sommers, C. (2000) *The War against Boys: How Misguided Feminism Is Harming Our Young Men.* New York: Simon and Schuster.

Holland, J., Ramazanoglu, C., Sharpe, S., and Thompson, R. (1992) Pleasure, pressure and power: Some contradictions of gendered sexuality, *Sociological Review,* 645–673.

Holland, J. , Ramazanoglu, C., Sharpe, S., Thomson, R. (1998) *The Male in the Head : Young People Heterosexuality and Power.* London: The Tufnell Press.

Hollway, W. (1984) Gender difference and the production of subjectivity. In J. Henriques, W. Hollway, C. Urwin, C. Venn, and V. Walkerdine (eds), *Changing the Subject: Psychology, Social Regulation and Subjectivity.* London: Methuen.

Hollway, W. and Jefferson, T. (2000). *Doing Qualitative Research Differently: Free association, narrative and the interview method.* Thousand Oaks, CA: Sage Publications.

Houldcroft, L. (2002) Bullying Girls who make lives a misery, *The Journal,* 11 November. http://icnewcastle.icnetwork.co.uk/lifestyle/health/page.cfm?objectid=12353895&method=full&siteid=50081 accessed 25 July 2004.

Hursh, D. (2005) Neo-liberalism, markets and accountability: transforming education and undermining democracy in the United States and England, *Policy Futures in Education,* 3(1): 3–15.

International Journal of Qualitative Studies in Education, Special Issue: Thinking with Deleuze in Qualitative Research, 23(5): 503–509.

Ivinson, G. and Murphy, P. (2007) *Rethinking Single-sex teaching: Gender, school subjects and learning.* Berkshire, Open University Press McGraw Hill.

Jackson, Alecia Youngblood (2010) Deleuze and the girl, *International Journal of Qualitative Studies in Education,* 23(5): 579–587.

Jackson, C. (2006) *Lads and Ladettes in School: Gender and a fear of failure.* Maidenhead, UK: Open University Press.

Jackson, D. (1998) Breaking out of the Binary Trap: Boys' Underachievement, Schooling and Gender Relations. In D. Epstein, J. Elwood, V. Hey, and J. Maw, (eds) *Failing Boys? Issues in Gender and Achievement.* Buckingham, UK: Open University Press.

Jackson, S. (1982) *Childhood and Sexuality.* Blackwell Publishing.

Jackson, C. and Tinkler, P. (2007) 'Ladettes' and 'modern girls': 'Troublesome' young femininities. *Sociological Review,* 55(2): 251–272.

James, A. (2010) Research briefing: School bullying. NSPCC http://www.nspcc.org.uk/inform/research/briefings/school_bullying_pdf_wdf73502.pdf.

Jeffreys, S. (2009) *The Industrial Vagina; The Political Economy of the Global Sex Trade.* London: Routledge.

Jones, A. (1997) Teaching post-structuralist feminist theory in education: Student resistances. *Gender and Education,* 9(3): 261–269.

Jones, L. (2011) Becoming-Rhythm: A Rhizomatics of the Girl, *Deleuze Studies,* 5(3): 383–399.

Kaufman, E. and Heller, K. J. (1998) *Deleuze & Guattari: New Mappings in Politics, Philosophy, and Culture.* Minneapolis: University of Minnesota Press.

Kearney, M. C. (2006) *Girls Make Media.* New York: Routledge.

Kehily, J. (2002) *Sexuality, Gender and Schooling: Shifting agendas in social learning.* London: RoutledgeFalmer.

Kehily, M. J. (2008) Taking centre stage? Girlhood and the contradictions of femininity over three generations, *Girlhood Studies*, 1(2): 51–71.

Kehily, M., Epstein, E., Mac an Ghaill, M., and Redman, P. (2002) Private girls, public worlds: Producing femininities in the primary school. Special issue 'retheorising friendship in educational settings', *Discourse: Studies in the Cultural Politics of Education*, 23(3): 167–177.

Kelly, A. (ed.) (1981) *The Missing Half: Girls and Science Education*. Manchester: Manchester University Press.

Kelly, L. (1988) *Surviving Sexual Violence*. London: Polity.

Kenway, J. (1997) *Will Boys be Boys? Boys' Education in the Context of Gender Reform*. Australian Curriculum Studies Association, Deakin West, ACT.

Kenway, J. and Bullen, E. (2008) The Global Corporate Curriculum and the Young Cyberflâneur as Global Citizen, pp. 17–32. In Nadine Dolby and Fazal Rizvi (eds), *Youth Moves: Identities and Education in Global Perspective*. New York: Taylor & Francis.

Kindlon, D. (2006) *Alpha Girls: Understanding the New American Girl and How She Is Changing the World*. Rodale Books.

Kitzenger, J. (1995) 'I'm sexually attractive but I'm powerful': Young Women Negotiating Sexual Reputation, *Women's Studies International Forum*, 18(2): 187–196.

Klein, R. (2009) The harmful medicalisation of sexualised girls. In M. Tankard Reist (ed.) *Getting Real: Challenging the Sexualisation of girls*. North Melbourne: Spinefex.

Kofoed, J. (2009). Emotional evaluations in cases recognized as cyberbullying. In Proceedings of conference 'The good, the bad and the challenging', Copenhagen, 13–15 May.

Kofoed, J., and Ringrose, J. (2012) Travelling and sticky affects: Exploring teens and sexualized cyberbullying through a Butlerian-Deleuzian-Guattarian lens. Special issue 'Education and the politics of becoming', *Discourse: Studies in the Cultural Politics of Education*, 33(1): 5–20.

Kristeva, J. (1982) *Powers of Horror*, trans. Leon Roudiez, New York: Columbia University Press.

Lacan, J. (1977) *Écrits* (trans. Alan Sheridan). London: Routledge.

Laclau, E. and Mouffe, C. (1985) *Hegemony and Socialist Strategy. Towards a Radical Democratic Politics*. London: Verso.

Lamb, S. (2002). *The Secret Lives of Girls: What Good Girls Really Do—Sex Play, Aggression, and their Guilt*. New York: Free Press.

Lamb, S. and Brown, L. (2006) *Packaging Girlhood*. New York: St Martin's Press.

Lambert, A. (2001) Is this what we meant by feminism?, *The Independent*, 1 March.

Lather, P. (1991) *Getting Smart: Feminist Research and Pedagogy Within/In the Postmodern*. London: Routledge.

Lauder, H., Brown, P., Dillabough J.-A. and Halsey, A. H. (2006) *Education, Globalization and Social Change*. Oxford: Oxford University Press.

Lawler, S. (2000) Escape and Escapism: Representing Working class women. In S. Munt (ed.) *Cultural Studies and the Working Class: Subject to Change*. London/New York: Cassell.

Lawlor, A. (2002) Teen guilty in bullying case. *The Globe and Mail*. 25 March, accessed 22 July 2002 from http://www.pwc.k12.nf.ca/PROJECTS/bullying/news_stories.htm.

Leach, J. (2006) Are girls worse bullies than boys? *The Guardian*, 8 March. http://www.guardian.co.uk/education/mortarboard/2006/mar/08/aregirlsworsebulliesthanb (accessed July 2008).

Leach, S. (2004). Behind the surge in girl crime, *The Christian Science Monitor* accessed 15 September 2004 from http://www.csmonitor.com/2004/0915/p16s02-usju.html.

Lerum, K. and Dworkin, S. (2009) 'Bad Girls Rule': An Interdisciplinary Feminist Commentary on the Report of the APA Task Force on the Sexualization of Girls, *Journal of Sex Research*, 46(4): 250–263.

Leschied, A., Cummings, A., Van Brunschot, M., Cunningham, A., and Saunders, A. (2000) *Female Adolescent Aggression: A Review of the Literature and the Correlates of Aggression* (User Report No. 2000–04). Ottawa: Solicitor General Canada.

Levin, B. (2004). Media government relations in education, *Journal of Education*, 19(3): 271–283.

Levin, D. E. and Kilbourne, J. (2009) *So Sexy So Soon: The new sexualized childhood and what parents can do to protect their kids*. Ballentine Books.

Levine-Rasky, C. and Ringrose, J. (2009) Theorizing Psychosocial Processes in Jewish Canadian Mothers' School Choice, *Journal of Educational Policy*, 24(3): 255–269.

Levy, A. (2005) *Female Chauvinist Pigs: Women and the rise of raunch culture*. London: Free Press.

Lingard, B. (1998) Contextualising and Utilising the 'What about the Boys?' Backlash for Gender Equity Goals: http://www.aare.edu.au/98pap/lin98245.htm.

Lingard, B. (2003) Where to in Gender Policy in Education after Recuperative Masculinity Politics? *International Journal of Inclusive Education*, 7(1): 33–56.

Livingstone, S. (2008) Taking risky opportunities in youthful content creation: teenagers' use of social networking sites for intimacy, privacy and self-expression, *New Media & Society*, 10(3): 459–477.

Livingstone, S. and Brake, D. (2010) On the Rapid Rise of Social Networking Sites: New Findings and Policy Implications, *Children and Society*, 24(1): 75–83.

Livingstone, S. and Haddon, L. (2009) *EU Kids Online: Final report*. LSE, London: EU Kids Online (EC Safer Internet Plus Programme Deliverable D6.5).

Livingstone, S., Haddon, L., Görzig, A., and Ólafsson, K. (2009) *Risks and Safety on the Internet: The Perspective of European Children. Full findings.* http://www2.lse.ac.uk/media@lse/research/EUKidsOnline/EUKidsII%20(2009–11)/EUKidsOnlineIIReports/D4FullFindings.pdf.

Lloyd, G. (2005) *Problem Girls: Understanding and Supporting Troubled and Troublesome Girls and Young Women*. London: RoutledgeFalmer.

Lucey, H. and Reay, D. (2002) Carrying the Beacon of Excellence: Social Class Differentiation and Anxiety at a Time of Transition, *Journal of Education Policy*, 17 (3): 321–336.

Lucey, H. and Reay, D. (2003) The limits of 'choice': Children and inner city schooling, *Sociology*, 37(1): 121–142.

Lucey, H., Melody, J. and Walkerdine, V. (2003) Uneasy hybrids: psychological aspects of becoming educationally successful for working-class young women, *Gender and Education*, 15(3): 28–299.

Luke, C., and Gore, J. (1992). *Feminisms and Critical Pedagogy*. New York: Routledge.

Lynch, K. (2006) Neo-liberalism and marketisation: The implications for higher education, *European Educational Research Journal*, (5)1: 1–17.

Mac an Ghaill, M. (1994) *The Making of Men: Masculinities, Sexualities and Schooling*. Buckingham, UK: Open University Press.

Mahoney, P. (1998) Girls Will Be Girls and Boys Will Be First. In D. Epstein, J. Elwood, V. Hey, and J. Maw, (eds) *Failing Boys? Issues in Gender and Achievement*. Buckingham, UK: Open University Press.

Malins, P. (2004) Machinic Assemblages: Deleuze, Guattari and an Ethico-Aesthetics of Drug Use, *Janus Head*, 7(1): 84–104.

Manago, A. M., Graham, M. B., Greenfield, P. M., and Salimkhan, G. (2008) Self-presentation and gender on MySpace, *Journal of Applied Developmental Psychology*, 29, 446–458.

Martino, W. and Kehler, M. (2006) Male teachers and the 'boy problem': An issue of recuperative masculinity politics, *McGill Journal of Education*, 41(2): 1–19.

Martino, W. and Pallotta-Chiarolli, M. (2003) *So what's a boy? Addressing issues of masculinity and schooling.* Maidenhead, UK: Open University Press.

Martino, W., Kehler, M. and Weaver-Hightower, M. (eds) (2009) *The Problem with Boys: Beyond recuperative masculinity politics in boys' education.* New York: Routledge.

Masny, D. and Cole, D. R. (2011) Special Issue: Education and the politics of becoming, *Discourse: Studies in the Cultural Politics of Education,* Routledge.

Massumi, B. (1987) Notes on the Translation and Acknowledgements. In Gilles Deleuze and Felix Guattari, *A Thousand Plateaus.* Minneapolis: University of Minnesota Press.

Massumi, B. (1994) *A Shock to Thought: Expression after Deleuze and Guattari.* London: Routledge.

Massumi, B. (2002) *A Shock to Thought: Expression After Deleuze and Guattari.* New York: Routledge.

Maxwell, C. and Aggleton, P. (2010) Agency in action – young women and their sexual relationships in a private school, *Gender and Education,* 22 (3): 327–343.

Maxwell, C. and Wharf, H. (2010) *Freedom to Achieve. Preventing violence, promoting equality, starting in schools.* IOE and Womankind.

Maxwell, C., Chase, E., Warwick, I., Aggleton, P. and Wharf, H. (2010) *Preventing Violence, Promoting Equality: A Whole-School Approach.* Project Report. London: WOMANKIND Worldwide.

Mazzei, L. and McCoy, K. (2010) Thinking with Deleuze in qualitative research, Editor's Introduction to Special Issue. *International Journal of Qualitative Studies in Education,* 23(5).

McCartney, J. (2011) Are 'Slut Walks' a backwards step? *The Telegraph,* 17 May.

McClintock, A. (1995) *Imperial Leather: Race, Gender, and Sexuality in the Colonial Contest,* New York: Routledge.

McIlhaney, J. and McKissic Bush, F. (2008) *Hooked: New Science on How Casual Sex is Affecting our Children.* Chicago, IL: Northfield Publishing.

McNay, Lois (2000). *Gender and agency: Reconfiguring the subject in feminist and social theory.* Malden, MA: Polity Press.

McNeil, R. and White, H. (2007) Sexist bullying and teenage attitudes towards violence, Paper presented at Gender Equality Duty: Are Schools Ready? Conference, Cavendish Conference Centre, London, 20 March.

McRobbie, A. (1991) *Feminism and Youth Culture.* London: Macmillan.

McRobbie, A. (2004) Notes on Postfeminism and Popular Culture: Bridget Jones and the New Gender Regime, pp. 3–14. In A. Harris, (ed.) *All About the Girl: Culture, Power and Identity.* New York: Routledge.

McRobbie, A. (2008) *The Aftermath of Feminism: Gender, Culture and Social Change.* London: Sage.

McRobbie, A. and Garber, J. (1976) Girls and subcultures. In S. Hall and T. Jefferson (eds) *Resistance Through Rituals: Youth Subcultures in Post-War Britain.* London: Hutchinson.

McRobbie, A. and Nava, M. (eds) (1984) *Gender and Generation.* London: Macmillan.

McVeigh, T. (2002). Girls are now bigger bullies than boys: Charity says increase in 'girl-to-girl' cruelty blights lives and is in danger of escalating out of control, 10 November, http://education.guardian.co.uk/classroomviolence/story/0,12388,837731,00.html (accessed 20 August 2004).

Mendick, H. (n.d.) Boy's underachievement, http://www.genderandeducation.com/resources/contexts/the-boys-underachievement-debate/ (accessed June 2011).

The Metro (2011) Croydon riot girls boast that looting was 'good fun'. 9 August. http://www.metro.co.uk/news/871891–croydon-riot-girls-boast-that-looting-was-good-fun#ixzz1oA4LcyLA (accessed September, 2011).

Millet, K. (1968) *Sexual Politics.* Granada Publishing.

Mirza, H. S. (1992) *Young, Female and Black.* London: Routledge.

Mirza, H. S. (2009) *Race, Gender and Educational Desire: Why Black Women Succeed and Fail.* London: Routledge.

Moretti, M. M., Odgers, C., and Jackson, M. (eds) (2004) *Girls and Aggression: Contributing Factors and Intervention Principles.* American Psychological Law Society Series. New York: Kluwer Academic Press/Plenum Publishers.

Morley, L., and Rassool, N. (1999). *School Effectiveness: Fracturing the Discourse.* Brighton and London: Falmer Press.

Motz, A. (2001) *The Psychology of Female Violence: Crimes Against the Body.* London: Routledge.

Mount, S. (1997) Research brief what about girls? Are they really not aggressive? *The Ohio State University Human Development and Family Life Bulletin: A Review of Research and Practice* 3(2), accessed July 2004. Available: http://www.canadiancrc.com/newspaper_articles/What_About_Girls_Aggression_Ohio_State_1997.aspx.

Murch, C. (2010) The sexualisation of young people: Moral panic? *Counterfire.* http://www.counterfire.org/index.php/features/38–opinion/4350–sex-sales-andmorality-tales-thesexualisation-of-young-people.

The National Post (2007) Rebelling against a culture of porn. 8 August. http://www.canada.com/nationalpost/columnists/story.html?id=d7155b2e-989d-4729–b02e-6c345aa41520 (accessed, June 2010).

Nayak, A. and Kehily, M. J. (2006) Gender undone: subversion, regulation and embodiment in the work of Judith Butler, *British Journal of Sociology of Education*, 27(4): 459–472.

Nayak, A. and Kehily, M. J. (2008) *Gender, Youth and Culture: Young Masculinities and Femininities.* Basingstoke: Palgrave.

Negra, D. (2009) *What a Girl Wants?: Fantasizing the Reclamation of Self in Postfeminism.* Abingdon: Taylor and Francis.

Noret, N. and Rivers, I. (2006) The prevalence of bullying by text message or email: Results of a four year study. Poster presented at British Psychological Society Annual Conference, Cardiff, April.

Northam, J. (1982) Girls and Boys in Primary Maths Books. *Education* 10, 1 (Spring): 11–14.

Nurka, C. (2001). Postfeminist autopsies, *Australian Feminist Studies*, 17(38): 177–89.

O'Donovan, D. (2006) Moving away from 'failing boys' and 'passive girls': Gender meta-narratives in gender equity policies for Australian schools and why micro-narratives provide a better policy model, *Discourse*, 27(4): 475–494.

Olfman, S. (2008) *The Sexualization of Childhood.* New York: Praeger.

Oliviero, H. (2004) Teen girls turn to cellphones, instant messaging to intimidate. *Rocky Mountain Telegraph*, 26 August. Available: http://www.healthyplace.com/Communities/Parenting/Site/articles/cellphones_intimidate.htm.

Olssen, M. A. and Peters, M. A. (2005) Neoliberalism, higher education and the knowledge economy: from the free market to knowledge capitalism, *Journal of Education Policy*, 20(3): 313–345.

Olsson, L. (2007) *Movement and Experimentation in Young Children's Learning: Deleuze and a Virtual Child.* New York: Routledge.

Oppliger, P. A. (2008) *Girls Gone Skank: The Sexualisation of Girls in American Culture*. New York: McFarland.

Orner, M. (1992) Interrupting the calls for student voice in 'liberatory' education: A feminist poststructuralist perspective. In C. Luke and J. Gore (eds.) *Feminisms and critical pedagogy*. London: Routledge.

O'Sullivan, S. (2006) *Art Encounters Deleuze and Guattari: Thought Beyond Representation*. London: Palgrave.

Osler, A. and Vincent, K. (2003) *Girls and Exclusion: Rethinking the Agenda*. London: RoutledgeFalmer.

Osler, A., Street, C., Lall, M., and Vincent, C. (2002) *Not a Problem? Girls and Exclusion from School*. London: Joseph Rowntree Foundation.

Owens, L., Shute, R., and Slee, P. (2000a) 'Guess what I just heard!': Indirect aggression among teenage girls in Australia, *Aggressive Behaviour*, 26(1): 67–83.

Owens, L., Slee, P., and Shute, R. (2000b) 'It hurts a hell of a lot ...' The effects of indirect aggression on teenage girls, *School Psychology International*, 21(4): 359–376.

Paasonen, S., Nikunen, K., and Saarenmaa, L. (2008) *Pornification: Sex and Sexuality in Media Culture*. Macmillan: Basingstoke.

Paechter, C. (2006) Constructing femininity/ constructing femininities. In B. Skelton, B. Francis and L. Smulyan (eds.) *The SAGE Handbook of Gender and Education*. Thousand Oaks, CA: Sage.

Paechter, C. (2009) *Being boys, being girls: Learning masculinities and femininities*, London: Open University Press.

Palmer, A. (2006) What turns a nice child into a 'brat bully'? *The Telegraph*, http://www.telegraph.co.uk/education/expateducation/4200059/What-turns-a-nice-child-into-a-brat-bully.html (accessed June 2006).

Papacharissi, Z. (2009) The virtual geographies of social networks: a comparative analysis of Facebook, LinkedIn and ASmallWorld, *New Media and Society* 11(1&2): 199–220.

Papadopoulos, L. (2010) *Sexualisation of Young People Review*. London: Home Office.

Parkes, J., Ringrose, J. and Showunmi (2011) *Evaluation of WOMANKIND Worldwide UK Education Programme 'Challenging Violence, Changing Lives' (2004 – 2011)*. London: WOMANKIND.

Patchin, J. W. and Hinduja, S. (2010) Trends in Online Social Networking Adolescent Use of Myspace Over Time, *New Media and Society*, 12(2): 197–216.

Pateman, C. (1988) *The Sexual Contract*. Bristol: Polity Press.

Paul, P. (2005) *Pornified: How Pornography is Damaging our Lives, our Relationships, and our Families*. New York: Times Books.

Pepler, D., Madsen, K., Webster, C. D., and Levene, K. S. (2003) *The Development and Treatment of Girlhood Aggression*. Mahwah, NJ: Lawrence Erlbaum Associates.

Peters, M. A. (2004) Editorial: Geophilosophy, Education and the Pedagogy of the Concept, *Educational Philosophy and Theory, Special Issue: Deleuze and Education*, 36 (3): 217–226.

Phillips, M. (2002) The Feminisation of Education. *The Daily Mail* 19 August. At http://pws.prserv.net/mpjr/mp/dm190802.htm.

Phoenix, A. and Pattynama, P (eds) (2006) Special issue of *European Journal of Women's Studies on 'Intersectionality'*, 13 (3).

Pini, M. (2001) *Club Cultures and Female Subjectivity: The Move from Home to House*. Basingstoke: Palgrave.

Pipher, M. (1995) *Reviving Ophelia*. New York: Ballantine.

PISA (OECD Programme for International Student Assessment) (2003) Available at http://www.pisa.oecd.org/pages/0,2987,en_32252351_32235731_1_1_1_1_1,00.html.

Pisters, P. (2003) *The Matrix of Visual Culture: Working with Deleuze in Film Theory.* Palo Alto: Stanford University Press.

Pitt, A. (1998) Qualifying resistance: Some comments on methodological dilemmas, *Qualitative Studies in Education,* 11(4): 535–553.

Pitt, A. (2001) The dreamwork of autobiography: Felman, Freud, and Lacan. In K. Weiler and L. Stone (eds), *Feminist Engagements: Revisioning Educational and Cultural Theory.* New York: Routledge.

Pomerantz, S. and Raby, R. (2011) 'Oh, she's so smart': girls' complex engagements with post/ feminist narratives of academic success, *Gender and Education* ISSN 0954-0253 print/ ISSN 1360-0516 online.

Popkewitz, T. and Brennan, M. (1998) *Foucault's Challenge: Discourse, Knowledge, and Power in Education,* New York: Teachers College Press.

Price, S. (2008) Boys' schools break barriers: single-sex success story, *The Sydney Morning Herald.* http://www.smh.com.au/news/national/boys-schools-break-barriers-singlesex-success-story/2008/10/11/1223145699338.html, (accessed June 2011).

Prince, R. (2011) David Willets: feminism has held back working men. *The Telegraph.* http:// www.telegraph.co.uk/education/educationnews/8420098/David-Willets-feminism-has-held-back-working-men.html (accessed June 2011).

Projansky, S. (2007) Mass magazine cover girls: some reflections on postfeminist girls and postfeminism's daughters. In Y. Tasker and D. Negra (eds) *Interrogating Postfeminism.* Durham, NC and London: Duke University Press.

Putallaz, M., Grimes, C. L., Foster, K. J., Kupersmidt, J. B., Coie, J. D., and Dearing. K. (2007) Overt and relational aggression and victimization: Multiple perspectives within the school setting, *Journal of School Psychology,* 45(5) October, 523–547.

Raby, R. (2007) School Rules, Bodily Discipline, Embodied Resistance, pp. 125–142. In C. Levine-Rasky (ed.) *Canadian Perspectives on the Sociology of Education.* Toronto: Oxford University Press Canada.

Rasmussen, M. (2006) *Becoming Subjects: A Study of Sexualities and Secondary Schooling.* Routledge, New York.

Reay, D. (2001) Spice girls, 'nice girls', 'girlies' and tomboys: Gender discourses, girls' cultures and femininities in the primary classroom, *Gender and Education,* 13(2): 153–166.

Reay, D. (2004) 'Mostly Roughs and Toughs': Social class, race and representation in inner city schooling, *Sociology,* 35(4): 1005–1023.

Redfern, C . and Aune, K. (2010) *Reclaiming the F Word: The New Feminist Movement.* London: Zed Books.

Reiss, M. J. (1998) The representation of human sexuality in some science textbooks for 14–16 year-olds, *Research in Science & Technological Education,* 16: 137–149.

Renold, E. (2005) *Girls, Boys and Junior Sexualities: Exploring Children's Gender and Sexual Relations in the Primary School.* London: RoutledgeFalmer.

Renold, E. and Epstein, D. (2010) Sexualities, Schooling and Schizoid Agendas. In L. Martinsson and E. Reimers (eds) *Norm-struggles: Sexualities in Contentions,* Cambridge: Cambridge University Press.

Renold, E. and Ringrose, J. (2008) Regulation and Rupture: mapping tween and teenage girls' 'resistance' to the heterosexual matrix, *Feminist Theory: An International Interdisciplinary Journal,* 9(3): 335–360.

Renold, R. and Ringrose, J. (2010) Phallic girls?: Girls' negotiating phallogecentric power, In Nelson Rodriguez and John Landreau (eds) *Queer Masculinities: A Critical Reader in Education.* New York: Springer.

Renold, E. and Ringrose, J. (2011) Schizoid subjectivities?: Re-theorising teen-girls' sexual cultures in an era of 'sexualisation', *Journal of Sociology,* 47(4): 389–409.

Reynolds, B. (1998) Becoming a body without organs. In E. Kaufam, and K. J. Heller (eds) *Deleuze & Guattari: New Mappings in Politics, Philosophy, and Culture.* Minneapolis: University of Minnesota Press.

Richardson, H. (2008) Poor white boys not catching up. BBC News, http://news.bbc.co.uk/1/hi/education/8485016.stm (accessed May 2010).

Riddell, S. (1989) reprinted 2005. Pupils, Resistance and Gender Codes: A Study of Classroom Encounters. In C. Skelton and B. Francis, (eds) *A Feminist Critique of Education.* London: RoutledgeFalmer.

Rigby, K. (1998) Gender and bullying in schools. In P.T. Slee and K. Rigby (eds) *Peer Relations Amongst Children: Current Issues and Future Directions.* London: Routledge.

Rimer, S. (2007) AMAZING +: Driven to Excel; For Girls, It's Be Yourself, and Be Perfect, Too. *New York Times.* 1 April. At http://select.nytimes.com/gst/abstract.html?res=F10912FD35540C728CDDAD0894DF404482.

Ringrose, J. (2003) Learning too late? A psychoanalytic reflection on the affective, defensive and repressive dynamics of learning about 'race' in Women's Studies, *Resources for Feminist Research,* 30(1–2): 33–50.

Ringrose, J. (2006a) A new universal mean girl: Examining the discursive construction and social regulation of a new feminine pathology, *Feminism and Psychology,* 16 (4): 405–424.

Ringrose, J. (2006b) 'Lines of flight': (Re)Interpreting a young woman's fantasies of social mobility, Exploring Deleuze and Guattari Syposium, Cardiff University, 6 December.

Ringrose, J. (2007a) Successful girls?: Complicating post-feminist, neo-liberal discourses of educational achievement and gender equality, *Gender and Education,* 19(4): 471–489.

Ringrose, J. (2007b) Troubling agency and 'choice': A psycho-social analysis of students' negotiations of Black Feminist 'intersectionality' discourses in Women's Studies, *Women's Studies International Forum,* 30(3): 264–278.

Ringrose, J. (2007c) Rethinking white resistance: Exploring the discursive practices and psychical negotiations of 'whiteness' in feminist, anti-racist education, *Race, Ethnicity and Education,* 10(3): 321–342.

Ringrose, J. (2008a) 'Every time she bends over she pulls up her thong': Teen girls negotiating discourses of competitive, heterosexualized aggression, *Girlhood Studies: An Interdisciplinary Journal,* 1(1): 33–59.

Ringrose, J. (2008b) 'Just be friends': Exposing the limits of educational bully discourses for understanding teen girls' heterosexualized friendships and conflicts, *British Journal of Sociology of Education,* 29(5): 509–522.

Ringrose, J. (2010a) Sluts, whores, fat slags and Playboy bunnies: Teen girls' negotiations of 'sexy' on social networking sites and at school, In C. Jackson, C. Paechter and E. Renold (eds) *Girls and education 3–16: Continuing concerns, new agendas.* Basingstoke: Open University Press.

Ringrose, J. (2010b) Introduction: Rethinking Gendered Regulations and Resistances, in *Education, Gender and Education,* Special Issue: Regulation and Resistance in Education, 22(6): 595–602.

Ringrose, J. (2011a) Are you sexy, flirty or a slut? Exploring 'sexualisation' and how teen girls perform/negotiate digital sexual identity on social networking sites. In R. Gill and C. Scharff (eds) *New Femininities: Postfeminism, Neoliberalism and Identity,* London: Palgrave.

Ringrose, J. (2011b) Beyond Discourse? Using Deleuze and Guattari's schizoanalysis to explore affective assemblages, heterosexually striated space, and lines of flight online and at school, *Educational Philosophy & Theory,* 43(6): 598–618.

Ringrose, J. and Eriksson Barajas, K. (2011) Gendered risks and opportunities? Exploring teen girls' digital sexual identity in postfeminist media contexts. Special issue 'Postfeminism and the Mediation of Sex, *International Journal of Media and Cultural Politics*, 7(2): 121–138.

Ringrose, J. and Renold, E. (2010) Normative cruelties and gender deviants: The performative effects of bully discourses for girls and boys in school, *British Educational Research Journal*, 36(4): 573–596.

Ringrose, J. and Renold, E. (2011) Teen girls, working class femininity and resistance: Re-theorizing fantasy and desire in educational contexts of heterosexualized violence, *International Journal of Inclusive Education*, http://www.tandfonline.com/doi/abs/10.108 0/13603116.2011.555099.

Ringrose, J. and Renold, E. (2012) Slut-shaming, Girl power and 'Sexualisation': Thinking through the Politics of the International SlutWalks with Teen Girls, *Gender and Education.*

Ringrose, J. and Walkerdine, V. (2007) Exploring some contemporary dilemmas of femininity and girlhood in the West. In C. A. Mitchell and J. Reid-Walsh (eds) *Girl Culture: An Encylopedia*. Greenwood Publishing Group.

Ringrose, J. and Walkerdine, V. (2008) Regulating the Abject: The TV Make-Over as Site of Neo-liberal Reinvention Toward Bourgeois Femininity, *Feminist Media Studies*, 8(3): 227–246.

Ringrose, J. and Willett, R. (2008) 'Click here to add friends': Sex, gender and social competition in young people's negotiations of online social networking sites. BERA, September 2008 Edinburgh, UK.

Ringrose, J., Gill, R., Livinstone, S., and Harvey, L. (2012) *A Qualitative Study of Children, Young People and 'Sexting'*. London: NSPCC.

Ringrose, J., Harvey, L., Gill, R., and Livingstone, S. (2011) Girls' bodies and the affective, racialised, visual economies of 'sexting. Pornified? Complicating debates on the sexualisation of culture conference, Institute of Education London, December 2.

Rivers, I., and Noret, N. (2010) 'I.h8 u': findings from a five-year study of text and email bullying, *British Educational Research Journal*, 36 (4): 643–671.

Rose, N. (1999a) *Governing the Soul: The Shaping of the Private Self*. 2nd edn. London: Free Association Books.

Rose, N. (1999b) *Powers of Freedom: Reframing Political Thought*. Cambridge University Press: Cambridge.

Ross, T. (2010) Eton head says UK education is failing boys, *The London Evening Standard*, http://www.thisislondon.co.uk/standard/article-23796870–eton-head-says-uk-education-fails-boys.do.

Rowland, P. (2006) The Little Miss Perfects who are plain trouble, Wales Online http://www.walesonline.co.uk/news/wales-news/tm_objectid=17066876&method=full&siteid=50082&headline=the-little-miss-perfects-who-are-plain-trouble-name_page.html#ixzz1oAF15B33 (accessed June 2006).

Rush, E. and La Nauze, A. (2006) *Corporate paedophilia: the sexualisation of children in Australia*. Behm: The Australia Institute.

Salkeld, L. and Hartley-Parkinson, R. (2011) Teenage paedophile who groomed up to 139 girls as young as 11 on Facebook has sentence reduced by top judges, *Mail Online*, http://www.dailymail.co.uk/news/article-2108081/Facebook-sex-abuser-Jake-Ormerod-sentenced-reduced-Torbay-paedophile-ring.html#ixzz1oRer27p0 (accessed June 2012).

Sarakakis, K. and Tsaliki, L . (2011) Post/feminism and mediated sex. *International Journal of Media and Cultural Politics* 7(2): 109–119.

Sarracino, C. and Scott, K. (2008) *The Porning of America: The Rise of Porn Culture, What It Means, and Where We Go from Here*. Chicago, IL: Beacon Press.

Sears, C. (2011) Policing the 'grotesque': The regulation of pornography in Canada, PhD Thesis, Vancouver: Simon Fraser University.

Segal, L. (1999) *Why Feminism? Gender, Psychology, Politics*. London: Polity Press.

Seidman, I. (1998) *Interviewing as Qualitative Research: A Guide for Researchers in Education and the Social Sciences*. New York: Teachers College Press.

Selwyn, N. (2008) Online social networks – friend or foe?, Teachers TV programme, http://www.teachers.tv/video/24687 (accessed 15 July 2008).

Semetsky, I. (2004) Introduction: Experiencing Deleuze, *Educational Philosophy and Theory*, 36 (3): 227–232.

Sex and Relationship Education: Views from Teachers, Parents and Governors (2010) http://www.durexhcp.co.uk/downloads/SRE-report.pdf (accessed June 2011).

Shain, F. (2003) *The schooling and identity of Asian girls*. Stoke-on-Trent: Trentham Books.

Shain, F. and Ozga, J. (2001) Identity Crisis? Problems and Issues in the Sociology of Education, *British Journal of Sociology of Education*, 22(1): 109–121.

Shalit, W. (2007) *Girls Gone Mild: Young Women Reclaim Self-Respect and Find It's Not Bad To Be Good*. New York: Random House.

Sheperd, J. (2010) Girls think they are cleverer than boys from age four, *The Guardian*, 1 Spetember. http://www.guardian.co.uk/education/2010/sep/01/girls-boys-schools-gender-gap (accessed July 2011).

Shilling, C. (1992) Reconceptualising structure and agency in the sociology of education: Structuration theory and schooling, *British Journal of Sociology of Education*, 13(1): 69–87.

Shute, R. H., Owens, L., and Slee, P. (2002) 'You just stare at them and give them daggers': Nonverbal expressions of aggression in teenage girls, *International Journal of Adolescence and Youth*, 10: 353–372.

Simmons, R. (2003) *Odd girl out: The hidden culture of aggression in girls*. New York: Harcourt.

Simmons, R. (2011) *Odd girl out: The hidden culture of aggression in girls* (revised, updated). New York: Marimer.

Skeggs, B. (1997) *Formations of Class and Gender*. London: Sage.

Skeggs, B. (2005) The making of class and gender through visualizing moral subject formation, *Sociology*, 39(5): 965–982.

Skelton, C. and Francis, B. (2008) *Feminism and the Schooling Scandal*. London: Routledge.

Slack, J. (2008) Menace of the violent girls: Binge-drinking culture fuels surge in attacks by women, *The Daily Mail*, http://www.dailymail.co.uk/news/article-1039963/Menace-violent-girls-Binge-drinking-culture-fuels-surge-attacks-women.html#ixzz1oA3fQWLy (accessed, June, 2011).

Smith, C. (2010) Review, Sexualisation of Young People Review, *Participations*, 7 (1), pp. 175–179, available at http://www.participations.org/Volume%207/Issue%201/papadopoulos.pdf.

Smith, P. and Sumara (2003) Evaluation of the DfES Anti-Bullying Pack, DfES Research Brief RBX06-03.

Smith, P. K. and Brain, P. (2000) Bullying in school: Lessons from two decades of research, *Aggressive Behavior*, 26: 1–9.

Smith, P.K., Mahdavi, J., Carvalho, M., and Tippett, N. (2006) *An Investigation Into Cyberbullying, its Forms, Awareness and Impact, and the Relationship Between Age and Gender In Cyberbullying*. Research Brief No. RBX03–06. London: DfES.

Smithers, R. (2004) Minister Backs Split-sex Lessons in Some Subjects. *The Guardian*, 17 November.

Smithers, R. (2008) Bebo named as best social networking site in survey. *The Guardian*, 4 January.

Spender, D. (1982) *Invisible Women: The Schooling Scandal*. London: Writers and Readers Publishing Cooperative.

SRE Core Curriculum for London (2009): *A Practical Resource*. P. Power and T. Procter for GOL and PSHE Association. www.younglondonmatters.org/uploads/documents/srecorecurriculumforlondonapracticalresourcepdfdocument.pdf.

St. Pierre, E., and Pillow, W. (2000). *Working the ruins: Feminist poststructural theory and methods in education*. New York & London: Routledge.

Statistics Canada (2004) The gap in achievement between boys and girls. http://www.statcan.ca/english/freepub/81–004–XIE/200410/mafe.htm.

Stepp, L. (2007) *Unhooked: How Young Women Pursue Sex, Delay Love and Lose at Both*. New York: Riverhead Press.

Stern, S. (2006) Girls Gone Wild? I don't think so…Spotlight on digital media and learning, available at: http://spotlight.macfound.org/blog/entry/susannah-stern-girls-gone-wild.

Stromquist, N. P. (2007) Background paper prepared for the Education for All Global Monitoring Report 2008 *Education for All by 2015: will we make it? The Gender Socialization Process in Schools: A Cross-National Comparison*. New York: UNESCO.

Swicord, J. (2006) Survey Finds Young Boys Failing in Schools Across the US. Available at http://www.voanews.com/english/archive/2006-04/2006-04-13-voa4.cfm?CFID=138742099&CFTOKEN=19806460.

Taft, J. (2004) Girl Power Politics: Pop-culture Barriers and Organizational Resistance. pp. 69–78 in A. Harris, (ed.) *All About the Girl: Culture, Power and Identity*. New York: Routledge.

Talbot, M. (2002) Girls just want to be mean. *New York Times Magazine*, 24 February, pp. 24–26. http://www.newamerica.net/index.cfm?sec=Documents&pg=article&DocID=752&T2=Article accessed 12 August 2004.

Tamboukou, M. (2008) Machinic Assemblages: Women, art education and space, *Discourse*, 29 (3): 359–375.

Tamboukou, M. (2010) Charting cartographies of resistance: Lines of flight in women artists' narratives, *Gender and Education*, 22(6); 679–69.

Tankard Reist, M. (ed.) (2009) *Getting Real: Challenging the Sexualisation of Girls*. New York: Spinifex Press.

Tasker, Y. and Negra, D. (2007) *Interrogating Postfeminism: Gender and the Politics of Popular Culture*. Durham, NC and London: Duke University Press.

Thomas, A. (2004) Digital literacies of the cybergirl, *E-learning*, 1(3): 358–382.

Thompson, K. (2010) Because looks can be deceiving: media alarm and the sexualisation of childhood – do we know what we mean?, *Journal of Gender Studies*, 19(4): 395–400.

Tolman, D. M. (2002) *Teenage Girls Talk About Sexuality*. Cambridge, MA: Harvard University Press.

Tozer, J. and Horne, M. (2011) Parties in stretch limos, catwalk shows and fake tattoos: The disturbing sexualisation of little girls revealed. http://www.dailymail.co.uk/femail/article-1360750/Revealed-Disturbing-sexualisation-girls-cocktail-parties-stretch-limos.html#ixzz1TD2WELDn.

Tsavdaridis, D. and Cummings, L. (2004) Pupils bullied in Cyberspace, *Daily Telegraph*, 20 August 2004 http://cyberbully.org/newsreports.html (accessed 24 August 2004).

Turkle, S. (1995) *Life on the Screen: Identity in the Age of the Internet*. New York: Simon and Schuster.

Twohey, M. (2004) Violent crimes by girls rising, but the reasons why remain unclear, 25 August, http://www.jsonline.com/news/state/aug04/254029.asp (accessed 17 September 2004).

Tyler, I. (2008) 'Chav Mum, Chav Scum': Class Disgust in Contemporary Britain, *Feminist Media Studies*, 8 (1): 17–34.

Unterhalter, E. (2007) *Gender, Schooling and Global Social Justice*. London: Routledge.

Vail, K. (2002) How girls hurt: The quiet violence in your schools. *American School Board Journal*, 189 (8). http://www.asbj.com/2002/08/0802coverstory.html (accessed 17 August 2004).

Vincent, C. and Ball, S. (2006) *Childcare, Choice and Class Practices*. London: RoutledgeFalmer.

Walkerdine, V. (1984) Some Day My Prince Will Come: Young Girls and the Preparation for Adolescent Sexuality. In McRobbie, Angela and Nava, Mica (eds), *Gender and Generation*. Basingstoke, Hants, UK: Macmillan Educational.

Walkerdine, V. (1988) *The Mastery of Reason*. London: Routledge.

Walkerdine, V. (1989) *Counting Girls Out*. London: Virago.

Walkerdine, V. (1991) *Schoolgirl Fictions*. London: Verso.

Walkerdine, V. (1997) *Daddy's Girl: Young Girls and Popular Culture*. Macmillan: Cambridge.

Walkerdine, V. (1999) Violent Boys and Precocious Girls: Regulating Childhood at the end of the Millennium, *Contemporary Issues in Early Childhood*, 1(1): 3–23.

Walkerdine, V. (2007) *Children, Gender, Video Games: Towards a Relational Approach to Multimedia*. London: Palgrave.

Walkerdine, V. and Ringrose J. (2006) Femininity: Reclassifying upward Mobility and the neo-liberal subject. In C. Skelton, B. Francis and L. Smulyan (eds) *The SAGE Handbook of Gender and Education*. Thousand Oaks, CA: Sage.

Walkerdine, V., Lucey, H., and Melody, J. (2001) *Growing up girl: Psychosocial explorations of gender and class*. Basingstoke: Palgrave Press.

Wallace, J. (2007) Inclusive Schooling and Gender. Paper presented at the Canadian Teachers' Federation conference. Ottawa. 4–6 May.

Walter, N. (1999) *New Feminism*. London: Virago.

Walter, N. (2011) *Living Dolls: The Return of Sexism*. London: Virago.

Weedon, C. (1987) *Feminist Practice and Poststructuralist Theory*. New York: Blackwell.

Weekes, D. (2002) Get your freak on: How black girls sexualise identity, *Sex Education*, 2(3): 251–262.

Weeks, J. (2003) *Sexuality*. London: Routledge.

Weems, L. (2009) M.I.A. in the global youthscape rethinking girls' resistance and agency in Postcolonial Contexts, *Girlhood Studies*, 2(2): 55–75.

Weiner, G. (1985) *Just a Bunch of Girls*. Milton Keynes and Philadelphia: Open University Press.

Weiner, G., Arnot, M. and David, M. (1997) Is the Future Female? Female Success, Male Disadvantage and Changing Gender Patterns in Education. In A. H. Halsey, P. Brown, H. Lauder, and A. Stuart-Wells, (eds) *Education, Culture, Economy and Society*. Oxford: Oxford University Press.

Werbner, P. (2007) Veiled interventions in pure space: honour, shame and embodied struggles among Muslims in Britain and France, *Theory, Culture and Society*, 24(2): 161–186.

Willett, R. (2009) 'As soon as you get on Bebo you just go mad': young consumers and the discursive construction of teenagers online, *Young Consumers: Insight and Ideas for Responsible Marketers*, 10 (4): 283–296.

Willis, J. (2009) Girls Reconstructing Gender: Agency, Hybridity and Transformations of 'Femininity', Rethinking Agency and Resistance: What Comes After Girl Power?, *Girlhood Studies*, 2 (2): 96–118.

Willis, P. (1977) *Learning to Labour*. Aldershot: Gower.

Wiseman, R. (2002) *Queen Bees and Wannabes: Helping your daughter survive cliques, gossip, boyfriends and other realities of adolescence.* New York: Crown.

Wittig, Monique (1969/1979) *Les Guérillères.* The Women's Press, London.

Wollstonecraft, M. (1792/1975) *A Vindication of the Rights of Women.* Miriam Kramnick, (ed.) London: Penguin.

Wolmuth, A. (2009) What are the challenges to school-based SRE being empowering to young people? Unpublished assignment for Gender, Theory and Practice module, Institute of Education., University of London.

Woods, S. and Wolke, D. (2003). Does the content of anti-bullying policies inform us about the prevalence of direct and relational aggression in primary schools?, *Educational Psychology*, 23(4): 381–401.

Worrall, A. (2004). Twisted sisters, laddettes, and the new penology: The social construction of 'violent girls', pp. 41–60. In C. Alder and A. Worrall, (eds) *Girls' Violence: Myths and Realities.* New York: SUNY Press.

Wright, J. E. (2001) *The Sexualisation of America's Kids: And How to Stop It.* Lincoln, NE: The Writers Club Press.

Youdell, D. (2006) *Impossible Bodies, Impossible Selves: Exclusions and Student Subjectivities.* London: Springer.

Youdell, D. (2010) Recognizing the subjects of education: engagements with Judith Butler. In M. Apple, S. Ball and L. A. Gandin (eds) *The Routledge International Handbook of the Sociology of Education.* London: Routledge.

Young, I. M. (1990) *Throwing Like a Girl and Other Essays in Feminist Philosophy and Social Theory.* Bloomington, IN: Indiana University Press.

Younger, M. and M. Warrington (2005) *Raising Boys' Achievement.* London: Department for Education and Skills. Research Report 636. Available at http://www.dfes.gov.uk/research/data/uploadfiles/RR636.pdf.

Younger, M. and Warrington, M. (2007) Closing the Gender Gap? Issues of gender equity in English secondary schools, *Discourse: studies in the cultural politics of education*, 28(2): 219–242.

Youth Justice Board (2009) Girls and offending: Patterns, perceptions and interventions. http://www.yjb.gov.uk/publications/Resources/Downloads/Girls_offending_summary.pdf (accessed September 2011).

Yuval-Davis, N. (2006) Intersectionality and feminist politics, *European Journal of Women's Studies*, (13)3: 193–209.

YWCA (2002) If looks could kill: Young women and bullying. http://www.ywca-gb.org.uk/newsarticle.asp?ID=106 (accessed March 2004).

Index

Aapola, S. *et al.* 4, 26, 65
abjection 73, 138
abstinence education 53, 55
affect 30, 77, 78–9, 80 *see also* desire;
    affective assemblages *see* assemblages,
    affective; affective economy 90, 100,
    133; affective turn in social sciences
    77–85; flow of affect/desire 78–9, 80–1,
    82–4, 118–19, 125, 126, 133; revisiting
    affective charge of postfeminist politics
    139–44
Affleck, Ben 117
agency, girls': binaries of 59, 61, 63–4, 69;
    and the body 85 *see also* sexual regulation
    of girls' bodies; and choice 57–69;
    debating 58–60; discursive agency 61,
    71, 72; governmentality research and
    postfeminist discourses of femininity
    64–7; narrative voice, power and 60–4,
    65; sexual *see* sexual agency, girl's
aggression, feminine *see* feminine aggression
Aguilera, Christina 140, 141
alcohol 120; mocktails 50
Ali, S. *et al.* 21, 59
Allen, L. 53
'almighty symbolic' 72
American Pie 125
American Psychological Association, report
    on sexualisation of girls 43, 47
anal sex 124, 125, 126
Appadurai, A. 13
Arnot, M.: *et al.* 14, 15; and Phipps, A.
    15–16
Arnot, M. *et al.* 21
ASBO girls 38–41
ASBO Teen to Beauty Queen 39
assemblages, affective 80–2, 114, 136;
    sexualised 116–31; social networking
    sites 114, 116–31 *see also* social
    networking
Attias, B. A. 84

Attwood, F. 123
Australia: child sexualisation 43;
    choice and neo-liberalism 67–8;
    feminine aggression 28; femocrats
    15; pornography education 147;
    postfeminist fears over 'feminisation' of
    schooling 19–20
Azam, S. 45, 125

Bailey, Reg 49–50
Bailey Review, *Letting Children Be Children*
    43, 44, 49–50, 55
Baker, J. 67–8
Ball, S. J. 3
Batchelor, S. 38
Bebo 114; offline effects of Bebo identity
    126–8; photos and producing a 'sexy'
    visual display 119–21, 122; and re-
    signifying 'slut' and 'whore' 122–8, 138;
    'skins' and applications 116–21, 123,
    125, 129–30, 131
Beck, U. 3, 149
becomings 83
Benjamin, S. 24
Bergen, V. 77
Besag, Valerie 29
Bjorkqvist, K. 31
black girls 37
Blackman, L. and Walkerdine, V. 4
bodily anxieties 127, 129, 130
body politics 127–8
Bonta, M. and Protevi, J. 81
Boom Chicka Wah Wah 117, 118
Bouchard, P. *et al.* 17, 18
Bourdieu, P. 58, 61, 83
Boxall, Rosimeiri 30
boyd, d.m. and Ellison, N. B. 114
boys: aggression in 32; 'failing' *see* 'failing
    boys'; and sex education 53–4
'Boys getting it right' report 20
Bracchi, P. 30, 38

Braidotti, R. 85
Brown, L. M. 90, 100
Buckingham, D. 58; and Bragg, S. 44
bullying: anti-bullying interventions 99–103, 134–6, 145; 'bullycide' 30; cyberbullying *see* cyberbullying; discourse 99–103, 104–7; and the feminine as pathological 105–7; gender blindness in early research 36; girl-on-girl 29–30, 34, 128; and naturalising middle class mean girls 35–8; and Ofsted 149–50; parental invocations of 103–5; physical 36; psychological 36; sexual 22, 36; zero-tolerance policies 37
Burman, M. J. *et al.* 31
Business Week 20
Butler, J. 61, 70–3, 84

Canada: education *see* Canadian education; sexualisation of girls 43, 48–9
Canadian Council of Ministers of Education 19
Canadian education 15; and feminine aggression 34–5; postfeminist fears over 'feminisation' of schooling 17–19; School Achievement Indicators Program 17
capitalism 3, 65, 78–9
Chesney-Lind, M. and Irwin, K. 32
childhood studies 58; girlhood and agency 58–60; 'girlhood' research problems 57–8
child sexualisation 43–7, 50; and class 45, 48, 50–1, 56; female *see* sexualisation of girls
choice, girls': and agency 57–69; 'choice biographies' 65, 67; choice discourse critique 65–8; in clothing 66 *see also* clothing, girls'; governmentality research and postfeminist discourses of femininity 64–7; and neo-liberalism 67–8; saying 'STOP' 94–5; and sexual pressures 63, 94; and the suffering of domestic abuse 68
class: and child sexualisation 45, 48, 50–1, 56; classed discourse of bullying 99–103; and educational achievement 21–2, 24, 25; and feminine aggression 30, 35–41; naturalising middle class mean girls 35–8; and the public/private split 100; and the sex industry 46, 48
clothing, girls': choice in 66; and cultural dynamics 146–7, 148; and molarity 82–3; 'tarty' 6, 96, 97, 142, 143

Cohen, J. 13
Cohen, M. 20–1
Collins, P. H. 5
complexes 74; Oedipal 78
'Confident, capable and creative: supporting boys' achievements' 22
Connell, H. 18
contraception 52–3
Cowley, P. and Easton, S. T. 17
Crick, N. R. 31–2, 33; and Grotpeter, J. K. 31
criminologists, feminist 39–40
cultural capital 25, 35, 61
cultural dynamics 6, 24, 26, 37, 57, 88, 95, 104, 146–7
cultural studies 5, 58
Currie, D. H. *et al.* 93, 97
cyberbullying 29–30, 35, 36, 114, 130–1; and Ofsted 149–50

Daily Mail 16, 49, 139–43
Daily Telegraph 2, 16, 17, 140, 141–2, 143
Davies, B. 59–60, 73, 110; and Bansel, P. 3; *et al.* 73
Deleuze, G. and Guattari, F. 61, 77–85, 123, 134; schizoanalysis 79–80, 84, 136
Demos 12
depression 36, 37, 45, 47
desire 53, 74, 78–81, 134 *see also* affect; control of 108 *see also* sexual regulation of girls' bodies; flow of affect/desire 78–9, 80–1, 82–4, 118–19, 125, 126, 133; as lack 78
desiring machines 79–80
determinism, discursive 69, 73, 77
deterritorialisation 83
developmental discourse 26
Direct and Indirect Aggression Scales (DIAS) 31
discursive agency 61, 71, 72
discursive constraints 57–60
discursive contradiction 72, 74
discursive determinism 69, 73, 77
discursive misfire/misrecognition 71, 73
discursive performativity 71, 73 *see also* performativity
discursive positioning theory 73
discursive psychology 73
discursive re-signification 6, 61, 71–2, 122–5, 126–7, 138
discursive subjectification 61, 71–2 *see also* feminine subjectivity
dis-identification 73
Dobson, R. and Hodgson, M. 47

domestic abuse 68
Dorries, Nadine 55
dress, feminine *see* clothing, girls'
Driscoll, C. 57, 59
Duits, L. and van Zoonen, M. 66–7
Durham, G. 44, 48
Dweck, Carol 32

eating disorders 22, 37, 45, 47
economic decline 2–3
Education Act (1944) 14
educational decentralisation 15
educational discourse 4–5; 'failing boys'
    discourse 16–23, 25; masculinist 17,
    19, 25–6; and moral panics 4 *see also*
    postfeminist panics/fears; relation with
    media *see* mediascapes; 'successful girl'
    discourse 12–26
educational equality 14–26, 149
educational feminisation 12, 14–16;
    postfeminist fears over 'feminisation' of
    schooling 16–20
educational mediascapes *see* mediascapes
educational policy-scapes *see* policy-scapes,
    educational
educational testing 24, 144
Egan, D. and Hawkes, G. 46–7, 49, 50
embodied resistance to sexual regulation
    86–112
emotion *see* affect
empowerment, female 4, 34, 46, 59, 65 *see*
    also agency, girls'; power; postfeminist
    masquerade of 65, 69, 146; vs
    victimisation 59, 64, 66
Empower Program for girls 34
energy flows 78–9, 80–1, 82–4, 118–19,
    125, 126, 133
Epstein, D. *et al.* 53
equal opportunities *see also* gender equality:
    educational 14–16; laws 14
Equal Pay Act (1970) 14
ethical axes 81
ethical issues research 156
ethno-politics 77
exclusion 22, 23, 24, 29, 33, 36, 131; and
    affective injuries from peer networks
    131–4; school exclusion 37; self-
    exclusion 37
Eyre, L. and Gaskell, J. 15

Facebook 114
'failing boys' 16–20, 25; discursive effects of
    discourse on UK policy scape 20–3
fantasies: fantasy space for trying out sexual
    identities 124 *see also* social networking;

gendered 13, 20, 40, 56, 74–5, 110–12,
    118, 124; pornographic 146; ruptures of
    dominant discourses in 61; subverting
    and pre- and postfeminist 110–12
Female Chauvinist Pigs (Levy) 46
feminine aggression 28–41; bullying *see*
    bullying; of deviant, low class, violent
    ASBO girls 38–41; indirect 31, 32, 33,
    34–5, 36, 37, 40; mediascapes of 28,
    29–30, 34–9; name-calling *see* injurious
    signifiers; naturalising middle class mean
    girls: UK media and policy context 35–
    8; new management strategies 33–5; in
    popular cultural domain 30; relational
    31–2, 33–4, 35; sexual cyber-aggression
    130–1 *see also* cyberbullying; and the
    signifier 'slut' 91–5 *see also* sluts
feminine pathology 8, 50, 56, 80, 91,
    105–7, 108, 110, 135–6, 138, 147;
    aggressive *see* feminine aggression; 'mean'
    girls 29–30, 34–5, 40–1, 89–91, 106–7
feminine repression 30, 32, 35, 37, 40, 54,
    56, 74, 78–9, 100, 106, 147
feminine subjectivity 40, 41, 70–85
    see also identity; sexual identity; and
    agency *see* agency, girls'; sexual agency,
    girl's; being 'known' 89–91; Butler's
    theories of subjectification 70–3; the
    contradiction of femininity 74, 91,
    106–7, 109–10; dilemmas of perfect and
    'nice' vs horrible and 'mean' femininity
    89–91; and discourse negotiation 74;
    discursive, psychosocial and affective
    theoretical–methodological approach
    70–85; discursive subjectification 61,
    71–2; and gender binaries 71, 80,
    89–91, 97, 118; girls entering and
    negotiating competitive heterosexualised,
    postfeminist femininity 86–112; girls
    negotiating postfeminist sexualised media
    contexts 113–38; and oedipalisation
    78; schizoanalysis and the pathologies of
    feminine binaries 80; and sexual agency
    see sexual agency, girl's; sexual identity *see*
    sexual identity; and 'sluts' *see* sluts; and
    social networking *see* social networking
feminine 'success' 3–5, 12–26; and 'failing
    boys' 16–23, 25
femininity, idealised *see* idealised femininity
femininity norms 66, 71, 78–9, 80, 106,
    117, 127, 134, 138, 146 *see also* idealised
    femininity; sexual regulation of girls'
    bodies; celebrity norms 121; injurious
    norms 126 *see also* injurious signifiers;
    lines of flight from *see* lines of flight

feminisation: of education *see* educational feminisation; of work and the labour market 12

feminism: 'bra-burning' 142; and economic decline (Willetts) 2–3; educational *see* educational feminisation; and feminine aggression 28, 34, 38–9; feminist political imaginary 147–50; postfeminist views of 142, 143; poststructural feminists 64; second wave 7, 14; sex-positive, anti-sexism feminism 146; and the sexualisation of girls *see* sexualisation of girls; third wave 5; using and abusing 23–6; ways forward for education and 139–50

feminist criminologists 39–40

femocrats 15

Fine, M. 53; and McClelland, S. I. 126

fitness 4; sexual health 126

flight lines *see* lines of flight

flows of energy 78–9, 80–1, 82–4, 118–19, 125, 126, 133

Foucault, M. 25, 71, 144; post-Foucauldian governmentality theories 64–7

Francis, B. 20, 60

Fraser Institute 17

Freud, S. 78

Froese-Germain, B. 19

Gender and education: the evidence on pupils in England 21–2, 36

gender anxieties: over 'failing boys' 16–23, 25; over feminine aggression *see* feminine aggression; over feminine 'success' 3–5, 12–26; over 'feminisation' of schooling 16–20; over girls' sexualisation *see* sexualisation of girls; Segal 4

gender bias in schooling 17 *see also* educational equality; educational feminisation; power relations 52; sex education 53–4

gender binaries 46, 61, 63–4, 69, 71, 80, 89–91, 97, 118

gendered behavioural issues 22 *see also* eating disorders; self-harming

gendered discourse of bullying 99–103

gendered fantasies 13, 20, 40, 56, 74–5, 110–12, 118, 124; subverting and pre- and postfeminist 110–12

gendered identity 22, 24–5, 51, 58, 65, 70; sexual *see* sexual identity

gendered power dynamics 43, 52, 56, 78–82

gendered violence 22 *see also* feminine aggression

gender equality: assumptions 1, 12; disruption of myths 148; gap 7, 14, 15–24; illusion 7; measuring 23–6; struggle for educational equality 14–16; UN Millennium Development Goals 26; as a whole-school approach 149; and worsening employment opportunities for men (Willetts) 2–3, 12

Gender Equality Duty 149

Genz, S. 5

geophilosophy 77–85

Getting Real: Challenging the Sexualisation of Girls (Tankard Reist) 45

Giddens, A. 58

Gillborn, D. 144

Gill, R. 5, 56, 66–7, 69, 125; and Scharff, C. 4, 5

Gill, Z. 20

girls: agency *see* agency, girls'; sexual agency, girl's; aggression of *see* feminine aggression; 'alpha girls' 12–13, 20; as benefactors and winners of globalisation 3; black 37; bodily anxieties 127, 129, 130; body politics 127–8; celebration versus crisis in girlhood 4; choice *see* choice, girls'; deviant, low class, violent ASBO girls 38–41; empowerment *see* empowerment, female; entering and negotiating competitive heterosexualised, postfeminist femininity 86–112; feminine subjectivity *see* feminine subjectivity; feminine 'success' and postfeminist panic 3–5, 12–26; friendships, conflicts and entry into heterosexualised dating cultures 86–112, 120–1, 122–4, 126–8, 131–6; 'girl effect' (Koffman) 26; girl power 22–8, 34, 38, 70–5, 103, 158; 'girlhood' research problems 57–8; girl-on-girl bullying 29–30, 34, 128; girl power 12, 26, 28, 34, 38, 39, 60, 62, 65, 93, 148; girl power discourse 12, 34; girl-to-girl cruelty 29; as human capital in developmental discourse 26; 'mean' girls 29–30, 34–5, 40–1, 89–91, 106–7 *see also* feminine aggression; naturalising middle class mean girls 35–8; negotiating postfeminist sexualised media contexts 113–38; negotiating 'reputation' 91–5; regulation of girls' bodies *see* sexual regulation of girls' bodies; 'riot girls' 30, 39, 40; at risk 26–7, 30, 36, 51–6 *see also* feminine aggression; self-commodification 115, 117–38; sexual agency *see* sexual agency,

girl's; sexualisation of *see* sexualisation of girls; sexually explicit representations of girls' bodies 114, 117–22; sexual objectification of 5, 45, 47–9, 109; 'slags' *see* slags; 'sluts' *see* sluts; social networking *see* social networking; split between personality and body 108; struggle for educational equality 14–16; victimisation *see* victimisation, female
'Girls and Offending' report 40
Girls Gone Mild (Shalit) 45, 48–9
Girls Gone Skank (Oppliger) 44–5
globalisation 23; girls as benefactors and winners of 3
Gonick, M. 73; *et al.* 60
Gorard, S. 14
Gove, Michael 23
governmentality theories, post-Foucauldian 64–7
Growz, E. 79
Guardian 17, 29

habitus 83
Hadley, M. 32, 33
Hamilton, M. 44–5, 46
Harris, A. 3, 26, 64–5
Hartley, Robbie 17
Hatton, Ricky 117
health 4
Hefner, Hugh 49
Henriques, J. *et al.* 74
Herbert Secondary School 88–9, 103–5; sexual regulation and embodied resistance at 88–112
heterosexism 22; heterosexist sexual politics 7, 43, 53, 57; heterosexualised matrix of power relations 70–3, 86–112
Hickey-Moody, A. and Malins, P. 85
Hilton, Paris 125, 141
Hoff-Sommers, C. 20
Hollway, W. 74; and Jefferson, T. 75
homophobia 22
Houghton, Keeley 30
'How girls hurt' report 35

id 79
idealised femininity 74–5, 89–91, 106, 117, 118, 121, 125, 141, 145; and feminine aggression *see* feminine aggression
idealised masculinity 117
identification 72, 73, 95
identity: being 'known' 89–91; gendered 22, 24–5, 51, 58, 65, 70; molar

encodings of 82–3; negotiating 'reputation' 91–5; online social networking sites, identity construction and gender 114–15; sexual *see* sexual identity
ideoscapes 13
The Importance of Teaching (White Paper) 23
indirect aggression 31, 32, 33, 34–5, 36, 37, 40
individualisation 3, 56, 64–5, 149
injurious signifiers 6, 71–2, 103, 122–5, 126–7, 128, 130, 131–7, 138 *see also* slags; sluts
intelligibility 71
Internet, social networking *see* social networking
interpellation 64, 71–2, 108, 147
intersectional approach 25, 56, 59, 69, 149–50 *see also* class; race
interviewing: (in-depth, individual and focus groups) 87–88, 115––16, 155, intersubjective space of the interview, 109
It's a Girl's World 30, 34–5
Ivinson, G. and Murphy, P. 14

Jackson, A. Y. 82–3
Jackson, C. 100
Jackson, S. 52
Jones, A. 59–60
Jones, L. 83
Jong, Erica 49

Kehily, M. J. 55
Kelis 117, 125
Kenway, J. 19
Keys, Alicia 117
Kindlon, D. 12
Koffman, Offra 26
Kristeva, J. 147

Lacan, J. 74
Ladette to Lady 39
lap dancing 46, 47, 48, 119, 146
Letting Children Be Children 43, 44, 49–50, 55
Levin, D. E. and Kilbourne, J. 44
Levy, A. 46
libido 78, 80 *see also* affect; energy flows
lines of flight 83–4, 85, 124, 126–7, 136–7, 149
Lingard, B. 19
Living Dolls: The Return of Sexism (Walter) 46

Liz Claiborne Foundation 34
The Lolita Effect (Durham) 44, 48
London Evening Standard 139–40
London Riots (2011) 39, 40

machines: desiring machines 79–80; dualism machines 79, 84; war machine 82
McRobbie, A. 1, 2, 5, 58, 65–6, 69, 145–6
mapping methodology 69–70, 77, 79, 80–1, 84, 123, 137–8
Marie Claire 125
Martino, W. and Kehler, M. 19
masculinity: idealised 117, 118; masculinist discourse 17, 19, 25–6, 117; norms 146
Massumi, B. 80, 81
matter, molar and molecular 82–3
Maxwell, C. and Aggleton, P. 61–3, 111
Mazzei, L. and McCoy, K. 77
Mean Girls 30, 34–5, 36, 83, 125
mediascapes 13–26; Australia 19–20; Canada 17–19; of child sexualisation 44–50; of girls' aggression 28, 29–30, 34–9; girls negotiating postfeminist sexualised media contexts 113–38; international 28; media sensationalism and the affective charge of postfeminist politics 139–44; postfeminist 13–26, 35; postfeminist fears over 'feminisation' of schooling 16–20; UK 16–17; US 20
media studies 5, 66, 77, 116, 146
mediatisation 13 *see also* mediascapes
Mendick, H. 24
Middleton, Kate 110
mimesis 83, 123, 125
Mirza, H. S. 59
misfires 61, 71
molarity 78–83, 134
molecularity 82–3, 138
Monroe, Marilyn 117, 118
moral panics 4; postfeminist *see* postfeminist panics/fears
Moretti, M. M. *et al.* 32
MySpace 114

name-calling: injurious *see* injurious signifiers; re-signification of *see* discursive re-signification
narrative voice 62–3, 65; 'choice biographies' 65, 67
National Curriculum 15
National Post 48–9
Nayak, A. and Kehily, M. J. 71–2
Negra, D. 110

neo-liberal discourse 3–4, 24, 60, 68, 142; and postfeminist discourse 3–4
neo-liberalism: and choice 67–8; ethos 3–4; as gendered 4; and individualisation 3, 65; neo-liberal logic 149; and the panic over feminine 'success' 3–5, 12–26; and school 'effectiveness' 23–4, 144; and the sexualisation of girls 56
new age 4
New Mills Secondary School 115–16
New York Observer 49
New York Times 20, 29

Observer 29
Odd Girl Out 30, 34–5
O'Donovan, D. 20
oedipalisation 78
Oedipal myth/interpretation 78, 111; schizoanalysis and 79
Ofsted inspectors 149–50
Oliviero, H. 29
online observation 116, 121
online social networking *see* social networking
Ophelia Project 33
Oppliger, P. A. 44–5
Oprah Winfrey Show 30, 34
oral sex 63, 67, 95, 117, 125
Oral Sex Is the New Goodnight Kiss (Azam) 45
Osler, A. 37
Owen, Michael 117

Palmer, A. 35
Palmer, Sue 16
Panorama 30
Papadopoulos, L. 43–4, 54–5
parental invocations of bullying 103–5
Pateman, C. 4
Pearson, Ian 12
peer groups 31, 37, 41, 54, 56, 82–3, 128; exclusions and affective injuries from peer networks 131–4; and girls entering and negotiating competitive heterosexualised, postfeminist femininity 86–112; social networks *see* social networking
peer nomination questionnaire 31
performativity 23, 24, 52, 54, 71, 73, 144; performance of confident sexual agency 125; performative logic 149; performative politics 71; performing digital 'slut' 121–2; performing Playboy Bunny 128–30; and re-

signification 124; school 'effectiveness' 23–4, 144; sexualised possibilities with Bebo applications 118–19
Personal, Social and Health Education (PSHE) 51, 55, 138, 144–5, 146, 148
Phillips, M. 16
Pipher, M. 33
Playboy Bunny 50–1, 56, 117, 118, 128–30
policy-scapes, educational 13–14; assessment-driven policies 24; discursive effects of 'failing boys' discourse on UK policy scape 20–3; naturalising middle class mean girls 35–8
pornography 46, 48, 56, 124; education 147; girls negotiating postfeminist 'pornified' media cultures 113–38; pornification 56, 125, 147; porno-chic 66, 119, 145–6; pornographic fantasies 146; porno-scripts 124
postfeminism: fears relating to *see* postfeminist panics/fears; meaning and nature of 1–7, 65; postfeminist, educational 'entanglements' 5; postfeminist femininity 86–112; postfeminist masquerade 65, 69, 146; relationship to education 1–7; revisiting affective charge of postfeminist politics 139–44; sexual politics of *see* postfeminist sexual politics; as a zeitgeist-shaping sensibility 5
postfeminist discourses 1, 5; deconstruction of 25, 26, 60, 67, 146; governmentality research and postfeminist discourses of femininity 64–7; and neo-liberal discourse 3–4; of sexual performance 107–10
postfeminist fantasies 110–12
postfeminist mediascapes 13–26, 35 *see also* mediascapes
postfeminist panics/fears: over 'failing boys' 16–23, 25; over feminine aggression *see* feminine aggression; over feminine 'success' 3–5, 12–26; over 'feminisation' of schooling 16–20; over girls' sexualisation *see* sexualisation of girls
postfeminist sexual politics: challenging postfeminist discourses of sexual performance 107–10; and educational attainment 24–6; heterosexist 7, 43, 53, 57, 86–112; regulation of girls' bodies *see* sexual regulation of girls' bodies; and resistance 6–7,

86–112; revisiting affective charge of 139–44; shaping through mediascapes *see* mediascapes; shaping through postfeminist panics *see* postfeminist panics/fears
post-humanist theories (Deleuze and Guattari) 61, 77–85
poststructuralism 5, 13, 59–60, 64, 73 *see also* intersectional approach
power: affective assemblages and the rethinking of 80–2; female empowerment *see* empowerment, female; gendered power dynamics 43, 52, 56, 78–82; girl power discourse 12, 34; heterosexualised matrix of power relations 70–3, 86–112; molar powers 78–83; narrative voice, agency and 60–4, 65; power relations in schools 52, 70; reduction 96, 102; ruptures to formations of 76, 78, 79, 85; sexual 6, 56, 128; space, matter and 82–4
prince/princess fantasies 110–12, 138
prostitution, teenage 45, 47, 48
PSHE (Personal, Social and Health Education) 51, 55, 138, 144–5, 146, 148
psychoanalysis 73–6; Deleuze and Guattari's critique of 78–9; and schizoanalysis 79–80, 84
psychosocial research 73–6; psychosocial and affective theoretical–methodological approach 70–85

qualitative research 75, 77–8
Qualitative Studies in Education 77

race: discourse of bullying 99–103; and feminine aggression 37, 39–40; and the *Gender and Education* report 40
Race Relations Act (1976) 14
'Raising Boys' Achievement Project' 21
Rake, Katherine 50
Rats and Bullies 30
Reay, D. and Lucey, H. 88
recognition 73, 137; discursive misrecognition 71, 73
relational aggression 31–2, 33–4, 35
Renold, E. 61, 84, 111; and Epstein, D. 144
repression, female *see* feminine repression
reputation 91–5
re-signification 6, 61, 71–2, 122–5, 126–7, 138
retrosexism 5, 6
Ringrose, J. and Renold, E. 61
'riot girls' 30, 39, 40

risk: bullying *see* bullying; and child
sexualisation 42–50; and feminine
aggression 30, 36 *see also* feminine
aggression; and individualisation 3,
64–5; protection and sexuality in girls'
schooling 51–4; the 'at risk' failing
girl 26; and school interventions 145;
of social networking 29–30, 35, 36,
114–15
Rocky Mount Telegraph 29
Rousseau, Jean-Jacques 14
Rowland, P. 35

Sanguinetti, Michael 6, 143
Sax, Leonard 19–20
schizoanalysis 79–80, 84, 136
School Achievement Indicators Program
(SAIP, Canada) 17
school 'effectiveness' 23–4
school exclusion 37
school space 82–3
Scottish Parliament report, *Sexualised goods
aimed at children* 54
SEAL (Social and Emotional Aspects of
Learning) education 55
Segal, L. 4
self-commodification 115, 117–38
self-exclusion 37
self-harming 22, 45
self-help 4
self-sexualisation, girls' 54, 114–15, 121–
30; self-commodification 115, 117–38
Sewell, Tony 16
Sex and Relationship Education (SRE) 43,
51–4, 55; 2010 report 51–2
Sex Discrimination Act (1975) 14
sex education 52–3, 55, 126; abstinence
education 53, 55; protectionist discourse
52–3; SRE 43, 51–4, 55
sex industry 46, 47–8, 56, 146 *see also* lap
dancing; pornography; stripping
sexism 2, 5, 6, 7, 15, 21, 22, 24, 146;
heterosexist sexual politics 7, 43, 53,
57, 70–3, 86–112; retrosexism 5, 6;
and the sexualisation of girls 46, 48, 49,
53–4, 55–6 *see also* sexualisation of girls
sex quizzes 118–19
sexual agency, girl's 63–7 *see also* sexual
regulation of girls' bodies; performance
of confident sexual agency 69, 125;
saying 'STOP' 94–5
sexual bullying 22, 36
sexual competition 89, 95–8, 101, 106,
110–12, 144–7
sexual cultures 95, 108

sexual desire *see* desire
sexual grooming 114
sexual health 126
sexual identity 51, 116 *see also* gendered
identity; and Bebo skins 116–19,
123, 129–30, 131; and bodily
anxieties 127, 129, 130; fantasy
space for experimentation 124
see also social networking; girls
entering and negotiating competitive
heterosexualised, postfeminist
femininity 86–112; negotiating
'reputation' and the signifier 'slut'
91–5; online 114–15, 116–30 *see also*
social networking; as 'slags' *see* slags; as
'sluts' *see* sluts
sexual innocence 44, 45, 48, 49, 51, 56,
95, 117, 125, 127, 130, 146
sexualisation of girls 42–56; and
corporate marketing 44–5; girls
entering and negotiating competitive
heterosexualised, postfeminist
femininity 86–112; implications
of debates for education 54–6;
mediascapes 44–50, 113–38;
negotiating postfeminist sexualised
media contexts 113–38; negotiating
'reputation' 91–5; new 'sexual contract'
(McRobbie) 65; and the popular press
47–50; and pornography 46, 48, 56,
66, 119, 124, 125 *see also* pornography;
public anxieties over child sexualisation
43–7; regulation *see* sexual regulation
of girls' bodies; risk, protection and
sexuality in girls' schooling 51–4; self-
sexualisation/self-commodification 54,
114–15, 117–38; and the sex industry
46, 47–8, 56; sexual objectification 5,
45, 47–9, 109
Sexualisation of Young People Review 43–4,
54–5
sexualised discourse of bullying 99–103
Sexualised goods aimed at children (Scottish
Parliament report) 54
sexualised insults *see* injurious signifiers
sexually explicit representations of girls'
bodies 114, 117–22
sexual objectification of girls 5, 45, 47–9,
109
sexual performance, postfeminist discourses
107–10
sexual pleasure 43, 125–6, 145, 146, 147;
and sex education 53–4
sexual politics, postfeminist *see* postfeminist
sexual politics

sexual power 6, 56, 128
sexual regulation of girls' bodies 6, 7, 53,
   54, 86–112 *see also* postfeminist sexual
   politics; and bullying 99–107 *see also*
   bullying; challenging postfeminist
   discourses of sexual performance 107–
   10; and embodied resistance 86–112;
   negotiating 'reputation' and the signifier
   'slut' 91–5; and online social networking
   displays 119–21; saying 'STOP' 94–5;
   sexual competition and the politics of
   'bad' fighting 95–8
Shalit, W. 45, 48–9
signifiers, injurious *see* injurious signifiers
Simmons, R. 33–5, 93
Skeggs, B. 115, 130
Skelton, C. and Francis, B. 14
Slack, J. 30
slags 91, 120, 123, 129 *see also* sluts; 'fat
   slag' 128, 130, 131–7; school response
   to fight over girl being called a 'fat slag'
   134–6
sluts 6 *see also* slags; performing digital 'slut'
   121–2; re-signifying 'slut' 6, 122–8,
   138; the signifier 'slut' 71, 91–5, 100,
   107–8, 122–8, 138; slut-shaming 93–4,
   100, 126; SlutWalks 6, 148–9
slutty pictures 119–21
SlutWalks 6, 148–9
Smith, C. 44
Social and Emotional Aspects of Learning
   (SEAL) education 55
social exclusion 22, 24, 29, 33, 36, 131
social fields 61, 72
social networking: Bebo and dominant
   gender/sexual discourses 116–19;
   cyberbullying *see* cyberbullying; identity
   construction, gender and 114–15;
   offline effects of SNS identities 126–8;
   performing digital 'slut' 121–2; photos
   and producing a 'sexy' visual display
   119–21, 122; and re-signifying 'slut'
   and 'whore' 122–8, 138; sexual cyber-
   aggression 130–1; 'skins' and applications
   116–21, 123, 125, 129–30, 131
So Sexy So Soon (Levin and Kilbourne) 44
space, striated and smooth 82
Spears, Britney 141
spirituality 4
SRE (Sex and Relationship Education) 43,
   51–4, 55
Stern, S. 114, 115
Strauss-Kahn, Dominique 148
stripping 117, 118, 119

structuration theory 58
subjectivity, feminine *see* feminine
   subjectivity

Taft, J. 18–19
Talbot, M. 34
Tamboukou, M. 82, 83
Tankard Reist, M. 45
Tarde, Gabriel 82
Tasker, Y. and Negra, D. 4
teenage prostitution 45, 47, 48
territorialisation 83; re-territorialisation
   61, 78, 83, 127
third wave feminism 5
Thirteen 30
Thornbury Secondary School 115
The Times 12–13, 16, 47
Times Educational Supplement 139
Toronto 'SlutWalk' 6, 148–9
Tozer, J. and Horne, M. 49
transcendental empiricism (Deleuze and
   Guattari) 77–85
Trimble, Doug 18

United States of America: abstinence
   education 53; bullying 35; and
   feminine aggression 28; mediascapes
   20

victimisation, female 6, 32, 47, 66;
   and bullying discourse 101; vs
   empowerment 59, 64, 66
violence, feminine *see* feminine aggression
Vuitton, Louis 117

Walkerdine, V. 90, 110; *et al.* 25, 73–4,
   75, 76
Walter, N. 46
Weekes, D. 95
What's Happening to Our Girls? (Hamilton)
   45
'whore', re-signifying the term 122–8, 138
Willetts, David 2, 12
William, Prince 110
Willis, J. 60, 111
Willis, P. 58
Wiseman, R.: *Queen Bees and Wannabes*
   34, 36
Wollstonecraft, Mary 14

Youdell, D. 71
Younger, M. and Warrington, M. 14
Youth Justice report, 'Girls and Offending'
   39, 40